I0605195

WARDS OF THE LEAGUE

TEXANS

Dallas Texans logo. Image used in cooperation with the National Football League and its representative NFL Properties LLC.

WARDS OF THE LEAGUE

The Untold Story of the First NFL Team in Dallas

Mike Cobern

Fort Worth, Texas

Library of Congress Control Number: 2024031141

TCU Box 298300
Fort Worth, Texas 76129
817.257.7822

Design by Bill Brammer

This book is dedicated to Giles E. Miller Sr., Connell R. Miller Sr., and the entire Miller family for letting me tell their story.

It is also dedicated to the few brave souls who came out to support the Dallas Texans in 1952.

CONTENTS

FOREWORD

"Well, Giles and I may have just bought a football team!"

That is a close approximation of what I remember my dad, Connell Miller Sr., announcing at the dinner table one evening a little over seventy-one years ago.

If you are reading this book, chances are pretty good that you're either an aficionado of the pigskin sport, a dedicated sports junkie, or maybe just a true history buff concerned with all things Texas. Whatever the case, I will assume you already know the ending to the story usually told about the "sad-sack team from Dallas that went bankrupt and only won one game in 1952." I can assure you there is much more to it!

I was contacted over two years ago by the author, Mike Cobern, who had an idea that there must have been a much bigger backstory to the founding and ultimate failure of not only the first professional football team in Texas but of the entire South.

I very much liked what he proposed: a complete history with the good, the bad, and the ugly—from the very beginning through a myriad of post-ending "what ifs." In other words, as Texans are often wont to say, "The whole enchilada!" I have read a number of magazine, internet, and newspaper articles and accounts over the years regarding the Texans, and they universally fall short of providing the famous line I've plagiarized from radio icon Paul Harvey, "And now you know the rest of the story."

Mike's sincerity and willingness to spend all of the time necessary to interview family members and anyone with even a remote connection to the team, its owners, or players, as well as his effort digging for every scrap of information available and taking it through the vetting process, caused me to sign on immediately.

In addition to providing Mike with everything I had regarding the Texans, I quickly gave him Giles Miller Jr.'s contact information. My cousin and I are only a month and a half apart in age, and as the oldest child in each family, we both probably have a few more memories of that year rolling about in our heads than our younger siblings. Outside contacts and other family members have also not been overlooked for any possible information that would be of help to the author in his quest for completeness and accuracy.

On a personal note, 1952 was a whirlwind year for this youngster as well, as Dad and Uncle Giles's plans to dip our families' toes into the unknown waters of professional football quickly worked their way into my consciousness.

That big dinner table announcement had not come as a complete surprise to me, as I'd been hearing snatches of conversations that my parents were having. Then, there were Dad's often lengthy telephone calls with his brother that led to his rushing out for meetings with agendas that included prospective investment group members, the press, representatives from the National Football League, and a myriad of others.

This, of course, was happening in the heyday of the Southwest Conference, where anytime our SMU Mustangs hosted a rival in the Cotton Bowl, the denizens of North Texas would respond with sixty to seventy thousand rabid fans passing through the turnstiles. I suspect this certainly must have fostered the germ of an idea with radio broadcasting savant Gordon McLendon to bring professional football to Dallas. Unfortunately, due to a conflict you will read about in this book, he had to back away, but he passed his thoughts and plans along to two of his best friends, Giles and Connell Miller.

Both of our families were more than just casual fans of the game. Train trips with friends to out-of-town games were the norm for our parents (no kids allowed), and many times when we were at the Cotton Bowl for an SMU game, we'd sit in the student-card section, holding up the correct numbered card as directed by a megaphone-wielding student on the sideline. (The downside was, of course, that we couldn't see what we had spelled out for the spectators on the other side of the field.)

We youngsters were also devotees of the pigskin sport. Giles Jr. and I were playing on a football team sponsored by the Park Cities YMCA and coached by my Uncle Giles. It was a time when almost every player wanted to have the number thirty-seven on his jersey, since that was the collegiate number of our hero, Doak Walker, SMU's three-time All-American and the 1948 Heisman Trophy winner. And you will hear more about a sorely missed opportunity with Walker in the book.

I was lucky, as Doak was a good friend of Mom and Dad's. When he and his first wife Norma would visit her parents, who lived near us, they would usually stop by. It was during one of those visits that my younger brother Alex and I were outside tossing a football around. Doak, now playing on Sundays as a Detroit Lion, noticed my passing technique and took a few minutes to show me the correct way to hold and throw the ball. Now with my fingers placed correctly on the lacing, I was soon throwing perfect spiral passes to Alex. Wow! Another time, Doak and Norma pulled up in their spanking-new 1953 Chevrolet Corvette, insisting that Mom drive it around the block . . . with me as a passenger. Another incredible moment!

After "The Doaker" retired as a player, I was at the Cotton Bowl for a game when, during a halftime ceremony, my old "passing coach" gave a very emotional speech to the crowd after the City of Dallas presented him with the keys to a brand-new Cadillac Eldorado.

And so you might guess that the sport of football was a rather important part of our lives, and you'd be right. However, it was Giles who first bought into Gordon's plan that, since Gordon was barred by the NFL commissioner from following through with his desires to own a team, his friends the Millers should do it. All I will say here is that Giles must have taken to the idea like a hungry bass jumping on a, well, whatever bait appeals to a hungry bass. Dad had a few reservations about it, my mother confided to me later; however, the brothers always went into projects fifty-fifty, and this particular one, albeit on a much larger scale, was no different. Now it was "Damn the torpedoes, full steam ahead!"

I can't imagine the turmoil that Dad and Uncle Giles endured during the days and months leading up to that first kickoff in the Cotton Bowl against the vaunted New York Giants on September 28, 1952. Besides running the very busy Texas Textile Mills for their father, the brothers were taxed with having to keep a wary eye on the developing postwar influx of cheap Japanese cotton fabrics coming in and threatening the American cotton industry. In addition, they were juggling all the pieces of the football puzzle that had to successfully come together. It undoubtedly took an incredible amount of time and skillful planning, but they each did their best to make sure their family wasn't forgotten in all the mayhem.

To prove my point, in May of 1952, just as Mom and Dad had finished building our new home in Dallas's Greenway Parks subdivision, the three of us went on a road trip up to the Indianapolis 500. Following that, I spent a month at Camp Tejas near Denton, Texas, where my counselors were twenty-year-old Lamar Hunt and his SMU teammate (and future NFL player and coaching great) Raymond Berry. Several years later, Lamar, of course, would found the American Football League as well as the second incarnation of the Dallas Texans that he would eventually move up to Kansas City.

Immediately after that camp session was over, we piled into the car again and headed to Colorado Springs for a few days of "R&R" at the Garden of the Gods Club. After checking into our room, Dad made a call to room service for something and, lo and behold, here comes Lamar Hunt, whom I had said goodbye to only a few days before. Not too surprising, though, since Lamar's sister, Margaret, and her husband, Al Hill, were the owners of this fabulous place.

Dad and I also had time to hop into his new MG-TD and watch our young friend, Carroll Shelby, compete in a sportscar race at the Marine Corps Air Station Eagle Mountain Lake west of Fort Worth. Around that same time, we also traveled up to the old WWII Army Air Corp training field at Caddo Mills, where I witnessed my very first organized drag race, put on by the North Texas Timing Association.

After that, it was all about football and our new team. Dad took me to a few of their practices at Burnett Field over in Oak Cliff, but we quickly saw less of him as he and Giles became totally involved with making this thing happen.

It's truly a shame that it didn't.

Depending on your usual proclivity for beverages while perusing a good book, either put on a pot of coffee or make sure that six-pack in the fridge is cold, settle back in your recliner, and enjoy the read!

Connell R. Miller Jr.
May 2022

INTRODUCTION

Keeping history alive never seems like hard work, when it is important. And recounting the past has been going on forever. Yet you do not have to go far to find someone who is unfamiliar with something that once happened. More often than not, the unfamiliarity arises because stories are buried or forgotten altogether.

This story has perhaps been both buried and forgotten.

The most repeated question that people asked me while I was working on this book was, "What made you decide to write about this?" My answer always varied somewhere between "Because no one ever has" or "No one knows about it."

Largely untold and unknown to many is that there was once a professional football team that existed for a brief moment, just one season, in a place where failure today seems unfathomable. Over the years, its chronicles suffered from a massive lack of attention and awareness.

And perhaps even more shocking, this team was important enough to have played in the National Football League, with the place they called home now residence to a franchise brand that carries a net worth of more than $9 billion. The city is Dallas, Texas.

Rhett Miller is an accomplished musician, known to many as the leader and founding member of the popular band the Old 97's. He described this tale maybe better than anyone ever has when he penned an article for *Sports Illustrated* that began: "In 1952 my grandfather pulled off quite a feat. He managed to go broke bringing professional football to Dallas. Yes, that Dallas, the city that is now a gridiron capital and proudly harbors America's Team."[1]

Miller's grandfather's team was the Dallas Texans of the NFL—with a major emphasis placed on NFL and not AFL. These were not the same Texans that most people remember, that began in Dallas in 1960 before relocating to Kansas City in 1963 and now play as the Chiefs. Even the most casual football fan knows the story of that American Football League team. But chances are that even the most diehard fan couldn't tell, or doesn't know, the story of these 1952 Texans. They only participated for one season, and spoiler alert, they didn't make it.

I first became aware of the 1952 Dallas Texans sometime during the early part of the 1990s when the Dallas Cowboys were back in the spotlight, beginning their run of Super Bowl titles. While watching an ESPN weekly show called *NFL Films Presents* that featured various chapters in football history, I saw a seven-minute story about this clumsy, inept team and its lone season in Dallas.

For whatever strange reason, I was immediately drawn into the drama around this sad-sack group. Like most football fans, I love to learn about the history of days gone by. Stories of how teams and players won it all, with the immortal glory that goes with it, appeal to me. But the story of this team had no glory attached to it; they were simply awful.

However, their on-field performance wasn't what intrigued me. Rather, my interest lay in the fact that my hometown of Dallas once had another team. A team that no one had ever really spoken of or even acknowledged, for that matter.

Maybe this lack of appreciation was because they were so bad, and anyone who knew of these Texans would rather forget about them? Or was it because they didn't last long? Or as time went on no one really cared, and they weren't relevant? Or was it because the game back then just wasn't the global phenomenon that it later became? I suppose the answer could probably be a mix of all these things.

I recorded the ESPN feature that day and kept the tape—on brilliant quality VHS, of course—and would sometimes watch it over the ensuing years. As the years flew by, I periodically came across articles, footnotes, or references about the team.

Then the internet arrived and changed everything. Throughout the

2000s, I casually searched even more, discovering listings of football cards or programs for sale, reading old newspaper accounts, etc. But as always, life took over, and I would usually find myself needing to get back to work and the daily routine that paid the bills. More time passed by.

Flash forward to 2019. One day while doing more cyber surfing, I came across a recently published article in *Texas Monthly*. It was titled "Right Place, Wrong Time: How the 1952 Dallas Texans Flamed Out after One Lackluster Season of Football." I thought, *Wow!* The article was great, giving an up close and personal account of what actually happened.

Right away, I saw that the story was written by a guy named Connell Miller Jr., who happened to be the son of one of the team's owners. This not only refreshed my interest but piqued it even more. I read the piece repeatedly, at least four or five times.

By now I was more hooked on this team than ever. In the coming days, I couldn't move past it, so I decided to touch base with the magazine's staff, just hoping to obtain a good quality print of some of the photos used. Surprisingly, they put me in touch directly with the source himself, Connell. Finding and contacting him was a gift sent from the heavens. After all, he lived through the whole damn thing.

A wonderful rapport developed quickly between the two of us, starting out with my annoying rapid-fire questions and requests. Connell was going to be the man who could tell me what happened, and more importantly, why it didn't work.

Not long into one of our first conversations, he pointed out, "Mike, I was only nine years old at the time."[2] Ouch. But while that was certainly the case, Connell was there at the dinner table and team practices with his dad, as well as every other step of the way. He set me off on the path to a better understanding, giving me leads and greater insight about the team than anyone else previously could. The routine calls, emails, and text messages between the two of us turned into a special friendship that continues to this day.

From that moment on, I spent more time collecting information, albeit still just for myself. My goal wasn't necessarily to become an expert on the unknown team. Who would want to own that distinction? I was simply curious and wanted to find out more.

I've always been an avid reader and student of the game, owning more books about football than I can count. Being somewhat of a dinosaur, for me any good book represents the road toward learning in a way the internet can't give you. If it's an important subject, then a book must have been written about it. So, with renewed focus, I set out to find what had been written about the Texans in book form or otherwise personal accounts.

I quickly discovered that locating any useful information about the franchise would prove to be daunting, if not impossible. The team was from a time so long ago that the likelihood of finding any real first-hand accounts would not be possible, seeing as all the players and staff associated with the team have left us.

Continuing further down the path, I threw out a wide net, expanding my searches. What I found, though, was a little shocking—meaning not much. Only magazine and newspaper articles. When it came to books, there were NONE to be found.

That is with the lone exception of the forty-eight-page, team-compiled media guide written in 1952 before the Texans' season took place. But it was basically a collection of statistics and facts about the players, staff, and schedule that contained no real narrative. The book was so small it could fit in your pocket.

Although the team was both terrible and short-lived, that there was never anything dedicated solely to the subject seemed baffling to me. Having found nothing so far made the story seem more mysterious and fascinating.

That is when it hit me: If I couldn't locate any books written about the Texans, why not write one myself? At least for now I would be able to stake a claim at having the best book ever written about the team.

Shortly after this revelation, it happened. Finally, something was found. Whether it had been hidden in plain sight or buried on purpose, a previously undisclosed book was uncovered.

Enter Rhett's grandfather, Giles Edwin Miller, who was also Connell's uncle. He and his brother, Connell Ransom Miller Sr., were the two young millionaires who were the primary owners of the failed venture, along with a handful of other investors. They worked in tandem, but Giles was the leader and was responsible for the formation of the team, bringing it to life and then ultimately to its death. Giles Miller was the face of the Dallas Texans. (There was an old series of television commercials for the Smith Barney investment firm that used the slogan, "They make money the old-fashioned way...They earn it." Well, for Giles, he made his money the *really* old-fashioned way...he inherited it, through his family's two fortunes.)

Giles himself had written a private book in 1972. He first considered writing his story in 1970 after the death of good friend Harlan Ray, an investor and board member of the team. The idea soon left Giles but resurfaced two years later, this time prompted by the death of former Los Angeles Rams owner Dan Reeves. Reeves worked very hard during the Texans lone season, and especially afterward, to maintain a friendship. He was the only fellow owner who stayed in touch over the years, and the fact that Reeves didn't turn his back on him once things went sour meant a lot to Giles.

With the passing of Reeves, Giles decided that the time had finally come to accurately tell the story for the record, and with no bitterness or regret. The tools he relied on were mainly his own memory, his desk book, some old newspaper clippings, and files obtained from his attorney. Any other corporate or team files were long gone and presumably nonexistent. This was truly a one-man project.

Once finished, the book would become even more unknown than the team, with a title that was longer than a football season: *The Dallas Texans Saga – or at the Time the New York Yanks Became the Baltimore Colts.* Indeed, quite a mouthful.

Written as a diary-style memoir, the project was meant as a gift or offering to his family and close friends. Not many, if any, outside of this circle ever read the contents. For those who received the book, all copies had some form of personal inscription. In the words of his eldest son, the book tended to be something of a confessional.[3] Self-published, printed in paperback, and extremely limited, by the publisher's own account there were less than fifty originally produced and by now certainly fewer said to be in existence.

Unfortunately, although I had discovered the existence of this treasure, I couldn't see what was actually in it. So, my takeaway was still that no book had ever really been written about the Texans because no one had access to Giles's effort in the first place.

Without the book, I was at a disadvantage, but by no means was I at a dead end. I realized that crafting this story meant that I had to get my hands on this long-lost ledger of secrets, and so I made it my new quest to locate a copy. The book represented the only legitimate perspective that would really matter. I was certain that it would give me all the answers as to why the team failed, and with Giles as the source, the information would be irreplaceable and undisputable.

So, I pivoted and started looking for the book, canceling all other research. I exhausted every avenue, even all of the Miller family heirs, and still no copy appeared anywhere. Then one day my luck took a big-time turn. I received one of the only known copies of the book on loan from Giles's son Ed for my research purposes and was under penalty of death if not returned.

I had been introduced to Ed earlier, and he claimed to have what was likely the only known copy left in the family. For years the book had been lost with no recollection of where it was. Ed just knew that he still had it somewhere. Trunks and boxes from his backyard storage building all the way to his attic were rifled through over time to no avail. Then finally one afternoon the book was accidently found in his home, literally sitting out in the open.

Some of the other family members had already forewarned me that if I were to get a copy, it would be a hard read, and I quickly found out why.[4] Opening up the box upon receipt, I immediately noticed that time had done a number on the old paperback. The pages had yellowed, some even coming loose, the edges and corners were worn, and the spine was very weak. It was fragile . . . and I was nervous.

Carefully opening the book, I realized that I was going to need much stronger reading glasses as the font was unbelievably small. Still, even if it was going to be a hard read, I had in hand what I thought was going to be the vital reference tool needed to finally record the complete story of how the Texans failed.

Once reading it, however, I found that the little book wasn't an easy-to-follow autobiography. There was no index and no chapter themes. Sadly, after immersing myself into page upon page, I found that Giles's writing was more a series of notes and individual short stories—recollections that took place in and around the days of the team's formation and subsequent demise. The book carried well-documented and detailed accounts of certain things like expenditures, meetings, and lunches, but nowhere was there any clear and definitive mention of what really happened.

The feeling was anticlimactic. Unfairly, I suppose that I expected to see a passage written on page 32 that read, *Mike, this is what, why, and how things went.* My path, understandably, wouldn't be that easy. Giles may have been a great millionaire, but he was no storyteller or professional writer.

Although hard to understand initially, eventually patience took over, and there was a lot gained between the lines of Giles's words. Along the way, remembering that the initial objective was to just find the book and obtain information, I quickly came to greatly appreciate it. Reading the words and knowing that he crafted them completely by himself, along with his reasons for doing so, made me even more appreciative and grateful to the man who showed the guts to bring pro football to Dallas.

In hindsight, the efforts that he put into his written account may not have definitively told me everything about the business side, but the recollections did enlighten me enough to fill in a lot of blanks.

The personal side of his words told me much more. Early on he wrote, "I will be the first to admit that the story which follows reads like fiction, but I assure you that it is factual all of the way. Even to a painful degree, and all that happened before, during, and after is real." Ultimately, setting the record straight brought him full circle and at peace with the team's failure. It no longer haunted him, and he never spoke about it publicly after writing the book.

One of my biggest takeaways from the book was how considerate and thankful Giles was to others. An example that oddly stands out most was one of the final sentences in the foreword of the book, where he gave recognition to NFL commissioner Bert Bell, whom he called a friend of Dallas and a great friend to him. The assessment of Bell's friendship

Giles Miller's 1972 privately published account of all things that happened surrounding the Dallas Texans' lone season. Photo courtesy of the author.

wasn't just a stretch, it was beyond naïve.

The Millers never received proper managing, tutoring, or advisement from Bell or anyone else who could have offered it. Yet Giles, a bigger man and still grateful for the opportunity, called Bell a friend in spite of it all.

Rhett Miller was ironically right about his grandfather pulling off quite a feat. He was the first visionary to see Dallas as a premier location for the NFL. Incidentally, Rhett's piece was titled, "We Could Have Been Cowboys." I am glad they weren't.

The Texans drama makes for a much better story.

PROLOGUE

On Friday, August 20 of 1920, at the corner of Second Street and Cleveland Avenue in downtown Canton, Ohio, a meeting was being held at the Ralph E. Hay Motor Company Hupmobile dealership. It was limited, as there were only four representatives in attendance, and they were not strangers to one another.

They had all been competing in an informal society known as the Ohio League of football. The circuit had been around since 1902 and, as the name indicated, consisted primarily of Ohio-based teams.

Each of the clubs had previously been made aware of the agenda and objectives that were being set forth in this special meeting. All but four opted not to participate because at the time they weren't interested in the disclosed intentions of upgrading the game of football, its rules, or adding any unwanted formalities.

The four men who did attend were from Akron, Canton, Cleveland, and Dayton, and they represented the strongest clubs. There to form a more professional football league, their intent was to set and raise the standards of play in every way possible, to eliminate bidding wars for players between rival clubs, and to have a fair and balanced formation of schedules where all teams would face equal competition.

The meeting's organizer was Ralph E. Hay himself. In addition to having the dealership, he was also the owner of the Canton Bulldogs. That day in his office, the group founded what would become known as the American Professional Football Conference. At this same meeting, Hay was elected as secretary of the new APFC. The decision was also made that the next step would be to reach out to neighboring informal leagues and pro clubs of the same caliber with invitations to join the new APFC.

The teams in this expanded group would be invited to the next planned assembly.

The following month on Friday, September 17, at the same location, another meeting was held. This time the gathering was to expand the league formation and set forth the purchase price required for each interested team to become a member. With representatives from the four Ohio organizations, plus six more combined from Indiana, Illinois, and New York, things became a little tight in the dealership's cramped quarters. Because some teams brought two representatives, Hay's office was too small to accommodate the more than ten people on hand, so the meeting was moved to his automobile showroom. Due to a lack of available seats, some participants had to sit on the running boards of the cars.

It's hard to fathom today that the entrance fee was set at just $100 to buy into the new league. One of the founding members, George Halas, famously recalled, "There wasn't $100 in the room" between the men who assembled. He continued, "But still each of us put up our part of the $100 for the privilege of losing money."[1]

By the end of the meeting, there were ten teams on board from four different states. Shortly thereafter, four more joined to make the final count fourteen teams in a five-state area. Although only one month had passed since its birth, the league was renamed the American Professional Football Association. Two years later in 1922, and for a final time, the alliance would rechristen itself—the National Football League.

After all the franchise entries came together and agreed on the initial formation, the first season of the new league began in the fall of 1920. The lineup consisted of the Akron Pros, Canton Bulldogs, Cleveland Tigers, Dayton Triangles, Columbus Panhandles, Muncie Flyers, Hammond Pros, Decatur Staleys, Racine Cardinals, Chicago Tigers, Rock Island Independents, Rochester Jeffersons, Buffalo All-Americans, and Detroit Heralds. The league then swelled to twenty-one teams in time for the 1921 season.

Through the first half of the roaring twenties, the NFL fluctuated between eighteen to twenty teams per season, but the number finally settled down to ten to twelve competitors per year toward the end of its first decade. The frequent theme the league couldn't control early on was the proverbial revolving door. Clubs would form fast and default even faster.

By the start of the 1927 season, only one of the four founding Ohio League teams was still in existence, that being the Dayton Triangles, who survived until 1929. They along with the Buffalo All-Americans, the Chicago Bears (originally named the Decatur Staleys), and the Chicago Cardinals (who started as the Racine Cardinals) would make up the only four franchises out of the original fourteen to last through the 1920s.

Several other teams tried unsuccessfully as well in those early years. Failure, both on and off the field, as well as not having an established fan base were the culprits. The NFL had a new product that wasn't as familiar as America's pastime, baseball. For years, seeing three new teams each season while four more folded was commonplace.

Then continuity arrived and things finally stabilized. Although the attempts and misfires by ownership groups continued to occur, they were fewer in number as times were slowly beginning to change for the better. Only four new teams were established during the depression era of the 1930s, and they too would all eventually fold. By 1940, at the end of its second decade, thirty-seven NFL franchises had already failed.

Over the years, yet another change would take place. In the early days, the common characteristic among the first generation of franchises was that many of them were not based in large, populous cities but rather in small-market areas. Most of those teams just couldn't draw enough fans to survive. Only one of the small-town franchises would stand the test of time, the Green Bay Packers. A growth and relocation shift evolved as the league moved into bigger, more urban cities.

Once this occurred, expansion followed, along with an increase in the game's popularity. The league's new additions were now thriving. The prosperity push also meant more teams being established to the west and to the south, and there was the arrival of new franchises from the merger with the All-American Football Conference in 1950.

By then, as the NFL entered its fourth decade, forty-five franchises had folded. Still, the league had matured. If anything, despite two more failures, the circuit was growing stronger.

However, one more failure would occur—the 1952 Dallas Texans. The Texans were a franchise that arose out of two prior failed attempts in other cities. The incarnation that had first toiled in Boston and later ended in New York, as the Yanks, had finally surrendered itself. Their owner sold, or rather dumped, the franchise back to the NFL at a bargain-basement price.

The Yanks had survived eight seasons while recording one of the worst track records in league history. But they did possess one thing—they occupied the NFL's twelfth slot, and that was important. NFL commissioner Bert Bell fully intended to keep the number of teams in the league at an even dozen. He needed a suitor, and he also wanted to venture into a new, untapped market. He found both in two young millionaires from Texas.

It began as a can't-miss idea but quickly spiraled into a series of disastrous blunders. The new owners were eager and willing, but they received no guidance on how to run a team. Consequently, the list of missteps soon became one of whys and what ifs. It all happened so fast that they couldn't foresee things coming and couldn't stop the damage once they did.

In hindsight, the team provided a historic blueprint on how not to run a team, and for good reasons they folded within the year they formed. No NFL story has ever held quite the low level of distinction as the story of the Dallas Texans.

From the period that began at that Canton automobile dealership in 1920 through today, the number of NFL franchises that were born grew to eighty-one. Presently there are thirty-two, only two of which are still in existence from that first season. That leaves a total of forty-nine other franchises that have failed over the league's first one hundred years. It happened forty-eight times in the league's first thirty-one years. It has happened just once in the last seventy-two. And it very likely will never happen again.

The Dallas Texans were not among the first or only NFL franchises to fail, but they were indeed the last.

Dallas Texans' ticket office. 1721 McKinney Avenue in Dallas, Texas, 1952. Photo courtesy of Ed Miller and the Miller family.

1

BEGINNINGS

EVERYTHING has a birthplace. The journey for the Texans began almost two thousand miles northeast of Dallas in the city of Boston, Massachusetts.

After spending five seasons and exhausting all efforts in Beantown, this forerunner team would seek a new lease on life with three more seasons in the bright lights of New York City. During this eight-year period, the performance and results of this franchise could frankly be defined as terrible—the team on the field and the track record off—thanks to an ownership that routinely made poor decisions.

The owner, Ted Collins, was born in the heart of New York City as the son of a physician, but he was orphaned at the age of nine and raised by his aunt. He served in the navy during World War I and upon returning to the states attended Fordham University.

Like many in the roaring twenties, he was a big fan of jazz music, and despite not having any musical training at all, became a salesman for the Columbia Phonograph Company. In a matter of just eight months, he worked his way up to sales manager and within a year had been promoted to recording manager.

While his main focus was on radio programs, which were the country's major source of entertainment during those days, Collins is best known for being the man who discovered singer Kate Smith in 1929. With Collins managing her career for more than thirty years, Smith became "The First Lady of Radio."

At Collins's urging, she popularized "God Bless America," helping to make it the iconic patriotic song that it still is today. Collins was also her producer and later her show announcer while still maintaining interest in other business and entertainment ventures, including sports.

The money he earned from his working relationship with Smith would certainly help Collins fund his endeavors. In 1944, he was forty-five years old but had already begun his brush with sports entertainment. He was a part owner with Smith in the New York Celtics, who were a barnstorming basketball team of sorts that primarily played in the American Basketball League during his tenure. The enterprise eventually failed. Collins also bought a half interest in a minor league professional football team, but the club and the league disbanded due to World War II.

By mid-1944, undeterred and extremely persistent, Collins had heard of an opportunity to own a new team that was to be fielded in the National Football League for the upcoming season. The circuit had already selected Boston as a new city but needed an owner.

Although a previous Boston franchise, the Redskins, had departed in 1937 for a new location in Washington, DC, the league believed professional football could still succeed in the New England area. Boston wasn't exactly Collins's preference. He had long envisioned owning and running a football team in New York and having them play in the city's old Yankee Stadium.

This, however, was not to be. The location had to be Boston … for now. But while the placement was not New York, as he had hoped, Collins paid the league an entry fee of $66,000 for control of the new franchise and dubbed his newfound team the Yanks. At least it was the name he always wanted.

On the field, the 1944 Boston squad, to put it lightly, did not enjoy a good first season. They finished 2–8, and those two victories came against the Brooklyn Tigers, the only team in the league that would finish with a worse record, going winless.

Year two in Boston would surely bring renewed hope, but when the franchise started up in 1944, the timing could not have been worse. The NFL awarded Collins the franchise right in the middle of World War II, a time when existing clubs were already struggling to find enough bodies to field rosters each week. Due to the shortage of players caused by the war efforts, the Yanks merged their team with the only opponent they had ever defeated, the Tigers.

For the 1945 season, this combined group would simply be called the Yanks with no identifying city named or mentioned. And they improved from their inaugural season, but only slightly. After getting off to a good start, things faded in the fall months, and the team finished just 3–6–1. With the Brooklyn merger negated after one year, the 1946 campaign then saw the Yanks take a step back from the advances made during their second season and drop to a disappointing 2–8–1 record.

The 1947 Yanks did bounce back to what was their Boston high mark of 4–7–1, and by the time the 1948 season arrived, there was increased optimism that the club would finally finish with a winning record and possibly qualify for a playoff spot. At the very least, breaking even with a .500 record seemed plausible. Instead, the team took yet another step back and went 3–9.

After continuously losing on the field and the money that goes with it, Collins appealed to the league and was finally allowed to move to New York City—after obtaining the much-needed consent of the New York Giants, of course.

In an effort to mitigate his ongoing deficits and put Boston behind him, Collins made a smart business decision. Rather than have a formal and official relocation, as was typically done, he requested that the league grant him a new franchise in New York and permit him to officially fold his franchise in Boston. In addition, the league was sensitive to his plight, so it let him retain all of the player talent—for lack of a better word—and their contracts. This was simply a formality on the business side in an effort to provide him with a federal tax write-off. The move was clever and calculated, helping the new franchise immediately.

As part of his team's clean slate, Collins would need to rethink some things. Most of the club's assets, excluding the player contracts, were not allowed to transfer due to the Boston franchise folding. Tangible resources were designated as collateral. This included both equipment and uniforms, so out were the green and gold colors of Boston and in were the new blue and silver hues chosen for New York. Although Collins still wanted his club to be known as the Yanks, he changed the name to Bulldogs in an effort to further distance his team from the previously failed effort.

Once again, hopes were plentiful going into the 1949 season. The team had used its first-round draft pick on Heisman Trophy winner and All-American halfback Doak Walker as a future pick. Still having another year of eligibility, Walker remained at Southern Methodist University, choosing to stay in college and continue playing for the Mustangs. In an unfortunate lack of foresight, the Bulldogs became short on patience and traded Walker's draft rights to the Detroit Lions before the next season began. Letting go of a future Pro Football Hall of Fame member who could have changed the direction of the team was just another day in the life of the franchise.

In spite of their new home and leadership, the Bulldogs carried some of their old Boston habits and bad luck with them to New York. These factors, along with poor execution on the field, led to an even worse year than any seen in their former stop. The 1949 squad finished the season with a 1–10–1 record, a new low. Things had actually become worse. For their last game, played at the Polo Grounds on December 11, 1949, just over four thousand fans showed up to see the Bulldogs lose 27–0 to the Pittsburgh Steelers.

A still unwavering Collins, with a drive to make it work in New York, positioned himself to move his team to Yankee Stadium in the fall months. Collins worked out a multiyear lease for what was then a better stadium than the Polo Grounds. The lease itself, however, would cause future issues.

Another turnabout decision was made. The Bulldogs nametag seemed to not stick or feel right, so Collins announced that with the move to Yankee Stadium, the team would go back to its earlier moniker and now be known as the New York Yanks.

There would only be four holdovers on the roster from the one-win 1949 Bulldogs. The 1950 Yanks were going to be an entirely different team, and they needed to be. And as the new season unfolded, finally something amazing occurred—the New York Yanks became winners! They entered their bye week in early November at 6–1 and could smell the playoffs. A rough four-game losing streak meant the team would finish the season at 7–5, but still it was a winning record, something that this franchise had yet to see and could build on.

They'd won almost as many games in 1950 alone as they had in the previous three seasons combined. After that taste of success, planning would soon begin on their next major step toward improving and becoming a winning organization in 1951. However, something terribly unfortunate occurred that would alter the team's positive direction.

By June of that year, head coach Norman Parker "Red" Strader began to develop heart issues. He was hospitalized for several weeks and could not fulfill his regular offseason duties with the team. His health concerns continued over the next two months, and as training camp neared, Collins, fearing that Strader could die on the sideline during a game, made a decision on August 5 that he felt to be the only way forward. In his mind, he gave Strader a leave of absence. In Strader's mind, he was fired. Either way, just seventeen months earlier, in January 1950, Collins had made the right hiring choice with Strader. Now with the 1951 season fast approaching, he was once again in need of a head coach to replace the only winning man the franchise had ever seen.

Having to make a move rather quickly as it was time for training camp, general manager Frank Fitzgerald brought Collins the name of James Phelan. He was not just at the top of the list—he was really the only name on the list.

Like one of his Yanks head coaching predecessors, Maurice "Clipper" Smith, Phelan was a Notre Dame man and had played quarterback on the same Irish team with Smith in 1917. He had been a proven winner in the collegiate ranks, having been the head coach at the universities of Missouri, Purdue, Washington, and St. Mary's with an impressive career record of 137–87–14. He had also served as head coach of one of the All-American Football Conference teams, the Los Angeles Dons. Ironically, it was Phelan himself who had replaced Strader at St. Mary's a decade earlier.

But a lack of time to get acclimated with the players and coaches proved costly for Phelan. The 1951 Yanks reverted and became the same old laughingstock they had been prior to the last season's success. They started out bad, and they finished bad. They would not win a game until

December, which would be the only victory of the season, beating another dreadful team, the Green Bay Packers.

The Yanks finished in their familiar spot of having the league's worst record at 1–9–2. Home attendance was equally worsening, as they averaged just more than fifteen thousand fans per game for the year. In the final contest of the season, on their own icy home field with chilling wind conditions and a game-time temperature of seventeen degrees, the Yanks were defeated in front of just 6,658 fans by the crosstown Giants.

The Giants would be the team that the franchise would face to begin its next season. That 1952 home game would be nine months away, where a game-time temperature of ninety degrees and a hot wind would be waiting.

By now, Collins had determined that he had lost more than $1 million over his eight-year span of owning the team, and he missed being able to devote all of his time to what he did best: show business. He was a considerably more successful man in the singing and entertainment industry than the world of football.

Collins had employed numerous coaches, and Red Strader, the only one who seemed worthy, he ran off due to fear and poor health. His teams had two different nicknames over the franchise's lifespan, and he tried in two cities, with neither one working out.

A third iteration was soon on its way, although this time it would not include him.

Originally published by *The Sporting News* in 1952, cartoonist Willard Mullin's illustration portraying Doctor Bert Bell's diagnosis of Ted Collins's sick Yanks player. Reprinted with permission from the Estate of Willard Mullin by Michael H. Powers, attorney for the Estate of Willard Mullin.

2

GORDON'S DREAM

AFTER the 1951 season ended, Ted Collins committed to escaping the burden of owning a losing NFL team and to quit throwing good money after bad. He had constantly faced financial difficulties. His dream of making it in the sports world in the bright lights of New York City had been just that, a dream.

The other teams in the league were being run by true football men who were born into the sport, not show business managers. On the other hand, these football men couldn't do what Collins could do. What was also obvious was that radio star Kate Smith wasn't getting any younger. Her career, success, and the money she brought in needed to be his focus from this point on.

Now at a crossroads, no longer wanting to own this money pit of a team and eager instead to focus on his moneymaker, he put the franchise up for sale. He hoped to see a flurry of interest develop and possibly even have a bidding war ensue, but reality soon hit as no buyer came forward. Not one.

After this realization, he quickly appealed to the NFL commissioner for help and sold the Yanks back to the league for $100,000. Not a bad return on investment when considering the initial purchase price of $66,000. That is, until one factors in the more than $1 million in upkeep money Collins spent to fund the operation over its lifespan with no profit ever seen. From Collins's point of view, the league would know better than anyone else how to position the next ownership group. Plus, the NFL's money was just as green as any he might receive from an outside buyer. He had just tried that avenue and had failed.

With the league now owning the franchise and no one in the Northeast offering to take the team over, the league opened itself up to exploring new, nontraditional locations. Enter one Gordon McLendon. His dream had always been to try to bring pro football to Texas. By trade, McLendon was the definition of a classic radio pioneer, entrepreneur, and broadcaster all rolled into one. At the age of twenty-six, he arrived in Dallas to start his new life.

That same year, he and his father, Barton McLendon, founded a radio station that would become one of the most popular in the country. The station was KLIF, known as The Mighty 1190, and was based in the Oak Cliff neighborhood of Dallas. There Gordon McLendon would revolutionize the Top 40 radio format in the 1950s, as KLIF was among the nation's first Top 40 stations. He quickly developed a reputation as one of the more creative minds the industry had ever seen, becoming known as "The Maverick of Radio."

McLendon branched out. Once again with his father's backing, he began to purchase movie houses and drive-in theaters, eventually owning more than forty. Prior to all this, however, sports entertainment was at the top of his list.

In 1948, McLendon launched a syndicated radio network known as the Liberty Broadcasting System. Unable to afford live baseball broadcasts, Liberty would air recreations of Major League Baseball games, which was done by following the action via a Western Union ticker machine. Rather than physically being at the game and broadcasting from a stadium press box, McLendon himself would sit in the studio and read the incoming results. For the most part, listeners were not aware that the broadcasters weren't there seeing the action live. Ultimately, his creation would find itself in 458 affiliate stations across the country.

McLendon adopted an on-air character known as the "Old Scotchman" for listeners, and as his network expanded, his crew would comprise future broadcasting legends Jerry Doggett and Lindsey Nelson, as well as Wes Wise, who later went on to serve as mayor of Dallas. The broadcasters even used realistic sound effects—the crowd noise, a crack of the bat, virtually everything a fan would hear at the ballpark. This was sports theater with a built-in delay.

Although enjoying initial success with Liberty, by late 1951 McLendon encountered some serious obstacles that threatened his short-lived network. Beginning in the spring of the 1952 season, there were several MLB teams that decided to begin broadcasting their own games outside of their areas through syndication. In addition, the commissioner of baseball raised Liberty's annual rights fee to broadcast the games.

Previously, McLendon only paid $1,000 per year for these rights but was now told the cost would increase to a whopping $225,000 per year. Liberty would also be prohibited from broadcasting in any city that had a minor league team airing games on the radio and could not broadcast in the northeastern and midwestern United States.

Another setback for McLendon was not being able to reach an agreement with his major incumbent sponsor, the Falstaff Brewing Corporation, who instead signed on with a competitor. By now well over one hundred stations had dropped out of the Liberty Network. In this short time period, the company had suffered a one-two-three blow almost simultaneously.

This was a disaster and simply too much for anyone to handle without breaking down into a total collapse. Facing what would be insurmountable debts, the network ceased broadcasting on May 15, 1952. By then McLendon had filed an antitrust lawsuit against Major League Baseball charging restraint of trade.

Desperate to resurrect his Liberty Network, McLendon came up with a solution he thought might be even better than his previous model: he could acquire his own sports franchise. This time, whether it be baseball or football, he could actually have profit at both ends of the scene. If he played his cards right, it might even be more lucrative than broadcasting only. He could air his own team's games and pay himself—taking money out of one pocket and putting it into another.

McLendon felt that if he were to find the right franchise situation, he might join the "in crowd" and then be able to broker with his fellow owners for their teams' national broadcast rights as well. After all, he knew how to do it. If you can't beat them, join them, and then try to endear yourself to them and gain something extra along the way.

McLendon soon came across information from a faraway place—the NFL's headquarters in Philadelphia. Through his contacts, he learned of a team that was said to be up for sale. The NFL's recent acquisition of the failed Yanks franchise was nothing more than a life vest. The league repurchased the franchise for a good price and was now able to maintain a balance of twelve teams while saving the slot for a new suitor. With no intention of keeping this asset to themselves, the NFL's goal was to find the right ownership group in a brand-new market that could support a team.

The then commissioner of the NFL, Bert Bell, was a tough and boisterous football lifer. Bell was a Pennsylvania-born, former college quarterback who had a gruff personality and ruled with a firm hand. Having once stated, "All I've ever wanted to be was a football man," he took over as the league's top administrator in 1946.[1]

Prior to being appointed, Bell had been the owner of the Philadelphia Eagles and then part owner of the Pittsburgh Steelers. He served as the head coach at times for both teams. Overall, he had a terrible record, owning the dubious distinction of a worse winning percentage than the Yanks over their eight-year run.

As commissioner, though, Bell shined. He introduced competitive parity into the NFL through scheduling, as he himself would compile the annual league schedule on his kitchen table using index cards. One of his first orders of business was to prepare the NFL for a costly struggle with the rival AAFC. He presided over the 1949 merger, agreeing to add the three clubs.

Throughout his years at the helm, he always had a strong antigambling stance where the league was concerned. Bell made tough conduct codes for the players, coaches, and owners. He would generally advise owners on how to run their franchises and would very often make decisions for them.

Through the many years of pro football's early days, Bell did more to save the league than anyone in its history. He enjoyed credibility and the owner's trust. Bell had power and he used it, the epitome of a one-man office.

When word circulated that the Yanks franchise was on the market, McLendon approached Bell with his idea of having pro football come to Texas. Bell believed initially that it was crazy enough to work, so he did not kill the idea as talks continued.

Although he never considered Texas an option for an NFL franchise, Bell had always thought the region was a football hotbed. Many of the league's best players came from the Lone Star State. That Texas could be a great potential site for future exhibition games to gauge fan interest was always discussed, but a full-time franchise could be risky.

College football in Texas was a huge draw, with fans attending in masses. Would they do the same for the pro game? Historically, there had never been a professional major league team in Texas from any sport. In regard to football, the closest team in spirit was the Washington franchise. There would be no doubt that Redskins owner George Preston Marshall would voice loud resistance to any team in the South, as he still felt that was his territory, even as far away as Texas. At the same time, the NFL had enjoyed recent success out on the West Coast with Los Angeles relocating from Cleveland and San Francisco entering the league via the AAFC merger.

The initial asking price for the Yanks was said to start at $100,000 for the team's assets and players. Bell would broker the deal and practically be the lone decision maker of the sale as far as who would get the franchise and where it would land. Dallas could open up a whole new world for the NFL's national growth, and Bell knew it. And because McLendon was not discouraged by the price tag, both sides believed this could be the start of a mutually agreed upon deal.

That is right up until the minute Bell discovered that McLendon had a lawsuit pending against Major League Baseball. Within a heartbeat, McLendon was unequivocally cut off from any further talks, and it was case closed. As fast as things had begun, they came to an immediate stop. Bell also suspected that McLendon's sole purpose was to make a profit and that he was not in it for the love of the game. After this revelation, Bell wanted nothing to do with him. In the end, Bert Bell was not at all against the idea of Dallas; he was simply opposed to Gordon McLendon being involved. He didn't trust anyone who would go against a major sports league.

McLendon was indeed the man who first came up with the vision of pro football in Dallas, but he would not be the beneficiary. He started the conversation and now found himself out of the running due to his lawsuit with baseball. The Dallas entry into the world of the NFL would need to develop from another direction. If the city was to be a landing spot, McLendon's ouster meant that the league would need to find another suitor who could fit the bill.

The names of Giles and Connell Miller would soon surface.

Taken during a party meeting of what was called the Bonehead Club. Gordon McClendon is pictured top left in the bowler hat. The man pictured far right, also wearing a bowler hat, is Giles Miller, who would soon prove to be an important figure. Photo courtesy of Connell Miller Jr. and the Miller family.

3

THE MILLERS

LONG AGO, prior to foreign countries taking over the world's clothing industry, there were actual garment manufacturers in the United States that provided varieties of textile products to people everywhere. It was every American's basic need to have clothing.

Like many other important commodities, these goods were generated in-country rather than being imported. In turn, the industry jobs brought livelihoods to people, and with those jobs came economic and societal growth. During the period of the industrial revolution, villages, towns, and cities across the US were born and often came into prominence because a factory, mill, or production facility had been built.

It was in the textile industry that the Miller family patriarch, Clarence Ransom Miller, became an inventive groundbreaker. He was a self-made man, born in the East Texas town of Ennis to a poor farmer who raised cotton. Beginning work as a young man driving cotton to market in a wagon, Miller became so good at selling his product that soon he was also taking the neighbor's cotton to market.

He arrived in the Dallas/Fort Worth area with fifteen cents to his name, but by the time he was finished, Miller had built a corporate empire. Throughout North Central Texas, he practically owned a textile mill monopoly.

Miller had started out in the business working at the Burrus Mill and Elevator Company in Fort Worth, but growing tired of making money for other people, he ventured out. In 1902, he joined up with his two brothers,

A trade advertisement from Texas Textile Mills featuring the Tex-Tex brand of denim blue jeans. Courtesy of Connell R Miller Jr., representing Texas Textile Mills, Incorporated.

Byron and Burnie, and after their father provided the $3,500 starter money needed, they set up their own factory operation in Fort Worth, the Miller Brothers Manufacturing Company.

Focusing mainly on the production of work overalls, the company later became the first in the country to offer women's sportswear made from denim. Clarence Miller had placed a lot of faith in work overalls, once stating that "overalls are the only thing that haven't changed in fifty years."[1] He knew it was a safe bet.

The company grew and expanded from Fort Worth to also include a processing facility built in McKinney, Texas. It was transformed into Texas Textile Mills, featuring the Tex-Tex brand. But because of World War I and the British blockade of neutral ports, there was a huge surplus of cotton crops produced in the US, which caused the price of cotton to collapse. In an effort to provide some relief to farmers, the state of Texas set a minimum price per pound stipulation and began a marketing campaign, devised by Governor James E. Ferguson, that became known as the "Buy It Made in Texas" push. Chaired by Miller, the initiative was the first of many Texas gubernatorial appointments that he would serve in over the next twenty years.

He was a natural at promoting the state's business interests, and the endless possibilities that Miller conceptualized caused him to change his path from simple clothing manufacturing to controlling the source of his raw material. This synergy would make Miller a very wealthy and respected Texas businessman.

Assuming his first mill would be built in the big city of Dallas would only be natural; however, it was actually constructed in Waco, which is about one hundred miles south. Waco would offer mobility for Miller by providing a small-sized town that would have an adequate pool of workers at lower but fair wages. In addition, its industrial district was located outside of the city limits near the Brazos River. Dallas would become Miller's home, as it was an attractive location, but the city did not really meet the criteria for a mill, with no close access to a water supply.

Miller studied the overall environment of the Waco area when designing his first textile mill. Instead of a typical plant built of nondescript wood, brick, and mortar—the general design at the time—he would do something different and hire an engineer named J. C. Hipp, who was well known for textile mill designs throughout the South and Northeast.

To oversee the construction of Hipp's design, a local company was a must for Miller. A Dallas construction firm, W. C. Hedrick Company, received the contract for the plant building, and the result was a grand facility that included a three-story concrete main building with a glass-

Another trade advertisement from Texas Textile Mills featuring the Tex-Tex brand of denim blue jeans. Courtesy of Connell R Miller Jr., representing Texas Textile Mills, Incorporated.

walled view of the cloth processing room, a small power plant to produce the energy needs, a machine shop, and a finished goods warehouse.

Once his first mill was fully operational, a statewide effort began to promote additional plant development. Texas became the new territory for the textile industry. The resulting success saw a large boom throughout the state, all with Miller's heavy involvement. Conversely, the effect was also felt in bordering states, who would all see their mills close as Texas advanced and replaced them.

Across the country, the roaring twenties were a time of prosperity and industrial expansion, and the increased variety of products that were bought and sold were all made in the US. Miller's textiles were a huge portion of the national industry growth.

Joining in with other cotton traders to build the historic Cotton Exchange Building in downtown Dallas, Miller was elected president of the Texas Cotton Association in May of 1925 as a reward for all his efforts in improving the state's industry. The Dallas Chamber of Commerce began calling Miller the "Cotton Mill King of the Southwest."

His personal success as a businessman was unparalleled in the 1920s. By 1927, his mills were overbooked. They had a seven-month backlog. He couldn't make the products fast enough to keep up with demand.

At the same time, he continued to aggressively market and expand his company across the northern US and into Canada. In August of 1928, he traveled to Detroit to sample durable fabrics to the Ford Motor Company, in hopes of breaking into the auto industry. He made his sales call, and Ford would later decide to purchase a sheeting material from Miller that would be utilized for seating in its automobile production.

Miller was essentially printing money. However, the recent mill-building boom eventually led to overproduction. At the same time, the development of overseas textile mills, followed by imports into the US, caused a reduction in domestic demand. This led to a collapsing value in the market. It was a good time for Miller to hunker down and sit on the money he had amassed.

When the stock market crashed in 1929 ruining both corporate and individual wealth, Clarence Miller had already become a self-made multimillionaire, with enough money to live two lifetimes in the lap of luxury. He did right in business, he did right by sitting on his money, and most importantly, he did right on all thing's family.

At home and away from the business that made him, Miller was called Pop by his children and grandchildren. His wife was simply referred to as Mom not only by her children but by her grandchildren as well. They were married on October 6, 1909.

She was born Queen Esther Connell in Sweetwater, Texas, on July 9, 1887, into the affluent and well-known Connell family fortune. Her

Patriarch Clarence Ransom Miller began with fifteen cents to his name on his way to becoming a self-made millionaire. Miller's fortune funded his sons' dreams of bringing the NFL to Dallas. Photo courtesy of Connell Miller Jr. and the Miller family.

great-grandfather was Samson Connell, who had been the wagon master for General Sam Houston's Army in the Texas revolution against Mexico in 1836. Later in the war he delivered food and essential supplies to soldiers before their final stand at the Alamo. Toward the very end of the conflict he oversaw the delivering of ammunition and food to San Jacinto, where the Texans won the battle and their independence after capturing Mexican dictator Santa Anna.

The new Republic of Texas was grateful for the contributions made by Samson Connell and gifted him large land grants in West Texas that were eventually passed on to Esther, through the Connell family trust, and then later on into the Miller family holdings once she married Clarence. These parcels of ranchland eventually became home to more than two hundred wells that were rich in crude oil, providing the trust with a steady flow of money in the future—enough to define them as both oil millionaires and cotton tycoons.

There were extremely hard times for everyone during the period of the Great Depression, except for those in the Miller household. There was a home and plenty of oil and fabric money to go around. Double what any other millionaire could claim.

Clarence and Esther Miller had two children in their marriage, both sons who were born in Dallas. Their first child was named Connell Ransom Miller, born March 1, 1918. His given name was to preserve Esther's family surname. Their second child came along seventeen months later, Giles Edwin Miller, who was born on August 2, 1920. He was named after Esther's father, Giles H. Connell.

The boys grew up in what could be called a mansion by anyone's standards—that is, by anyone who did not live in the Dallas neighborhood known as the Swiss Avenue district, an area that could boast being the first in the city to have paved streets. The grand homes that lined those thoroughfares were the residences of Dallas's finest and wealthiest.

Like most in the vicinity, the home was originally built in the early 1900s, but after being partially destroyed by fire in 1926, it was purchased by Miller and commissioned to be completely rebuilt the following year. Sitting at 5112 Swiss Avenue, the house had two lawns large enough to enjoy all sorts of activities, especially football.

Growing up in Dallas, Connell and Giles's childhood was like that of many other kids, with one notable exception—one unlikely for the times. One of their closest friends as boys was someone who worked for the family for many years, an adult African American man named Earl Goins. Clarence Miller had initially hired Goins in 1925 to work as a landscaper for the mansion grounds. Along the way he was promoted to butler and went on to become a trusted extended family member.

When he was younger, Goins had been a light heavyweight boxing champ in France during World War I. He would work out, train, and play sports with the boys like one of them, making sure they went on routine daily runs in the morning before breakfast. Though their keeper, a nanny of sorts, Goins would serve as a coach and scoutmaster as well.

As part of his responsibilities, he was charged with getting the young Millers off to school and back, and was also given full authority to discipline them when they misbehaved, which with boys was more than

Pictured left is Earl Goins with his wife, Rosie, in front of the Millers' Swiss Avenue mansion. Photo courtesy of Connell Miller Jr. and the Miller family.

occasionally. While it was common practice then to "take a switch" to a child, Goins would cut switches small so that they did not hurt as much, while still making the point.

When the boys were out of high school, Goins went on vacation to see the Windy City of Chicago in 1938. While there, he was critically injured in an automobile accident, and Clarence Miller immediately flew up to be at his bedside. Fearing the worst, Miller asked him if there was anything at all he could do. Goins responded, "Mr. C.R., fly them boys up here. I want to see them before I die."[2] Thankfully, Goins did not die. A few months passed, and he returned to the Miller home.

Goins was not just a domestic worker for the family. He was a lifelong friend of the boys and their parents. His being in their lives greatly shaped both Connell and Giles's character as adults.

Growing up, Giles Miller, with the aid of Goins's training, was an amateur boxer. He had the build of an athlete. With a stout chest, thin waist, and short legs, his frame was perfect for a boxer, but football was his number one focus, having once described himself as an insatiable fan. Like many in Texas, as a boy Giles idolized legendary players of the Southwest Conference like Davey O'Brien and "Slinging" Sammy Baugh. And although he suffered from chronic asthma, he played football at both the high school and junior college level.

When World War II came around, both brothers served in the US Navy with Giles training at the Naval Intelligence School in Boulder, Colorado. He learned and served in the area of Japanese language translation prior to being discharged early due to severe allergies that were affecting his asthma.

Because he was released from the navy prior to Connell getting his release, Giles got a bit of a head start in the family's textile enterprise. He would wind up going to Southern Methodist University and working toward a law degree. Giles also took additional language courses, as it was in the back of his mind to perhaps become a diplomat if the family trade did not work out. But it eventually did, and his career settled on helping run his father's business.

In the time before his service, Giles attended Dallas's top prep school, the Terrill School for Boys. Longtime headmaster Sam Davis claimed Giles was a good boy, but you had to watch him, particularly when he was the editor of the school newspaper. Davis once recalled being startled to find an advertisement for a nightclub on the outskirts of town that declared, "We cater to Terrill students. Fifty beautiful hostesses."

While at Terrill, Giles put his other training with Goins to use as a mile runner. He never won a race, but he did make quite an impression on a young Betty Jane Stewart while competing in one particular meet. She came to see a duel between Terrill and a team from nearby Garland, and the Garland runner finished his four laps of the mile before Giles could even complete three. Despite the race concluding and the crowd celebrating the winner, Giles continued his snail's pace and completed the final lap.

Betty in the stands later said that she did not even know who Giles was before that track meet, but after witnessing him struggle his way through the last lonely leg, she could not get him out of her mind. So it was there where they met, and it turned out to be just the beginning.

They were married in 1942. In typical Texas tycoon fashion, the couple would settle into a modest twenty-room house in the neighborhood of Highland Park, directly across the street from the Dallas Country Club, where they were also members. Together, the Millers had three children, all boys: Giles Edwin Jr., who would be known as Ed, Stewart Ransom, known as Randy, and finally Donovan Connell, known as Donny.

Connell's path was a little different than that of his brother Giles. He would began his college education at Baylor University. After he was involved in an auto accident, his father Clarence insisted that he return to Dallas and attend Southern Methodist University to be closer to home. It was there that he met his future wife, who was also attending SMU. Martha Ruth Burns had originally been born in Wyoming and moved to the Southwest by way of Oklahoma, where she was brought up by her grandmother and grandfather, who was a banker. She graduated high school at Nashville's Ward-Belmont and then came to SMU on a music scholarship.

During his days in college, Connell was an avid photographer doing freelance shoots, but he was also making money on the side by photographing events at some of the SMU fraternities and sororities. While taking photos of the 1940 pledge class at the Delta Gamma Sorority, someone caught his attention. He started talking to a cute nineteen-year-old freshman who was sitting in the middle of the front row. She introduced herself as Martha, and they started dating. They later were married in July of 1942.

About that same time, during World War II, Connell joined the US Navy. After entering officer candidate school, which was held at the University of Notre Dame, Connell became a lieutenant junior grade and served aboard the USS *Crosby* in the South Pacific. Upon the end of the war, his active service had him return to Dallas and complete his commitment in the Naval Reserve while finishing off his degree at SMU.

Eventually, Connell and Martha settled a few blocks away from Giles and his family. They lived on a large, one-acre corner lot in the neighborhood overlooking Greenway Parks. In true brotherly fashion, they too were members of the Dallas Country Club, and they had three children, again all boys. They were Connell Ransom Jr., who would be known as

Taken during Christmas of 1946 at Clarence Miller's Swiss Avenue home, *left to right*: Clarence Ransom Miller, Esther Connell Miller, Betty Jane Stewart Miller, Giles Edwin Miller, Martha Burns Miller, Connell Ransom Miller. Photo courtesy of Connell Miller Jr. and the Miller family.

Ranse, Alexander Felts, known as Alex, and finally Burns Giles, known as Burnie.

The Miller brothers were once described as the youngest millionaires in America, and together the foursome of Giles and Betty, along with Connell and Martha, would be the founding members of a crazy idea perhaps ahead of its time. They would need some help and additional partners, but Dallas's entry into the sports world was about to come to fruition.

4

THE SALE

AS THE CALENDAR turned to 1952 at the league offices, work began on finding a suitable replacement for the abandoned New York Yanks franchise. Having had his eyes recently opened by radio pioneer Gordon McLendon to the idea of Texas being a potential home, NFL commissioner Bert Bell uncharacteristically had Dallas fresh on his mind. Although McLendon himself had been dismissed and was completely out of the running for the potential Dallas ownership sweepstakes, he did still have local connections and friends whom he could match with the league. The question was, who would want to buy and lead a historically money-losing franchise with a cursed lineage?

The person who fit that bill was the high-ranking chief of the fun-loving Bonehead Club of Dallas. To be clear, the club was no joke. There was truly an official Texas state chapter of this organization created in 1919. Membership consisted of wealthy businessmen, doctors, lawyers, and other professionals. Over the years, members of this exclusive organization kept the same purpose and philosophy that their founders set forth, embedded in their mission statement: "OUR AIM: NOTHING. OUR PURPOSE: NOTHING. OUR INSPIRATION: NOTHING. MOTTO: TO LEARN MORE AND MORE ABOUT LESS AND LESS UNTIL, EVENTUALLY, WE SHALL KNOW EVERYTHING ABOUT NOTHING!"[1]

Beyond their mission statement, the sole principle of the Bonehead Club was for its members to relax, have fun, and to forget the seriousness of the outside world that made them the money needed to practice this self-imposed foolishness. Some of their high-spirited projects included sponsoring a wedding between two camels in the Dallas Zoo, planting a large oak tree in the center of the busy intersection of Akard and Commerce streets, officially closing the state fair the day before its actual opening was set, and having Christmas parties in April.

The members were successful, prominent, and professional men who just wanted to enjoy adolescent humor on occasion—rich goofballs. It was said that the organization was so determinedly screwy that for their regular Friday night sessions, they would use a clock that ran backwards, so that the meeting would finish before it began.

Very early into the new year of 1952, Bonehead member McLendon introduced one of his closest friends to the prospect of obtaining a professional football franchise and setting up business locally. That friend was thirty-two-year-old Giles Edwin Miller, who along with his partner and brother, thirty-four-year-old Connell Ransom Miller, would soon begin work on forming the syndicate that would make a play at purchasing the league's ailing Yanks franchise. If their plan came to fruition, the deal would make them both the league's newest and youngest owners.

At about that same time, the NFL's current owners were holding their annual winter meetings at the Hotel Statler in New York City. On the final day of the gathering, Bell revealed some news that stunned most of those in attendance. It was announced on Sunday, January 20, that Yanks owner Ted Collins had decided to call it quits, and that the league would repurchase the franchise asset back for $100,000. Just moments later, though, Bell further disclosed that the NFL was already engaged with a potential ownership group in the South. Days earlier, he had been introduced to Giles Miller, and the two instantly hit it off.

Bell told all on hand that the league office would complete the workings of a deal with a new owner very soon. He declined to specify any particular names, but he did indicate that it would be a group headed up by a wealthy textile entrepreneur, saying, "Let's just call him Mr. X for now."[2] He added that the targeted goal would be to expand the NFL footprint into Texas.

Bell later explained, specifically regarding Dallas, that "we are not seeking a profit," and "we are interested only in the right group and the right

Young thirty-two-year-old millionaire Giles Miller, originally identified as Mr. X by NFL commissioner Bert Bell, was recruited to be the face of the Dallas Texans franchise. Although Miller was full of both energy and new-fangled ideas, sadly things spiraled out of control faster than they were assembled. Photo courtesy of Connell Miller Jr. and the Miller family.

site for our franchise, and Dallas appears to qualify on both scores."[3] He would also say, "I have been informed that this Texas group is willing to assume any and all obligations the Yanks may have, pay off everyone, and then set up a new business in Dallas."[4]

With this statement, Bell clearly did not intend to simply recoup the $100,000 league buyback expenditure. His intentions were to clean up all outstanding issues and liabilities that were left over from the failed Collins ownership. Unfortunately, in the end this would become a much larger expenditure than originally thought.

Connell Ransom Miller always partnered fifty-fifty with his younger brother Giles. The Dallas Texans were no different, as he experienced every joy and misery 1952 brought. Photo courtesy of Connell Miller Jr. and the Miller family.

Meanwhile, back in Dallas, Giles and Connell were both becoming increasingly optimistic about their prospects. They were quickly assembling a plan to reach out and accumulate enough investors through friends, colleagues, and family to make up a syndicate of owners. Being young millionaires, the Miller brothers had the connections. They also were ambitious, assertive, aggressive, and exuded that customary Texas swagger and bravado.

Throughout their business life, Giles and Connell had always been fifty-fifty partners in their ventures. This one would be no different. With this new NFL franchise, the younger Giles would take the lead management position, as Connell had some reservations, though he still supported the idea. His belief was that this would be a risky move, buying a rather sad-sack football team from New York that had a dismal record both on and off the field. But the prospect of bringing professional football to Texas, abetted by Giles's enthusiasm for the project, eventually won Connell over, and they jumped into the deal together.

However, word of a new stipulation quickly came down from the NFL offices. Bell was now demanding that any purchase or transfer of ownership to the Texas syndicate, or any other bidder for that matter, would have to include a provision for an additional $200,000. This money was earmarked to pay off the eight years remaining on the original ten-year lease of Yankee Stadium for home games, as negotiated by Collins with Yankees owner Dan Topping.

Bell's position was based on integrity, that the NFL would pay its debts. The league wanted to be on equal standing with baseball, and thus, he reasoned, would never take any handouts.

This would at least triple the NFL's original asking price of $100,000 to a sum total of $300,000. Although the news proved to be an unexpected turn of events, the Miller brothers remained undeterred and vowed to persevere by covering this added obligation with the investor syndicate.

Bell was very adamant from day one that any and every potential owner would be checked out thoroughly by him first. After his review, they would then be either approved or withdrawn from consideration. He wanted to know not only the background of the primary ownership individuals, but also the history of each syndicate owner or investor. And even then, he might decide to delve into their resources further. This was his standard way of conducting business and not necessarily unique to this particular deal.

Giles met earlier with Bell and roughed out an estimate of approximately $230,000 for a realistic player payroll and coaching staff for the first year. Bell had advised the need to keep the budget low, but not too low as to become uncompetitive, which would lead to failure. The commissioner had also advised that, based on the last two seasons, the Western Division, where the team would likely be placed, would more than cover the guaranteed payout for road games—just as long as this new Dallas squad drew in reasonable crowds as visitors in other cities.

During that initial conference, Bell confirmed that there would be twelve regular league games scheduled, advising him to plan accordingly. But he also informed Giles that he would always give thought and consideration into consolidating the travel schedule in order to save costs, meaning slating the 49ers and Rams games back-to-back as well as the Packers and Bears series.

While Giles requested that his team's opener be played at Washington in hopes of forming an early rivalry, Bell quickly barked back that it was far too early to even think about something like that now. After all, Miller and his syndicate had not even finalized the purchase yet. Nothing would be considered or approved until Bell said so. In fact, he didn't believe Dallas would likely play Washington in its first season.

Giles and Connell's circle of friends were highly successful people, many of whom were equally charitable philanthropists . . . and they would need to be in this deal. The brothers' next step was to quickly bring together and then consolidate these interested parties in order to raise the needed funds to complete the purchase. This phase of the plan, that being the initial league transfer of the franchise to the Millers as an ownership group, was not at all difficult. The obstacles would come later.

In addition to Giles and Connell, there were twelve more primary investors who signed on to form the syndicate:

- Don Stewart, Giles's father-in-law, and his brother, Harry E. Stewart. They were co-owners of The Stewart Company, which was a farm implement firm.
- J. Harlan Ray, an oilman and part owner of the Ray-Harris Drilling Company.
- David Harold "Dry Hole" Byrd, a successful oilman who would later sell his company to Mobil Oil and also hold deep financial investments in Ling-Temco-Voight.
- J. Curtis Sanford, a close friend of the Millers and an oil magnate who conceived of and funded the New Year's Day Cotton Bowl Classic.
- Grady H. Vaughn of G. H. Production Company, another oil company.
- George Leighton Dahl, the architect who oversaw the creation of Fair Park's Art Deco buildings for the 1936 Texas Centennial.
- John J. Coyle, vice president of the investment banking firm Rupe & Son.
- William Russell "Fritz" Hawn, a successful real estate developer and thoroughbred racing king.
- Jack Roy Grady, an executive with the Oak Cliff area paper company Fleming & Sons.
- Joe C. Thompson, the long-term president of the Southland Corporation.
- Leonard Nichols, owner of Nichols Bros. Garage and Auto Parking.

Needless to say, a who's who in Dallas business made up the fourteen major investors. There were a lot of names, but more importantly, there was a lot of money in the background.

Having assembled enough partners to complete their purchase alliance, and with all the background checks blessed by Bell, the Miller brothers' dream of bringing professional football to Texas would now be put to a league vote. Once done, the outcome was not even close. With a total of twelve teams casting ballots, including Bell's proxy vote for the league-owned former Yanks, the Millers passed by a result of eleven for, one against. Unsurprisingly, the one negative vote came from Washington, "territorial domain" again being the justification.

NFL commissioner Bell announced on Thursday, January 24, 1952, that the league was approving Dallas as the new home for the formerly known Yanks franchise, and that a group in Texas headed by brothers Giles and Connell Miller would be awarded the team upon the close of the purchase. Reports followed the next day from news services across the country. Through the national print media, several NFL owners applauded the move, including San Francisco 49ers owner Tony Morabito and Pittsburgh Steelers owner Art Rooney, who predicted that Dallas would triple the attendance the Yanks had seen in New York.

Chicago Bears owner George Halas also proclaimed that the "Dallas entry gives the league a true national flavor," noting that a home-and-home series between the Texans and his Bears would develop into a spirited and interesting challenge in the Western Conference of the NFL.[5] "Our intersectional rivalry with the Los Angeles Rams and the San Francisco 49ers has grown to the point where the games are as appealing to Chicago fans as our games with traditional foes, the Green Bay Packers," Halas commented to the *Daily Times Herald*, "I expect the series with Dallas to do the same."[6]

Newspapers around the US opined that the NFL's union with the money and oil-rich state of Texas would truly make professional football more of a national sport. Oddly enough, however, in the local Dallas media, news of the franchise coming to town was not exactly front-page material. In *The Dallas Morning News*, the main headlines that day were "Alger Hiss Seeking a Retrial" and "President Truman's Expressing Optimism about the Fall Elections." The arrival of pro football to Dallas was relegated to a small area of the sports section, where sports editor Bill Rives did sound optimistic when he wrote: "Although the club might be hard-pressed for a few years, professional football eventually should become well-established here. The NFL in looking for a place to move its New York Yankee franchise couldn't have found a better location."[7]

The NFL was so obscure to Dallas that Rives didn't even get the team's name right, calling them the Yankees. He went on to write that the franchise needed strong management support and must earn at least a .500 record in order to succeed with the locals. Undoubtedly, the public and media would have to familiarize themselves with the new team and new league.

The purchase was fully funded on January 29 and completed around Bell's home dinner table the next day with Giles and his wife Betty in attendance. Dallas would be recognized as a brand-new franchise after buying all of the remaining Yanks tangible assets from the NFL. That included the roster of players, equipment, supplies, and uniforms. Hopefully, the Millers would leave the losing disposition behind in New York with the establishment of fresh expectations, new habits, and sound management in Texas.

The Miller brothers were determined to prove to the NFL world that there was more to Dallas than just a reputation for pretentiousness. They wanted to show that the city and its fans were both deserving and knowledgeable.

The college game still may have overshadowed the pro league, but when questioned about whether the NFL would be received with anything close to the same level of support and interest the collegiate level enjoyed, Giles Miller declared, "There is room in Texas for all kinds of football."[8] He knew that the entire state had an ongoing love affair with amateur football, and he believed that the pro game would be an automatic and natural fit.

In the days that followed, once word had finished circulating through the press that the Millers had pulled off the unthinkable, Giles immediately started receiving letters by the bagful from people across the country requesting money or looking for some sort of handout. Most of the

Dallas Texans stockholders. *Left to right. Front row:* J. Harlan Ray, Connell Miller, Giles Miller, D. Harold "Dry Hole" Byrd, and Harry Stewart. *Back row:* John J. Coyle, J. Curtis Sanford, Don Stewart, Fritz Hawn, and Jack C. Vaughn. Photo Courtesy of the *Fort Worth Star-Telegram* Collection, Special Collections, The University of Texas at Arlington Libraries.

solicitors likely believed that if Miller and his brother were rich—and crazy enough to invest their family fortune in a football league where forty-seven of the first fifty-eight franchises had failed—then perhaps they had money to burn and give away.

Giles later told *The Saturday Evening Post* that he considered each letter "a vote." He then laughed and added, "Electing me the nation's Number One Chump of 1952."[9]

Whether these letters were a sort of praise or nod to his stupidity, the deal had finally happened. Dallas had its first professional football team.

5

ESTABLISHING THE ORGANIZATION

AFTER THE MILLERS and their syndicate's purchase of the NFL's defunct Yanks franchise was completed, and the details of the transaction were released to the media, the *Los Angeles Examiner* published a cartoon in its sports section of a cowboy playing a guitar while singing a parody of the song "Home on the Range":

"Oh, give me a home where the millionaires roam,
And three hundred grand is just hay;
Where seldom is allowed a discouraging crowd,
And the Cotton Bowl's jammed every day!"

As the calendar turned to February of 1952, one of the first orders of business was to somehow recover the added Yankee Stadium obligation of $200,000 needed to secure the franchise. The plan was to have this taken care of in small annual payments over time, so Giles and Connell Miller decided that the best way to raise the monies was to establish additional shares of stock to be sold to investors. There would be 11,500 shares issued $10 per share, and the shares would be divided into available purchases of twenty-five blocks. As part of that, the twenty-five investors also had to contribute another $4,600 for every stock block purchased, which would bring in an extra $115,000. The total would surpass what was needed, so some of the investments would be used as seed money after the Yankee Stadium debt was responsibly paid off.

At Love Field in Dallas, a then-confident group of syndicate investors board a flight to Chicago for a get-acquainted retreat. Pictured from left to right are Fritz Hawn, John Coyle, Jack Vaughn, Frank Fitzgerald, Harlan Ray, and Giles Miller, all being shown off by head coach Jimmy Phelan. Photo courtesy of GEMCO Press and the Miller family.

Needing even more operating funds, Giles Miller offered $150,000 in bond certificates backed by debenture unsecured loan certificates placed with close friends and local businesses. In typical millionaire fashion, this was accomplished easily and was intended to take care of the initial start-up expenses.

For the organization's ongoing funds, Miller believed that revenues from ticket sales, the team's portion of away game guarantees, concessions, and radio broadcast rights would easily pay for their in-season expenses. Giles was quoted as saying, "We're confident in good bottom-line numbers for the team's first season."[1] Owning and managing an NFL franchise seemed like it was going to be easy.

Now on the agenda was to appoint a board of directors, and for this there would be a groundbreaking move in the male-dominated world of sports. The franchise would change the fabric of the league by hiring two women to serve among the team's leadership. The thought initially came about when Giles's wife Betty and Connell's wife Martha, both smart and savvy in business, rightfully decided that they could bring something to the table and contribute new and original ideas. Not only were they co-owners with their husbands, but together they became the first females to sit on the governing board of an NFL franchise.

There was no hesitation whatsoever from commissioner Bert Bell, as he was all for the move and quickly approved it. He respected family and applauded their initiative. With that, the board of directors was set. Along with the fourteen syndicate investors, the following eight additions made up the twenty-one board members:

- James Blanchette
- James Hudson
- Neth Leachman Sr.
- James H. Stewart
- Leonard Green
- Jack C. Vaughan
- Mrs. Betty Miller
- Mrs. Martha Miller

The next of the many tasks ahead was settling on the team's name, which the syndicate originally charted by applying for the franchise to be called the Texas Rangers. One of the board members made the suggestion, as the moniker had just the right jingle to it. But after some thought, Giles Miller weighed in, making it known that he wanted to be more aligned with his hometown of Dallas. He wanted fans to be focused on the actual city where they played and not so much the state, so the group quickly decided that the team would lead with Dallas. Still, the word Texas was extremely important to their identity, leading to the obvious conclusion to make the club's nickname "Texans." With that, the succession of the New York Yanks was finally complete. The NFL's newest franchise would be branded the Dallas Texans.

Miller was asked by one newspaper writer if he planned to outfit the new squad in vivid colors, or if there would be a more conservative theme. His wife, newly appointed board member Betty, answered, "Well,

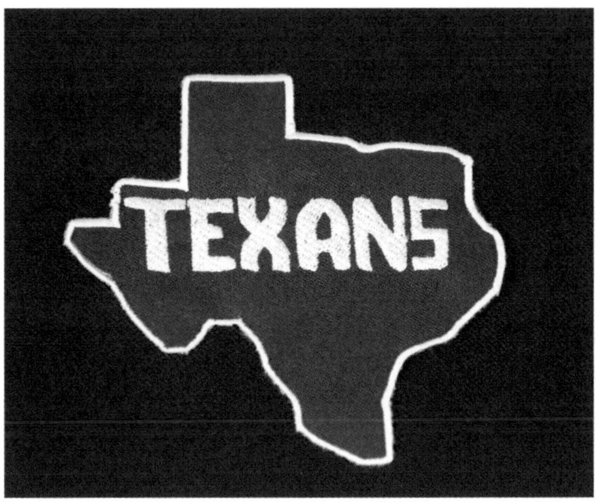

The patch worn on the right sleeve of both blue and white Texans jerseys. Photo courtesy of the author.

what do you think we'd do in a town where women sport blue jeans and mink coats?"[2]

Consequently, dressing the team on the field with a unique look was the next order of business. This was a serious matter to the brothers. Initially, they did not want to overthink it, so for whatever reason, whether it was thriftiness, keeping with the league's color mix, or simply the ownership's desired choice, the new color scheme did not change from its New York days. The primary colors would stay navy blue and white with an accent of silver.

The thought was to keep the colors but incorporate something innovative. Home jerseys would be blue with white block numbers and no striping on the sleeves. There was a patch placed on the left shoulder sleeve with the name "Texans" displayed inside an outline of the state. The road jersey would be an almost exact replica of what was worn in New York: white with three evenly placed blue stripes on both sleeves and the same Texas state logo.

An idea was conceptualized to have the pants designed with an outline of holsters and pistols stitched into the sides. Thankfully, that notion was quickly abandoned due its complexity. Instead, simple white pants with one blue stripe down the side of each leg would be worn with both the road and home jerseys. On certain occasions, there would be silver pants donned.

A little-known fact lost to time was a detail included on the hooded raincoat capes worn on the sideline. Much like the rest of the league, they were a simple and durable one-color gray with the team's name stenciled in blue, with "Dallas" arched over the top and "Texans" lined straight across the mid-back level. In between the two words was a precursor of things to come. The opening was just the right amount of space for a simple star logo, placed to represent the Lone Star State. The Texans did not intend to use the star as any type of primary insignia, but of course it would later become the prominent symbol of another NFL franchise, the Cowboys.

For the all-important headgear, a little art deco design took over. The glossy blue helmet remained but was highlighted by a uniquely wide white stripe that began over the entire front portion of the shell and moved across the top of the head to the rear, where it tapered into a thickness of just one inch. Prior to the use of helmet logos, the Texans would certainly stand out, at least style-wise. When seen in images and on film, fans would know who the team was.

There was much more to be done. By virtue of not bringing any management staff from New York, the Miller brothers would need to build an organization from scratch and do so rather quickly. The lack of holdover experience, though, turned out to be a blessing in disguise. Had any of the previous staff been included with the acquisition, they would have been an undesirable option since Giles and Connell wanted a fresh start. They didn't need the potential headache of having relocated, disgruntled employees. However, there was one man being pushed hard by Bell, who wanted to keep a close eye on the progress of the new franchise. Bell needed a mole.

Bell was very concerned with the young owners having no experience in the world of sports management. Wanting to install someone with prior industry knowledge to deal with running the football operations, he convinced the brothers to move holdover general manager Frank J. Fitzgerald into a key management position. That way Bell could keep a better eye on things from his faraway perch in Philadelphia.

The Texans' innovative helmet featured a unique wide stripe that began over the entire front portion and tapered across to the back side. Prior to the use of logos, the design stood out. Photos courtesy of the author.

Incidentally, Fitzgerald was Ted Collins's son-in-law. With encouragement from Bell, he was hired, but the marriage was short-lived. It did not take long before Fitzgerald began butting heads with some of the new staff and board members, including the brothers themselves, over office procedure and player acquisition moves. Within a hot second, Fitzgerald packed his bags and left Texas in a blaze on his way back to New York City, never acclimating himself to the Dallas way of life. He never even received the ten-gallon hat that was promised to him.

For the team's next hire, enter Hamilton Prieleaux Bee Maule, more commonly known as Tex. The brothers wanted a big promotional push for their new team, and having seen what had happened in Los Angeles and the success gained there, they sought out Maule, who was the number two marketing man in the Rams organization to Tex Schramm. The Millers offered an employment agreement of $7,000 for one year, paying him as much as Schramm was receiving from the Rams, with a change in title to publicity director, thus making his move a promotion of sorts. Maule could call his own shots while having the potential to move up the ladder to a general manager role later.

Florida born, Maule played college football at St. Mary's University before going into the navy as a merchant seaman during World War II. Upon leaving the military, he was a trapeze artist for the Ringling Bros. and Barnum & Baily Circus until landing with the Rams in 1946. His training in the world of entertainment would turn out to be beneficial for Maule, because soon the Texans franchise would be masquerading as a professional football team when in reality they were closer to being clowns.

Just as with the board of directors, the hiring of the capable Maule also met the approval of Bell. But the commissioner was not always agreeable, and he meant what he said when he decreed that he would need to okay everything and everyone.

The time had come to find a radio broadcast sponsor, and Connell insisted on driving this project. Of course, both he and Giles wanted to have their friend Gordon McLendon involved. His Liberty Broadcast Network, along with his local station KLIF, would be the perfect marriage. Acquiring a good and stable sponsor would bring top dollars to the club, so it was important for them to find someone with whom the franchise would be comfortable.

It was public knowledge that the brothers were close to McLendon, who was almost like family; however, Bell was more than apprehensive. He was dead set against the team being involved with him due to a lingering lack of trust. Already planning to come down to Dallas in the very near future to conduct an orientation meeting, Bell told the brothers to hold off on any decisions until they could all meet in person and discuss the issue. But before the trip happened, and much to Bell's satisfaction, McLendon's Liberty Broadcasting venture was thrown into an involuntary bankruptcy.

For Bell, it was problem solved. Of course, what was good news to him was bad news for Giles and Connell, who were upset over how this turn of events might affect the broadcast agreement they wanted.

With Fitzgerald gone, Bell had made it clear that he wanted to only use Giles Miller as his point person for all things related to the Dallas franchise, but on this occasion he reached out to the newly hired Maule for any potential damage control. Bell wanted to have a conservation with both Maule and Miller to discuss how to handle the whole subject of the Liberty scandal. The new owners had taken over a previously bankrupt team and did not need any further guilt by association with their "undesirable friend," as he put it.

Bell said to lead with the simple message that "there was no contract between the Liberty Broadcasting Network and the Dallas Texans and there never would be."[3] Beyond that, he let Miller know that he really needed to deemphasize any sort of relationship between himself and McLendon to the public. Bell's charge to Miller was to let Maule do his job in finding an adequate and honest broadcast partner that he could present to the both of them for approval. He added that Miller's focus should be on ticket sales.

Throughout all of this, McClendon continued to put out feelers in an attempt to copartner with another provider to obtain the game broadcasts. His hope was to somehow still share in the revenue stream. But as a man of his word, Miller began to distance himself from the situation, not wanting to get on Bell's bad side this early. Miller wanted Maule to look for other broadcasting possibilities and quickly get the issue wrapped up to avoid any confrontation between McLendon and the commissioner.

Maule carefully thought through the situation and saw that the problem wasn't with the station itself; the obstacle was McLendon and his perceived attachment to the endeavor. Ultimately, Maule was able to broker a pact, convincing the commissioner to soften his stance and let McLendon's KLIF radio station broadcast the games, as it was the one of the best in the country. But at the same time, McLendon would have no part of any sponsorship or operational involvement.

Listening to reason, Bell proclaimed that the station itself would be approved, but he wanted McLendon nowhere near the team or its ownership. Maule had overcome a huge hurdle, Bell was able to impose his will, and the brothers got the partner they wanted in KLIF.

By mid-February 1952, the league released all of the Yanks' leftover assets and shipped them down to Dallas. There was excitement and anticipation building as an allegedly full truckload of supplies, player contracts, records, and equipment came rolling down south to their new home. The Millers were about to receive the world's largest Christmas present. The assumption was that the tractor trailer carried the contents of a ready-made team.

Upon arrival, the brothers and staff were taken aback when the door was opened. It was like some sort of practical joke. The truck was virtually empty. There was nothing remotely resembling anything close to football contents, aside from a couple of file cabinets and a few boxes of old paperwork. Unbeknownst to Bell, the weight room and field equipment, along with everything else, had been sold off by Collins in an attempt to recover his losses. While Connell and Giles didn't anticipate receiving anything that was bolted down in New York or a lifetime supply of ankle tape, they did expect to at least be sent one football. They weren't, which meant this was going to be yet another set of unplanned expenses.

Even before the truckload setback, a myriad of details still lingered. On February 18, a board meeting was held where it was proposed and approved to lease club and ticket offices at the corner of McKinney Avenue and North Akard Street for $500 a month from J. Curtis Sanford, the same J. Curtis Sanford who was on the team's board of directors.

Once it became apparent that there were no real assets, such as office supplies or furniture, Giles Miller went on a shopping spree. He went with Sanford and fellow board member Jack Vaughn to the Kathy Office Supply store nearby and purchased all the necessary equipment for the new office setup on credit terms. In fact, he bought more than they needed.

After all the furnishings had been delivered, a few others in the organization started to bring in some high-end additions of their own. Vaughn provided an ancient Etruscan couch to the merriment of everyone there. The place was filling up fast, and eclectic quickly became tacky.

Contributing to all the mad spending, Sanford commissioned a king-sized, framed portrait of Doak Walker attached to the lobby wall over Vaughn's antique sofa. This unlikely mismatch was located directly adjacent to the framed Certificate of Membership issued by the league.

Next was securing a lease to use Burnett Field, a ten-thousand-seat minor league baseball park, as the team's practice site. South of Dallas in the Oak Cliff neighborhood, the grounds were centrally located and close enough to everything. Of course, the team would share the facility with some other occupants. Because the field was close to the Trinity River, rats had set up a base camp in the locker rooms, an unpleasant problem that lasted for decades.

There was only one option available for the team to use on Sundays, and it was a good one. The Cotton Bowl was a jewel nestled in the heart of the Fair Park area of Dallas and was only twenty-two years old, although recent expansions over the previous four years meant that 40 percent of the stadium was practically brand-new. Unlike many of its NFL counterparts, the stadium was specifically built for football and could be considered the best field in the league going into the 1952 season. The Cotton Bowl also had plenty of seats, instantly becoming the second largest in the NFL in terms of capacity. The brothers negotiated an attractive deal with the city and Fair Park officials to lease the stadium for a mere fee of $60,000 for their six home games. Having an adequate NFL-caliber facility was one thing that could easily be checked off as completed.

While some observers questioned the league's decision to place a pro team in an area that was so predominantly devoted to the college game, others questioned the Miller brothers' sanity. Either way, most saw it as a futile attempt to achieve different results with the pieces and parts that had failed in two other cities.

To help in this matter, many newfangled thoughts on how to market the team were being thrown about. One idea was that during pregame introductions, each Texans player would ride out on horseback. Seemingly not considered was that several of the players had never been on a horse before, or that the horses might soil the field. What could possibly go wrong? Another idea was that when replacement players came in as substitutions during the game, they would run onto the field carrying the Texas state flag, passing it off to the player headed to the sidelines.

For traveling, the Miller wives had planned on outfitting the team in full Western wear with cowboy boots and hats. They commissioned Ripley's of Dallas Supreme Quality Tailors to design snap-button shirts in the club's colors with the logo and team name prominently displayed. The balance of the ensemble would come from Fort Worth Stockyard clothing merchants. Onlookers would know who the Texans were, never mind that the team could not play in these "uniforms."

In late February, Commissioner Bell traveled down for the first of his several preplanned status checks. Originally, he was to spend two working days in town. He would wind up staying longer.

During the offseason, it was almost unheard of for Bell to travel outside of his Pennsylvania base. Traveling to see games during the season was one thing, but afterward he simply did not like to take trips and usually would go no farther than Atlantic City. But for this venture, since creating the Dallas franchise was primarily his own doing, he wanted to take on the added oversight.

With Bell arriving at the railroad station late on a Wednesday night, Giles arranged transportation for him to check in at one of Dallas's finest locales, the Baker Hotel, courtesy of the team. The next morning, the Millers went to the Baker and met the commissioner for breakfast. There was a Salesmanship Club of Dallas press conference being held there later that morning to announce the sponsorship of a Texans exhibition game with the Detroit Lions. Bell was impressed that the brothers had taken initiative and already made a good football decision that would also

Western-themed shirts were commissioned by Connell's wife, Martha. They were worn by family and board members as game-day apparel and by the players when traveling. Pictured is Martha's shirt, which she wore to every game. Photos courtesy of Connell Miller Jr. and the Miller family.

benefit local charities. He couldn't wait to hear what else they had accomplished.

After attending the press conference, Bell wanted to see some of the city, so Giles Miller took him on a drive around town. They went aimlessly through neighborhoods and by area attractions. Their conversation started out strong, as they were able to avoid telephone calls and other interruptions. But while riding along, Bell asked about the plan for other summer games before the final Detroit matchup. Miller told him that he had agreed with Washington just the day before to play in San Antonio at some point. Quickly agitated, the commissioner bellowed, "Fine. That's two. What about the rest?"[4] Bell let him know that both the Eagles and Steelers had already made all their arrangements.

Given the very short amount of time Miller had been involved with the team, Bell's question took him by surprise. Although a quick starter, he felt he should not be expected to have everything already laid out like the established teams that had been in the league for years.

As the drive continued, the commissioner then inquired about training camp sites. When Giles responded that he didn't yet have any idea where they would go, Bell barked, "You should have known from the first outset," before also adding, "I've counted on you being a full-time owner on the job."[5]

Sensing that their discussion would consistently turn to what he had not done so far, Miller explained that he never considered devoting more than part of his time to the operations of the team and that he would appoint some fellow board members and staff to become more involved with the day-to-day functions. He wanted to utilize his talents to promote and market.

Bell again voiced that he expected to communicate with only one person in Dallas and that Miller could not perform his necessary duties if he was spending his time on other affairs. The air was tense throughout the afternoon, and Miller felt like crashing the car. After starting the day out so well and attending the press conference, the old commissioner had raised his expectations to a higher level than where they should have been. He wanted seasoned perfection that Miller did not see coming.

Bell's tough love approach just did not work, at least from Miller's perspective. He was a beginner. What he really needed was more guidance and less criticism.

After the drive was finally over, the two returned to the hotel where Bell changed his clothes and got ready for the evening. A team-hosted buffet dinner awaited at the Brook Hollow Country Club. Day one had started out with optimism but ended with criticism.

Day two would bring a tour of Fair Park's grounds. Having never seen the stadium in person, Bell wanted to get an up close look at the Cotton Bowl. His plan was to wait out the morning at the hotel, working on other league business, and arrive there in the afternoon. This was so that he could personally see how the venue would appear during actual game times. He was more than impressed with the facilities, particularly with the large number of available lower- and upper-deck sideline seats. The Cotton Bowl was completely devoted to football, unlike the baseball stadiums most of the league utilized, which often had obstructed views, bad seating angles, and lacked ample seats between the goal lines. Seeing the Cotton Bowl firsthand was something even the gruff Bell could find no fault with.

Later that evening another dinner event was held, this time at the Mercantile National Bank Building with over one hundred businessmen and professionals in attendance. Once again, however, Bell became critical. He wondered why, with all of this income available under one roof, the team didn't have any sort of season ticket or sales plan presentation for an event where people received a free dinner that they could have easily paid for. A nondrinking man himself, he huffed, "You're getting rich people liquored up and not taking advantage of them spending money to help the league cause."[6] He left the event early while the rest of the party stayed and talked football, enjoying his absence.

By Saturday morning, Bell had decided to stay longer. He went to see the team's offices and hoped to spend much of the day discussing ticket policy. After seeing the layout of the Cotton Bowl, Bell wanted to understand what their thoughts were regarding the potential of premium pricing for the side seats of both decks.

Miller was ready for the pop question, but the answer didn't go over well. He commented to Bell that basically two-thirds of the seats were between the goal lines and would be sold as reserved. It was his intention to set the end zone area prices at half the rate and as nonreserved. All those reserved seats would be the same single price, first come, first serve.

Bell was quick to agree on the end zone discounting while explaining his point of view that those fans provided noise and rang the cash register at the concession stands. Spending less on their ticket, they could spend more on food and drink.

Before Giles could get around to disclosing that the end zones would be primarily segregated seating for African Americans, something that Bell did not know, the commissioner got off on a tangent as to why a seat three rows up on the 50-yard line would sell for the same price as an upper-deck seat midway up on the 20-yard line. He then took a seating diagram and practically set the price for the tickets himself. Miller decided to withhold any further input, accept Bell's points, and call it a day. He did not follow the bracket-pricing advice, however, instead going with his gut.

Talking civilly wasn't going to happen. Bell still believed that Miller and company should already know how to run a franchise.

The following day, Sunday, was to be a full board of directors meeting held in the game room of Giles's home. Bell had already decided to show up and was invited to attend. He had never seen any NFL owner with a residence as large and palatial as Miller's twenty-room mansion.

After listening to the agenda and commentary play out, Bell asked to speak to the group. He expressed his opinion about ticket prices and pointed out the urgency to get sales underway immediately. He also wanted to let everyone know, from his mouth, that a massive opportunity had been missed two nights ago at the Mercantile dinner event.

He went over the key rules of the league and the quirky rules of his own. For someone who was steadfast in his desire to only deal with one person, it seemed odd to Giles that Bell was basically training the Texans staff on how to approach and deal with him. In typical fashion, and with class, Miller let it go and didn't challenge the loud voice of the league. He bid the commissioner farewell and safe travels, offering Earl Goins to take him to the station. Bell left on a late afternoon train, having put in a full four days of work in Dallas. The visit was the first time where he demonstrated his art of micromanaging and criticizing.

REPRESENTING DALLAS IN THE NATIONAL CONFERENCE OF THE NATIONAL FOOTBALL LEAGUE

The Dallas TEXANS

FOOTBALL CLUB, INC.

1721 McKinney Avenue · Dallas 1, Texas RIverside 5836

Of all the start-up purchases the organization made, perhaps the most sensible was the teams stationery. Shown here is the letterhead used at the team offices. Photo courtesy of the author.

After passing the first test with Bell, optimism returned. Whether or not the brothers could be considered visionaries, courageous, fools for punishment, or just plain crazy, they nevertheless remained completely confident and enthusiastic in what they were doing. Giles Miller prophetically proclaimed, "There is room enough in Texas for all kinds of football," whether it be at the high school, college, or pro level.[7] He also added, "The Texans are going to field a stem-winder of a team next fall."[8]

In order to field that team, they now needed a coach. It was the one big decision still pending.

6

SETTING UP THE STAFF

AN IMPORTANT CALL WAS LOOMING—who would be the on-field face of the team, its head coach? Determining this would be perhaps the most important item on the to-do list. A qualified candidate had to be found quickly, as player decisions would soon need to be made.

Wanting a well-respected name, someone who was accepted by the locals, Giles Miller created excitement with rumors of hiring up-and-comer Paul "Bear" Bryant. He would one day become a legend as the head coach at the University of Alabama. There was also talk of bringing in Blair Cherry, who recently had enjoyed tremendous success at the University of Texas, where he took the Longhorns to three bowl games over a four-year span from 1947–50 while never experiencing a losing record.

Sammy Baugh was a local hero from Texas Christian University and was winding down a hall of fame career with the Washington Redskins. He had recently expressed interest in becoming a full-time head coach or even a player-coach and would have been the perfect selection for the Texans, had owner George Preston Marshall released him from his contract in Washington.

Alas, none of these were to be, and frankly, none had any interest in joining a team that no one had ever heard of. Tex Maule continued spreading word around the country regarding the search for a big-time name, attempting to create the illusion that this was a highly sought-after position. But there were just no takers.

Standing patiently on the sidelines, watching and waiting, was Yanks holdover head coach James Phelan. Since the start of the rumored relocation in January, he had wondered about his future and if he would have one with the new team. Phelan seemed to be the only man in the country who actually wanted the job.

So by default, Miller quickly made the decision to retain Phelan's services, convincing the coach that he had been the top choice from the beginning. The whimsical Irishman, known to all as Jimmy, was the only man with the luxury of understanding just what he was getting into, having overseen these players during their last year in New York.

A proven winner prior to the Yanks, Phelan was ready to put the indignity of the previous season's 1-9-2 record behind him. He had been a head coach for half of his life and was not accustomed to losing. As a college player at Notre Dame, his assistant coach was Knute Rockne, and he quarterbacked the Fighting Irish to sixteen victories out of twenty appearances. When he began coaching, it was no different. With stops at Missouri, Purdue, Washington, and Saint Mary's, he had an overall career win-loss record that few could match, a 136-82-14 mark.

In the collegiate ranks, he had never suffered through a season like 1951. Up to that point, it was the most monumental disappointment of his career—emphasis on *up to that point*. Phelan would need to build a new staff in Dallas that could mold this team of no-name talent into something respectable. However, he would soon have more responsibilities than just being a coach.

In order to fill the void left by Frank Fitzgerald's departure and save payroll dollars, Phelan was also given the additional title of general manager. He was not particularly thrilled with the move, as there would be no salary increase to take on the added responsibilities. Business dealings were not his forte; on the field activities were.

His desire to find his own coaching staff was most important to him. Staffs were smaller in those days, and very often the assistants would teach and oversee multiple positions. The previous season in New York, Phelan had inherited a staff and had no opportunity to implement any sort of plan. He used most of his time to become acclimated with the players he was given. In Dallas, the situation would be different. None of his three assistants in New York would be making the move south, although admittedly he not only didn't want them, but they didn't want to prolong their own agony either.

As GM, Phelan took over supervision of Maule, and he quickly hired Al Ennis to become the business manager of daily operations. Mat Corley was then brought on as ticket manager to handle the team's gate distribution with John B. Chester being named the team physician. The Texans did not want to employ a full-time doctor, so he was subcontracted. For the financial responsibilities, those would go to two board members who would report directly to the Miller brothers. J. Curtis Sanford was given the title of franchise general secretary, while Fritz Hahn became treasurer.

With the administrative roles now set, coaching positions were next. First up was the line coach, which in New York had been under the guidance of Shelby Calhoun. The Louisiana transplant and former player had been on the staff for two seasons prior to Phelan taking over. Calhoun would be replaced by a young Alex Agase. Agase was a three-time All-American guard and linebacker at the University of Illinois before finding a successful pro career with the Cleveland Browns, winning three championships. Illinois born and raised, he served as a marine in World War II and was still only twenty-nine. This was his first coaching opportunity.

The ends coach in New York was Nick Susoeff, who had only one year of coaching experience. A former end himself, he played for the San Francisco 49ers, accumulating good statistics there. Susoeff would be followed by forty-year-old William Thomas "Willie" Walls. Born in Arkansas, Walls, as the old saying goes, "Got to Texas as soon as he could." After attending TCU, he served in the navy during World War II and then went on to play six seasons in the NFL for the New York Giants. Before joining the Texans, Walls had been a head coach at both the high school and junior college levels.

The position of backfield coach usually ranked as the highest among the assistants. In New York, Joe Sheeketski had served in the role and was the elder statesman at forty-four years of age. A former Notre Dame man as well, he had been a head coach at two universities and actually served as an FBI agent during the war. Like the others, he wouldn't be making the move, so the opportunity presented itself to Cecil Isbell.

Houston-born Isbell was a thirty-seven-year-old future College Football Hall of Famer. Coming out of Purdue, he was a first-round draft selection of the Green Bay Packers and learned the art of offense under Curley Lambeau, the legendary head coach, who took Isbell under his wing and taught him the game's finer nuances. Upon retirement as a player, Isbell became an assistant at Purdue and later was the Boilermakers' head coach. He moved to the new All-American Football Conference, serving as the Baltimore Colts bench boss, before returning to work as an assistant under Lambeau with the Chicago Cardinals. Isbell had trained under one of the NFL's founding icons; by the time he moved to Dallas—and finally found his way home to Texas—he was by far the most knowledgeable member on the Texans staff, becoming Phelan's right-hand man.

For his final coaching hire, Phelan added another young and bright local man to a newly created position. Bruce Alford was a thirty-one-year-old former TCU player who was twice named All-Southwest Conference as well as the Most Valuable Player of the 1942 Orange Bowl. Like many, he too served during World War II, then afterward returned to the game, playing for the Yanks. No doubt he would be uniquely qualified and already familiar with the players. Alford's formal title was simply assistant coach, and he would be a Swiss Army knife of sorts, the low man on the staff. It did not matter to him, though, as he was very happy to be the only assistant to have transferred with the team, albeit as a former player turned fresh-faced, first-year coach.

The Texans would also need a new trainer to replace August G. Mauch, who had handled the duties in New York and would not be making the move. He was older and had no wish to relocate south, but his assistant with the Yanks was an acquaintance of Phelan's from his college days.

Raymond West, also known as "Chief," was a full-blooded Cheyenne Indian who had attended and graduated from the Haskell Institute in Lawrence, Kansas, which was a Native American school. He played sports, mainly basketball, and was once on an all-star traveling team with the legendary Jim Thorpe. Marketing themselves by using Thorpe's name, the team toured the country playing against anyone they could line up. In addition, Chief had held training positions at the universities of Florida, Georgia, and finally Saint Mary's College while also serving as an assistant basketball coach at each.

Phelan's final move would be to find someone to handle the equipment and supply duties. He didn't know anything about the equipment manager he brought on board, Willie Garcia. In fact, Phelan wasn't even sure Garcia had ever actually seen a football game. Nevertheless, Garcia knew the Millers. At the time, he was managing a Mexican restaurant that the brothers owned. He was a hard worker who would carry out the duties of cleaning, upkeep, inflating the balls, mending uniforms, and just about anything else that needed attention. Notably, Garcia also had a wooden leg that would wind up serving him well during the team's upcoming training camp.

The sideline leadership was set, led by the cranky, silver-haired Phelan with his many years of football knowledge and head coaching experience. He had now appointed four new assistant coaches, all but one having native Texas ties and each younger than his predecessor. These relative greenhorns were now a unit. Things were coming together, at least on paper.

When Phelan finally arrived at the team's offices for the first time, he was completely aghast upon seeing the Doak Walker wall. Glancing toward the opposite wall, he saw the team's membership declaration, "Dallas Texans Football Club, Inc."—so he knew he had to be in the right place. With a strong voice directed toward everyone, he howled, "Doak is a Lions star, not a Texan!"[1] Standing nearby, Sanford responded that everyone in Dallas knew and admired Walker, and it was a big improvement over the bare wall. Furthermore, he didn't know any of the team's players yet.

Although he disagreed, Phelan managed to live with the framed annoyance. And not just because Sanford was one of the highest-ranking board members with a financial interest in the franchise. More importantly, the painting was adhered to the wall—it simply wasn't coming off.

The Walker infatuation continued and led to yet another bold, or naïve, scheme to make a Texas-sized splash and push ticket sales. Giles's proposition was to present an offer of $250,000 in cash to the eventual 1952 champion Detroit Lions as a contract buyout for the services of the local legend. Translated, it meant that the Texans would assume Walker's contract, still paying him what was already agreed upon, after also paying the Lions the substantial sum to acquire him. Never mind how, and if, they could come up with the money. The possibility of having Walker come home and play on the same field where he starred in college, in a stadium that had come to be known as the house he built, was as good as any guarantee that all their games would sell out. Some media outlets around the country even began to circulate bogus reports that the agreement was a done deal between the teams. PR man Maule may or may not have planted that information himself.

The thought of Walker being brought to Dallas was put to the ultimate test one afternoon when Jack C. Vaughn, who at twenty-seven was the youngest of the millionaire owners, dropped by the McKinney Avenue offices for a chat with Coach Phelan. He wanted to be involved and talk about the players to gain a better understanding of what they had talent-wise. Once the conversation turned to the position of halfback, he propped his feet on the coach's desk and said, "You know, Jimmy, it's a shame that a fine Dallas boy like Doak Walker, probably the greatest football player who ever lived, has to work for the Detroit Lions. Why, if we don't do something quick, Doak will be down here playing against us in Dallas."[2]

He then stood up and proclaimed, "Here's a starter amount to use," as he rummaged through his pants pockets, finally locating a stack of one-hundred-dollar bills that he flipped onto the coach's desk. Vaughn told Phelan that he was opening up the money pot with $8,000, adding in reference to his fellow board members, "You get the other boys to match it, then you'll have about $100,000 and you can hop up to Detroit and buy Doak's contract."[3]

Calmly, and very wisely, Phelan gathered up the pile of money, restacked it, and slid the wad of bills back over to Vaughan. He then said, "No use in going to Detroit because the Lions would not make that trade unless we gave them the $100,000 and someone to take his place. Right now, we don't have anybody here who would interest them."[4]

Giles Miller *(center)* and Frank Fitzgerald *(right)* finalizing terms with head coach Jimmy Phelan *(left)* at the Texans offices. Photo courtesy of Ed Miller and the Miller family.

After Vaughn got up and departed from the offices, his $8,000 back in his pocket, Phelan glanced over at Isbell, who had heard the entire exchange. He looked at his assistant and shook his head in disbelief, saying, "What's money? It can't buy halfbacks."[5]

The cash-for-player transfer, as well as the pool that Vaughn had attempted to put together, was unheard of—both the trade idea and sum of money. After all, the syndicate had only paid $300,000 for the entire franchise. Once the reality hit Phelan that the Millers were serious about acquiring Walker, and this wasn't a prank, the potential of a deal happening was put to rest. There was absolutely no interest from either Detroit or Walker to participate in the charade. Thankfully, Phelan had managed to protect the brothers from their own ignorance.

Giles and Connell Miller continued to generate a plethora of ever-changing ideas while dabbling in some of the general manager duties they had placed on Phelan. Meanwhile, the old coach rolled up his sleeves and began the work of assembling the on-field product that the brothers had bought the privilege to lose money on.

7

FILLING THE ROSTER

THE ROSTER-BUILDING PROCESS had already begun in earnest, if you count the failed publicity attempt by Connell and Giles Miller to lure Doak Walker to Dallas. Ironically, he could have been back in his hometown had Ted Collins and the Yanks not foolishly traded away his draft rights three years prior as they were rebranding themselves the New York Bulldogs. At that time, Walker had another year of eligibility remaining at SMU, and Collins could not wait for the sure thing. Their loss was Detroit's gain.

To add further insult to injury, the player they acquired in the trade of Walker to Detroit—John Rauch, who was drafted second overall in 1949, one spot ahead of Walker—was no longer on the Yanks roster either, having been traded away himself midway through the 1951 campaign. So the Dallas Texans not only would have no Walker, they had no Rauch as well.

Exactly thirteen days before the franchise purchase was made, the NFL draft had been held on January 17 at the Hotel Statler in New York City. Featuring twelve teams, the selection process covered thirty rounds. With its exemplary record of 1-9-2 in 1951, the franchise would be selecting at the top of the list in nearly every round. But because the ownership change had yet to occur, the Yanks staff made all of the team's choices that were later assigned to the new ownership group in Dallas.

Although long and arduous, the draft was marked by quality over quantity, as the Yanks staff did a much better job at selecting new talent than their cohorts had done on the field in developing it. The New Yorkers tabbed three men who would eventually become Pro Football Hall of

Famers. Two of them would earn the honor with other teams, and one would get there by way of an administrative role later in life, rather than what he did on the field. As for the two recognized by their on-field performance, one would be traded away without contributing so much as to one single play in Dallas, while the other would stay and become a future cornerstone of the franchise.

Twenty-eight college players were taken by the club over the thirty rounds. One player, their first pick, was traded while nine would eventually be signed for training camp. These ten players were:

• Round one (2nd overall)—Les Richter, Guard, University of California. Twice a consensus All-American at the University of California, Berkley, Richter played guard and linebacker for the Golden Bears and could also be called on to serve as the backup kicker. But in the largest trade for a single player in NFL history, the Texans sent Richter away that summer prior to their inaugural 1952 season for a hefty return. It would later prove to be a mistake if ever there was one. Over his nine-year career, Richter would earn eight trips to the Pro Bowl and four first-team All-Pro honors on his way to the Pro Football Hall of Fame.

• Round two (14th overall)—Gino Marchetti, Defensive End, University of San Francisco. A massive defensive end and offensive tackle, Marchetti was born in West Virginia and raised in California as the son of Italian immigrants. He enlisted in the US Army upon graduating high school and fought in the Battle of the Bulge during World War II as a machine gunner. Afterward, he attended Modesto Junior College for one year and then joined the football program at USF. If anything, his accomplishments as a pro were actually more impressive than Richter's. Marchetti went to the Pro Bowl eleven times and was an All-Pro in nine seasons. A hall of famer as well, he was also named to the NFL's 100 All-Time Team.

• Round five (53rd overall)—Mel Sinquefield, Center, University of Mississippi. A Mississippi native, Sinquefield developed into a star lineman in high school, earning a scholarship to Ole Miss. He was named the top-rated center in the Southeastern Conference and was awarded a spot on the Senior Bowl in 1952.

• Round seven (74th overall)—John Petitbon, Back, Notre Dame. Petitbon was a legendary high school player from Louisiana where he was a three-sport athlete.

• Round nine (98th overall)—Jim Lansford, Offensive Tackle, University of Texas. This brought the team a native Texan. Lansford was a much sought-after high school recruit who chose to stay close to home and play for the Longhorns.

• Round ten (110th overall)—Jim Hammond, Back, University of Wisconsin. A high school star athlete in three sports, Hammond was known for his versatility. He was a legend at Wisconsin as a member of the famous "Hard Rocks" defensive team while also being named a Badgers team captain.

• Round eleven (122nd overall)—Pat Cannamela, Guard, University of Southern California. Three different publications selected him to All-American teams.

• Round eighteen (206th overall)—Les Molnar, Offensive Tackle, University of Buffalo. Much like the others, his college playing career had been interrupted in 1950 by being drafted into the US Marine Corps.

• Round nineteen (218th overall)—Gene Felker, End, University of Wisconsin. He had been a college teammate of Hammond's, playing receiver and defense for the Badgers' "Hard Rocks" unit.

• Round twenty-six (302nd overall)—George Young, Defensive Tackle, Bucknell University. Very late in the draft, the team selected this little-known prospect. After becoming an outstanding lineman in high school, Young attended Bucknell University and had a three-year varsity career with the Bisons, serving as a team captain in his final season. Young gave football his all as a player, but he had many other backup interests that included coaching or even something in sports administration should life as a defensive tackle not work out. This is exactly what happened. Young would one day become a member of the Pro Football Hall of Fame after earning NFL Executive of the Year honors five times as the general manager of the New York Giants.

The soon-to-be Texans franchise did not own a pick in rounds three, four, and eight, as they all had been previously traded away. This left eighteen remaining players who were selected over the course of the affair. None of them would take the next step and be signed to attend training camp.

Those players included:

- Round five (50th overall)—Jack Jorgenson, Offensive Tackle, Colorado.
- Round six (62nd overall)—Dave Cianelli, Center, Maryland.
- Round twelve (134th overall)—Jim Mutscheller, End, Notre Dame.
- Round thirteen (146th overall)—Bill Ward, Guard, Arkansas.
- Round fourteen (158th overall)—Paul Williams, End, Texas.
- Round fifteen (170th overall)—Jack Bighead, End, Pepperdine.
- Round sixteen (182nd overall)—Vince Kaseta, End, Tennessee.
- Round seventeen (194th overall)—Dick Horn, Back, Stanford.
- Round twenty (230th overall)—John Adams, End, Texas.
- Round twenty-one (242nd overall)—Harry Hugasian, Back, Stanford.
- Round twenty-two (254th overall)—Dean Schneider, Back, USC.
- Round twenty-three (266th overall)—Chet Freeman, Back, LSU.
- Round twenty-four (278th overall)—Bob Ward, Guard, Maryland.
- Round twenty-five (290th overall)—Jim Monihan, Back, Rutgers.
- Round twenty-seven (314th overall)—Gil Bartosh, Back, TCU.
- Round twenty-eight (326th overall)—Doug Moseley, Center, Kentucky.
- Round twenty-nine (338th overall)—Russ Hudeck, Offensive Tackle, Texas A&M.
- Round thirty (350th overall)—Ray Suchy, Guard, Nevada-Reno.

Ordinarily, the most valuable asset transferred with the sale of a team would be the people—the existing squad. The 1951 Yanks carried only thirty-six players on their roster during their final year. For a team that won only one game, it was a given that these castaways were not a group loaded with much talent.

Head coach Jimmy Phelan understood that the Texans simply inherited bodies, and not the league's best. From the thirty-six players, he and his staff decided to bring only some to Dallas for consideration, one of whom was Bruce Alford, moving to assistant coach. Of those who arrived, only fifteen plus Alford stuck around through training camp to make the opening-day roster. Some left of their own volition; others were cut by the team.

In need of whatever local talent they can find, the coaching staff watches a spring practice at TCU. Left to right are assistant coach Will Walls, head coach Jimmy Phelan, business manager Al Ennis, and assistant Bruce Alford. Photo courtesy of the *Fort Worth Star-Telegram* Collection, Special Collections, The University of Texas at Arlington Libraries.

Included in the group of sixteen was Don Colo, a brilliant player from Massachusetts entering his third season. He had served in the navy for three years and upon discharge went to Brown University where he earned All-Ivy League honors. Colo was a defensive tackle who had played his first season with Baltimore in the AAFC before joining New York.

Bennie Aldridge was one-quarter American Indian and from Oklahoma. He attended Oklahoma A&M and had tremendous speed as a kick returner and at his primary position of defensive back. Aldridge had spent two seasons in New York.

At twenty-seven years old, Sisto Averno was slightly older than most of the returning men. He was an Italian immigrant from New Jersey who served three years in the navy. Upon his discharge, he became a two-way player as an offensive guard and defensive tackle for tiny Muhlenberg College.

Brad Ecklund was a center known as "Whitey" because of his white hair. He too had served in the navy before enrolling at the University of Oregon, where he became a team captain. Ecklund originally began his pro career in the AAFC until his team was merged with New York. He had three years of pro experience.

Dan Edwards was Texas-born, raised in Gatesville. He attended the University of Georgia and was a great pass catcher in college, ranking second in the nation at one point and earning All-SEC honors in two of his years there. Edwards was drafted into the AAFC by Brooklyn in 1948 and was later assigned to the Yanks. In 1950, his first NFL season, he ranked second in receptions with fifty-two. He would be entering his fourth year.

Tough guy Barney Poole was a two-way player from Mississippi. With a large frame, he could play receiver, although his primary position was on defense. Poole was one of the only players in the history of college football to earn All-America honors four times. Moreover, it was not done in four consecutive years. He began his collegiate career at Army West Point, playing under legendary head coach Red Blaik for two seasons. As a junior who had to transfer after skipping the 1946 season, he played for the University of Mississippi for his final two years.

Another military man, Joe Soboleski was a Michigan-born offensive guard who played ball for Great Lakes Academy. Upon discharge, he attended the University of Michigan and made All-Big Ten. He had been with New York for one season after playing with Chicago of the AAFC as well as for the NFL's Washington Redskins and Detroit Lions.

Art Tait was from Tennessee and had starred at defensive end and as team captain for Mississippi State. He had one year of pro experience in New York and was entering his second season.

Nicknamed "Tugboat," Zollie Toth was a tough fullback out of Virginia who had attended LSU. He had been in New York for two seasons and had a sensational rookie year, finishing sixth in the league in rushing yards, totaling 636.

John Wozniak was the senior member of the New York transplants. Originally from Pennsylvania, he had been a four-year captain at the University of Alabama. He was a reliable offensive lineman and would be an important locker room presence, bringing much-needed veteran leadership.

For the all-important position of quarterback, Bob Celeri proved to be the only one still on the New York roster. A classic competitor and overachiever, he had attended the University of California, Berkley after serving two years in the navy. Celeri was entering his second season, having started the most games (eight) during the team's final year in New York. As a rookie, he had been called the "Cinderella Man" going into the 1951 season after narrowly escaping being cut by Phelan.

Mike McCormack was a University of Kansas guy who could walk into any room and command attention. Entering his second season as an offensive tackle, he had great physical size. He started all but one game in his first year and earned the unusual distinction of being named to the 1951 Pro Bowl squad as a rookie. After the season, due to the events around the Korean War at the time, McCormack enlisted. With his name placed, it was not known yet when he would be called up for duty or if there would even be a 1952 football season ahead for him. For now, Phelan loved what he saw in McCormack and hoped he would be a big part of their team should things work out favorably.

All the relocating players were important, but one under special consideration was a man who would become one of the key contributors in the franchise's history. He was truly a character who became legendary as one of football's greatest late bloomers—Arthur James Donovan Jr.

Known as Art or Artie, he had been completely at home living in New York. Bronx-born and a self-admitted fat guy who played tackle, he could take up a lot of room on the defensive line. Donovan had begun his college career at Notre Dame but quit after only one semester. He then joined the marines in 1943 and served three years during World War II, based in the Pacific theatre. Upon his discharge, he resumed his amateur career at Boston College.

He got his pro start with the AAFC's Baltimore Colts, and once the league was dissolved, the Cleveland Browns owned his rights. But because the fun-loving Donovan did not mesh with head coach Paul Brown's disciplinary approach, Brown promptly traded Donovan to the Yanks.

Before he ever signed his first contract to play professional football, Donovan asked a longtime family friend for career advice. The man replied, "There's no future in the pro game in general," and he went further, stating, "and there's no future for YOU in this game in particular."[1] However, jokester and novelty that he was, Donovan would be a huge part of the upcoming season, both literally and figuratively.

All the player assessments had been made, and only a couple of former Yanks remained. The last two on the list, though, were going to require special handling, as they would resist the establishment of the day.

Not overlooked, but also not fully considered beforehand, were the two African American players left on the roster. The city of Dallas at that time, along with all of Texas, was still segregated and retained strict laws. The Texans would be by far the most southern franchise on the NFL map. The next closest, promoted as a southern team by their owner George Preston Marshall, was the Washington Redskins. He was once infamously quoted as saying, "We'll start signing Negroes when the Harlem Globetrotters start signing whites."[2]

In the pioneer days of the NFL there were certainly Black players in the game; however, only two remained and were still playing at the start of the 1933 season. They were both out of the league by the end of the year. Most observers would come to realize that this silent lockout of Black players coincided with the entry of Marshall into the league in 1932. He openly refused to have Black athletes on his teams and pressured the rest of the NFL owners to follow suit.

No Black players were in the league from 1934 until 1946, when the Rams finally broke the color barrier with the addition of Kenny Washington. Later that same year, Los Angeles added yet another player, Woody Strode. After the 1946 season, racial integration was very slow to come to the NFL, as no team followed until Detroit signed two African Americans for the 1948 season.

Around the same time, the rival AAFC formed and proactively signed many Black players, as the league was considered a friendly oasis for opportunities. In the NFL by comparison, only three of its twelve franchises, Los Angeles, Detroit, and the Yanks, carried a Black player on their rosters before the 1950 season. Green Bay followed suit in 1950, and then all but one remaining franchise eventually signed Black players. Washington was still the lone holdout—and now potentially Dallas.

But the Millers made their move.

Dallas and the entire region maintained Jim Crow laws, which mandated racial segregation at all public facilities. This included hotels and restaurants within the city limits and meant any visiting teams would be required to seek separate accommodations for their Black players at Black-only boarding houses. This would apply to the Texans players as well. It was not possible for a Black family to own a home in certain neighborhoods. Apartment communities also had the same set of rules. Even the team's stadium, the city-owned Cotton Bowl, was classified as a public facility and enforced segregated seating. African Americans could only sit in the designated end zone areas.

This was an abnormal issue for the NFL, since the situation had never needed to be addressed. No football team in the Southwest Conference had ever navigated through segregated accommodations or seating. They simply had no Black players to begin with, and therefore no conflicts.

Word of the pending situation began to leak locally, and the media quickly raised questions about the new Black presence. *The Sporting News* claimed that this "posed perhaps the biggest color problem in the history of modern-day sports." The local African American community and its press had a significant interest in the possibility of the Texans having Black players, as this would give them someone to root for, a reason to become invested in the new team. There was a clearly defined color line that had yet to be crossed, but that demarcation could be manipulated.

From day one, both Giles and Connell Miller made it no secret that they wanted the squad to have a local flavor and as many players from the surrounding area as they could possibly get. The entire situation of bringing in Black players appeared to them a nonissue. Having been partially raised by Earl Goins, the family's African American butler, people were human beings in their eyes, and they saw no difference or divide.

When asked if he planned to trade either of these men, Giles went against the majority and replied that they would absolutely remain on the roster unless he found more talented players to replace them. When questioned by one *Fort Worth Star-Telegram* reporter, he responded, "We've already been asked several times about that and our feeling is this: We don't care about race, creed, nationality, or color. We think the vast majority of fans will judge by ability on the field, and if they can make the team, they play."[3]

This was his mindset in any business, so the decision was final. These two men were a part of the Texans, period. Besides, Giles knew deep down that this would be yet another avenue for PR man Tex Maule to promote the team within the Black community of Dallas. Their money was just as green as anyone else's when it came to gate revenue.

The players themselves were both quite talented. Together, Claude Henry Young, known to all as "Buddy," and his backfield partner George Taliaferro were now Texans. As far as he was concerned, Phelan saw the matter as a nonissue, bluntly stating his personal feelings: "I don't give a damn whether they're black or white. I'm interested a helluva lot in the way they play football."[4]

Their arrival marked a significant moment, as Young and Taliaferro would become the first Black players in Texas history to compete in a professional sport against white athletes. In addition, the Texans would not only be the first pro team in the state but also the first integrated of any in the southern US.

For his part, Young was an exciting and gifted athlete. He had been referred to as the "Bronze Bullet" because of his tremendous speed, which he needed as he did not possess size, standing just five feet four inches tall and weighing only 175 pounds. To this day, Young is one of the shortest men ever to play in the NFL.

Young played halfback, appropriate since he seemed about half the size of Art Donovan. His team bio would read that he was "the only player in the world who can block you at the knees without bending down." A track star, Buddy held the world record for the 45-yard dash, and twice tied the 60-yard dash record. After receiving several scholarship offers, he committed to the University of Illinois. As a freshman, he was named an All-American, but like many, he was drafted into the navy during World War II, which interrupted his college playing career.

Once discharged, he had an alluring offer to transfer west to UCLA but declined and stayed true to Illinois. Upon graduation, he played in the College All-Star Game against the reigning NFL champion Chicago Bears in front of 105,000 people and was named the game's MVP. After going undrafted but still wanting to play, he signed with the AAFC New York squad and played two seasons. Following the merger, he moved to the Yanks, where he spent two more years. On every team, Young was always one of the most-liked members.

Equally important was Taliaferro, who had been one of the club's leading rushers in New York. He was extremely versatile, having played halfback, quarterback, and punter, as well as two defensive positions where his specialty was forcing fumbles.

In college he was a three-time All-America standout at Indiana University, leading the Hoosiers to their only undefeated season in program history in 1945. But to his dismay, his time there was soon interrupted. Although World War II was essentially over when he entered college, Taliaferro was surprised to learn in early 1946 that he had been selected in the draft. Unsure of how long he would have to serve, he was on his way to report when he found out that he had been penciled in to play on the base's football team. Unhappy about the situation of having his college career uprooted, he was initially defiant and refused to play.

Learning this, the base's commanding officer summoned him to his office and advised him that he had two choices: he could either go to officer candidate school, which meant an automatic three-year enlistment period, or he could play football. It took no time for Taliaferro to respond that he would see him later on the practice field.

He would only need to serve one year in the army before returning to Indiana, where he finished a standout collegiate career. Like Young, Taliaferro concluded his amateur days in the College All-Star Game against the defending NFL champ, this time the Philadelphia Eagles. What happened to Taliaferro next, though, was of historic significance.

Growing up in Gary, Indiana, Taliaferro's childhood dream was to someday play for the nearby Chicago Bears. Around the same time he returned to Gary after college, the league had begun integrating Black players. Although the shift was happening, the number of players was small, and they were added only through walk-on tryouts. No Black player coming out of college had ever been drafted by an NFL team. Owners appeared to just not take the matter seriously enough.

Naturally Taliaferro felt that he or any other Black athlete had no

Seen here between Chief West *(left)* and Don Colo *(right)*, Buddy Young *(center)* was one of the smallest men to ever play pro football. NFL record books list his measurements at five feet four inches and 175 pounds, although those who played with him, without exception, said he was at least ten pounds lighter and more than an inch shorter. Photo credit: Johnson Publishing Company Archive. Courtesy of J. Paul Getty Trust and Smithsonian National Museum of African American History and Culture. Made possible by the Ford Foundation, J. Paul Getty Trust, John D. and Catherine T. MacArthur Foundation, The Andrew W. Mellon Foundation, and Smithsonian Institution.

chance whatsoever of being drafted. With this expectation, he signed with the Los Angeles Dons of the AAFC two weeks before the NFL Draft for what he called "all the money in the world," a salary of $7,000 plus a $4,000 bonus.[5] Later, no one was more surprised than Taliaferro himself when he was selected in the thirteenth round of the 1949 NFL Draft by his Bears.[6]

The big news didn't travel fast. He found out the next day when visiting Chicago to have lunch with three friends, one of them Buddy Young. After waiting at the restaurant for the third friend, the door suddenly opened, and he heard, "Guess who was drafted by the Bears?" The table of friends started to guess the names of all the well-known college players of the day, all of whom were of course white. It never occurred to any of them that a Black player would be possible until a copy of the *Chicago Defender* newspaper was produced. His name was spelled out in three-inch letters. The long-awaited and much-needed day had finally happened, and it had happened to Taliaferro. On top of that, the team that drafted him was his childhood favorite.

Unbeknownst to Bears owner George Halas, though, Taliaferro planned to honor his contract with the Dons. Halas was disappointed by Taliaferro's decision and was quoted as saying that him not joining the NFL was a shame because "he was the first African-American player I felt could make the team."[7]

Fulfilling his commitment, citing that a man's word was his bond, Taliaferro played one season with the AAFC before moving to the NFL after the merger and being assigned to the Yanks. Now heading south as he entered his fourth year, Taliaferro had already been part of a groundbreaking event in NFL history. And the Texans had a genuine multifaceted contributor.

As March arrived, all the initial player transactions had been completed. Phelan did not have the luxury of being choosy. In the coming months, he would need to acquire more players through free agent signings or by trade, but he felt that surely the Texans would be able to win more than just the one game the previous squad had achieved in 1951.

For now, this would serve as a starting point. There was still much more work to do.

8

THE TRADE

THE OFFSEASON was always the time for talent acquisitions, and the Texans desperately needed more. After vetting through the original roster, everyone involved was ready to explore any and all possibilities to get better.

The inheritance of veterans and rookies the new Dallas franchise received from the Yanks was, suffice to say, not an embarrassment of riches. However, the January draft had at least yielded one reward—and it was huge.

Les Richter.

Throughout the Texans' first couple of months, the staff pondered how to improve the roster and what should be done with this exceptional player they were gifted, one who was the second selection overall in the 1952 NFL Draft. They knew most coaches dreamed of finding a prospect like the two-time All-American.

Physically, Richter was a giant, standing six feet three inches tall and weighing 245 pounds with massive hands. The elite athlete had the mental toughness to play through injury, pain, or anything else. He possessed a competitive drive to be the best, as well as the maturity to put in the extra work it took to get there. He was smart, too, as the valedictorian of his graduating class. Any team could build around someone like Richter. He could be the windfall the Texans needed, possessing all the traits needed except for one—availability.

After finishing college, Richter visited Dallas and met with Coach Phelan in late April to get acquainted. His first impression was that he really did not like the area; he was a West Coast guy. Knowing nothing about the team aside from its poor record the year before, he pondered just giving up on football or simply not agreeing to terms.

However, by the time he thought things through and made his feelings known publicly, Richter was called to active duty during the Korean War. Because of his strong physical abilities and mental aptitude, he was named a lieutenant officer in the US Army and was stationed at Fort Lewis in Tacoma, Washington. As was custom in those days, there was a base football team assembled, the Ramblers, to compete with other military bases down the Pacific Coast. Richter, of course, was named team captain and coach.

Meanwhile, as Richter was playing base football, hundreds of miles away the Texans came to accept that their prized treasure would be serving in the military for at least two years and had absolutely no interest in joining their team upon his eventual discharge. They needed to decide if they should wait out what seemed an eternity and hold onto the hope that Richter might change his mind, or cut their losses and move on.

Maybe the time had come to salvage the situation and use this highly sought-after jewel to accumulate some real value. Obviously, the Texans needed a lot of help. Not just one great player but rather several good players. If they could only find a suitor.

The Los Angeles Rams were the defending NFL champions and had been runners-up the prior two years. Since relocating to the West Coast from Cleveland, they had never suffered through a losing season and routinely led the league in attendance. The Rams had a high-flying offense that was ranked first in the NFL and fielded eight Pro Bowl players. Like a Los Angeles department store at Christmas, the team was stocked with talent, most of it on the offensive side of the ball.

Knowing the scuttlebutt surrounding Richter, the Rams kept an interest in him should there be an impasse with Dallas. After all, he was a California product and had an existing friendship with businessman and fellow Cal Golden Bears alum Edwin Pauley, who was a minority co-owner of the Los Angeles club. Not having the opportunity to draft Richter, the Rams became eager to poach him away from the Texans to further enrich their robust roster.

Pauley was instrumental in aligning the Rams brass on the idea, and then in late May leading the suggestion back to Giles Miller that, should Richter become available, they might be interested. A deal could be beneficial for both teams' objectives.

Miller immediately got word to Phelan that, for the very first time, the Texans might actually have something of value and could gain from it. Phelan's assignment was to assess and prioritize what the immediate roster needs were and determine what the Rams had that Dallas could use. Here the Texans were, needing help in every area, and the solution was right in front of them.

For their part, the Rams would be willing to wait out the time required for Richter to fulfill his military duties. A player like this did not come around every day, and two years was not at all long in the grand scheme of things, given their winning position in the league.

Anticipating that the Rams were desperate to get his coveted player, Phelan believed they would be willing to give up an awful lot. For the sake of appearances, if the Texans were to make this bold move, he wanted a big splash to show the rest of the league that they were for real. He quickly let it be known that a player of Richter's stock should basically command a king's ransom, a virtual lineup of players, which to him meant eleven to be exact—offense, defense, or both.

After opening the possibility up for discussion, Pauley's work was done. The Rams were run by a structured committee and the primary owner, Dan Reeves, who was always involved with decisions. Reeves had hired Charles "Chile" Walsh to be the team's general manager, and under his direction the franchise had not seen a losing season in eight years. Walsh's contributions were many, like the hiring of future hall of famer Joe "Jumbo Joe" Stydahar to be the head coach. So along with Reeves, Chile and Jumbo Joe put together a blockbuster trade proposal for Phelan and the Miller brothers.

The deal was the biggest and most lopsided trade to date, and it is still one of the largest in NFL history. The Rams assembled a laundry list of exposed players from which the Texans could choose, granting them a total count of nine to eleven players depending on whom they selected.

The Texans nervously studied through the list and made their picks. The Rams confirmed and agreed to all the names. Both sides thought they won. Time would tell.

On June 13, Reeves announced that the Rams had traded eleven men for just one, Les Richter. Later that afternoon, the *Los Angeles Times*'s longtime and colorful sportswriter, Frank Finch, described the trade as "unquestionably the biggest shift of pigskin personnel in National Football League history."[1] For their part, the Texans received a massive haul that could have an immediate impact. In exchange, they surrendered one player who was not eager to join them and couldn't have played for the next two seasons anyway. At the time, the Texans were credited with getting the better end of the first megatrade in NFL annals.

When the announcement was made, Stydahar was ecstatic and quick to praise the hometown Richter, wishing that he had a whole team just like him, and careful not to mention the names of the eleven he just gave away. He proclaimed, "The Rams have always regarded Richter as one of the country's greatest football players, and we're sure he'll be a tremendous help to us." Concerning the Texans, he said, "We regretted giving up many of the boys, and I feel they will be a definite help to Dallas."[2]

In return for Richter, the most notable among the group of eleven was thirty-year-old Dick Hoerner, by far the Rams' most valuable asset that was given up. Having been in the NFL for five seasons, he had spent his entire career with Los Angeles and was considered one of the hardest running fullbacks of his era. Originally hailing from Dubuque, Iowa, he played for the University of Iowa Hawkeyes. After he initially signed with the Rams, the *Los Angeles Times* touted his potential: "When you find a six-feet, four-inches 220-pounder that can move, you have something. But when you run across one who is downright fast, can handle himself like a 160-pounder and can kick and pass to boot, then you have Lester (Dick) Hoerner the Los Angeles Rams' great fullback prospect."

Off the field, he wore eyeglasses. On the field, he wore a mean expression with a disposition to match. Sidelined with a broken foot as a rookie, Hoerner had fully recovered by his second year to become the Rams' leading rusher. He quickly built a reputation as murderous and unstoppable. Even with his hard-hitting ways, he was the fastest man on the team.

Up until the trade, Hoerner had been coveted by several other teams after greatly contributing to the Rams reaching the championship games in 1949 and 1950. Although they lost both, in his final year he once again led them back, and this time the Rams won the NFL title. He was also named a starter in the inaugural Pro Bowl game of 1951.

Hoerner devoted his first five seasons to the Rams and was leaving as the team's all-time rushing leader. Deemed a replaceable luxury in Los Angeles, he would be a necessity to build around in Dallas. Hoerner would bring much-needed skills to a team that did not have much, if any.

Entering his prime, Tom Keane would also arrive. Keane was an average-sized but versatile two-way player as a defensive back and an end on offense. He had played all four of his NFL seasons with the Rams. Originally from West Virginia, Keane started his college career at Ohio State University before serving in the navy for twenty months during the war. Upon his release, he returned home to the University of West Virginia and for a time was a star quarterback, though he soon shifted to end, where he excelled. The Rams had visions of using his athleticism exclusively on defense, which worked out well, netting him thirty-two interceptions. Now in Dallas, Keane was seen as easily the most productive defensive prospect who could be used on offense in a pinch as a receiver or even a backup quarterback.

Despite playing only one season of professional football, Dick Wilkins had an interesting background. Born and raised in Oregon, he was primarily a basketball player who later turned to football. Wilkins joined the marines during World War II but received an early discharge due to being hit in the eye with a shell casing while on maneuvers.

Moving on to the University of Oregon, Wilkins became what some called the greatest athlete ever to play for the school. But the recognition came from basketball, as he played four years for the Ducks. Not until his senior year was he convinced to try out for both baseball and football. Although he played only one season of college football, he led the team in receiving and helped the Ducks earn a top-ten ranking and a 1949 Cotton Bowl invitation. Like many others, he opted for the AAFC, signing with the Los Angeles Dons and playing brilliantly for one season. After the league merger, he was then selected by the Rams in the dispersal draft.

Prior to reporting, and despite his poor eyesight, he was recalled by the Marine Corps and missed the next two seasons in order to finish out his service. Though he never actually played a game for the Rams, he was still their property. Coming to Dallas, he would get a much better opportunity to showcase his receiving skills in lieu of fighting for a backup roster spot in Los Angeles. Wilkins was a good talent and needed the change of scenery.

Next was a very bright halfback, Billy Baggett. Average in size at five feet eleven inches and 175 pounds, he was born in nearby Greenville, Texas, with his family later moving south to the gulf city of Beaumont. There he became a high school football star. Upon graduation, he enrolled at LSU with high scholastic aspirations and played for the Tigers from 1948 to 1950. He was one of the school's biggest offensive weapons, leading the team in rushing his final two years. During his senior season, he averaged an amazing 6.5 yards per carry after gaining almost 200 yards in a game against Ole Miss.

Drafted by the Rams in 1951, Baggett had forsaken any attempt to play in Los Angeles. California was just too far away, so he chose instead to concentrate on earning a law degree after graduation. Not surprisingly, being part of the trade package suited Baggett. He would be closer to home and have a higher probability of playing time. He would also be able to continue his studies at LSU or even transfer to the SMU School of Law in Dallas.

Another arrival in the trade was second-year man Joe Reid, who had been with Baggett at LSU at six feet three inches and 225 pounds and was a good-sized player for his position. Coming off his rookie season with the Rams, he had played both center and linebacker. Like Baggett, Reid was accomplished in his studies, graduating second in his engineering class. He also was named student body president by his classmates. But unlike Baggett, Reid had been a part of the 1951 Rams championship team and would bring with him a winning attitude.

Twenty-six-year-old Dick McKissack, a local product, was also one of the names coming over in the trade. Having already served in the navy, he

The Texans coaching staff, from left to right: Alex Agase, Cecil Isbell, Will Walls, and Jimmy Phelan. Photo courtesy of NBC5/KXAS Television News Collection, University of North Texas Special Collections.

enrolled at SMU after his commitment and playing alongside Doak Walker for three years was once considered the best fullback in the Southwest Conference. He was of course overshadowed but still earned all-conference honors in both his junior and senior seasons. Given the statue of the SWC at the time, that was just a step away from being an All-American.

If they could not have Walker, the Texans would settle on his old backfield mate. Standing sturdy at six feet two inches and 208 pounds, McKissack was a high draft pick, selected by the Rams in the fifth round of the 1950 draft. However, while working a job in the Texas oil fields during the summer prior to his first training camp, he suffered a back injury that prevented him from reporting to the team. After a two-year layoff from football, no one was sure if he still had anything left. The Rams training staff advised Phelan that he was in perfect playing condition now, but for all intents and purposes, McKissack was a rookie coming to Dallas, albeit an older and injured one.

In terms of the sheer number of players given up by the Rams, the Texans received a lot for Richter. But in the end, they got very little in return. Aside from the six additions of Hoerner, Keane, Wilkins, Baggett, Reid, and McKissack, none of the remaining group of eleven would make any contribution. Five names would be lost to the folklore of one of the biggest trades in NFL history—only a footnote. A deal that appeared to be so lopsided toward the Texans later tilted heavily in the Rams' favor.

Of the five noncontributors, only two would even attend training camp. Rookie Arkansas A&M quarterback David Anderson was one of them. The other was a fellow rookie, an offensive lineman out of SMU named Jack Halliday. The three remaining players were Aubrey Phillips, a rookie center out of Texas Tech; George Sims, a third-year defensive back from Baylor; and finally Vic Vasicek, a linebacker from the University of Texas who would have been entering his fourth season.

The common thread was that each one of these five players had a Texas background, which fit perfectly the team's strategy of where they wanted to draw talent from. No doubt Phelan and company took some bad advice from the Rams, though. The headline in June read advantage Dallas. By training camp the headline was more like Los Angeles picked their pocket. The Texans had been duped.

Richter was destined to stay and succeed in California. Once he became a Ram, all he ever did was deliver. Without question, the franchise that drafted him made the right selection. They just didn't have the forethought to keep the future Pro Football Hall of Famer and decided to take the magic beans instead.

9

TRAINING CAMP

TEXANS have an old adage that goes, "If you don't like the weather here, stick around for five minutes and it'll change on you." However, in the summer the weather never really changes. Unless you count when the temperature is hot, and then it just gets even hotter. In some areas during the sweltry dog days of summer, the thermometer can hit one hundred degrees by ten in the morning.

As the organization entered the second half of July, the furnace and drought enveloping the North Texas area was in full force. Although the heat was bad, at least Dallas usually felt better than parts farther south.

A decision was still pending on where the franchise would set up accommodations and stage its training camp base for the upcoming first season. In their infinite wisdom and ignoring common sense—staying close to home in the slightly cooler climate of North Texas—the Miller brothers selected the small town of Kerrville, a site about three hundred miles southwest of Dallas. Kerrville had a population of only 7,600 residents and sat about an hour northwest from San Antonio and about two hours west of Austin. Kerrville was closer to the Mexican border than it was to Dallas.

A classic example of Texas flatland, Kerrville's lack of irrigation and frequent long dry spells would not allow for much of anything to grow, except prairie grass and dirt. The prairie grass was so stubborn the heat couldn't kill it, and the dirt would simply blow away in the hot summer winds. The area might have been considered more populous if only the snakes, grasshoppers, and ants were counted as inhabitants.

To keep the players focused, the Millers and their staff secured the tiny Schreiner Institute and its surrounding grounds. Schreiner was set up to operate as a military prep school. It was an all-male private Presbyterian university offering two-year programs to prepare young boys for their next steps in life. The players would occupy Delaney Hall, a modern dormitory that was only three years old. There would be no temptations or distractions at Schreiner. If the players did not die from the heat, they might very well do so from boredom.

Although the megatrade drama was now behind them, that did not mean the end of talent acquisitions. The roster still needed help in virtually every area before starting training camp, so the brothers and head coach Jimmy Phelan went on a trading spree. They accumulated eight additional veterans, none of whom were previous starters with their former teams, and in each of these deals the Texans only gave up draft picks, thus leveraging their future.

Next up was the task of combing through the "best of the worst" players still available on the market. With the league operating at only twelve teams, and no longer having the rival AAFC as an option, there were plenty of eligible but lesser-talented men around. And this lot was not choosy, as most were looking for any landing spot on an NFL roster. Located close to home for many, Dallas represented an attractive opportunity, one where they would be able to make an immediate impact. Out of this group, four more veteran players and fourteen undrafted rookies were signed by the team.

With the opening camp roster now set, there was still one more addition that remained. By way of a Green Bay Packers roster cut, there became available a massive six-feet-two-inch, 330-pound human named Forrest Porter Grigg Jr.

For as long as anyone knew, people called him "Chubby." The nickname fit. He was a capable player, but he overate which was affecting his career. With his backwoods accent, wavy strawberry-blonde hair, and giant gap-toothed smile, Grigg was quite the package. He was one of the first known men in pro football to play at over three hundred pounds.

Born in the Arkansas hills, he grew up in Texas and attended the University of Tulsa. Undrafted, Grigg signed as a free agent with the AAFC's Buffalo Bisons in 1946, but when he reported to his first training camp, the head coach gave him an ultimatum: he needed to reduce his weight to a maximum of three hundred pounds or he would not make the team. Once workouts started, in an effort to provide either humor, humiliation, or motivation, the coach told the players that in lieu of taking routine laps around the field, they could opt to run around Grigg instead.

He did lose some weight during camp, but did not reach the set goal. Out of necessity, though, he was kept and started the first few games of the season before being benched when the pounds came back. Reportedly, Grigg formed a habit of getting team trainers to retrieve four hot dogs for him to eat at halftime, hiding them under his parka even during warm, early-season games. This behavior was the reason he could never maintain a suitable weight.

Not utilized by the Bisons, and of course eating too much, his rights were sold to the Chicago AAFC club before his second season, where he again played only sparingly. Before his third year, Grigg was dealt to Cleveland, the reigning champs and the best team in the AAFC. Aware of his tendencies, legendary head coach Paul Brown still saw a potential he believed outweighed Grigg himself. Brown thought all the player needed was discipline and the right environment, one that only he would be able to provide. Brown's goals were to uncover Grigg's hidden abilities and then drop the Chubby nickname. For a time, it worked.

In his first year with Cleveland, Brown offered him a bonus if he weighed in at 278 pounds before the season. Grigg accomplished this, but then ballooned back up to 317 pounds by season's end. The following year, Brown again gave him another offer to arrive at 275 pounds. Again, Grigg hit the mark and was promised additional money if he were to keep the weight off for the rest of the season. Instead, he gained even more than the season before, up to 322 pounds.

Brown finally gave up on Chubby after his four seasons of yo-yoing in Cleveland and packaged him in a trade to Green Bay in April of 1952. Grigg never played a down for the Packers, being cut prior to camp for the same previous weight reasons.

So Phelan claimed him off waivers. Thinking a fresh start may do him well, the Texans decided that they were going to capitalize on and market who they saw as a huge cartoon character. It was brought to the team's attention that Grigg owned a side business—a rickety, two-pump gas station in East Texas—so Tex Maule's media machine planned to present the mammoth to the public as an "oil executive" by trade in the offseason who dominated opponents in the fall.

With that, reporting time for training camp had finally arrived. Sixty-three players, along with most of the staff, assembled in Dallas on two buses for the seven-hour road trip to Kerrville. There were some exceptions, as a handful of players were in the active military and would miss some or all of camp due to service commitments. Two other notable absentees were fullback John Petitbon and defensive lineman Gino Marchetti. Both were rookies who had been selected to play in the College All-Star Game in Chicago against the NFL defending champion Los Angeles Rams. They were to join the team immediately after the game.

Coach Phelan, along with the assistant coaches, head scout Gil Haynes, and trainer Chief West had already arrived at the Schreiner Institute. West would take care of the players' basic medical needs while Dr. Chester stayed behind in Dallas, on call if needed. Also making the trek down south were board members Jack Vaughn and Harlan Ray. Business manager Al Ennis and Maule were driving themselves down, along with team photographer Squire Haskins. And finally there was equipment manager Willie Garcia, who would prove to be worth his weight in gold over the next six weeks of camp.

Everything had come together. They were a real football unit and not just a bunch of crazy ideas.

The cash outlay for the summer was budgeted by treasurer Fritz Hawn and approved by the board. From accommodations to the all-important food and beverage budget, everything was seemingly covered. It was almost like they had done this all before. What could go wrong?

Father and family patriarch Clarence Miller had never publicly shied away from his opinion of Giles and Connell's reckless sports venture. He thought the Texans were simply an expensive hobby, one that would only lose money. At one point, he made a remark about operating expenses

Head coach Jimmy Phelan kicks off the first day of training camp in Kerrville, addressing the team while the snake infected prairie grass lurks behind them. Photo courtesy of NBC5/KXAS Television News Collection, University of North Texas Special Collections.

relative to feeding the players. Connell reminded him of his stable of racehorses and how much they ate, to which the elder Miller replied, "My horses eat hay. You'll be feeding your guys beefsteak!"[1] Given the size of certain players, particularly Art Donovan and Chubby Grigg, the brothers were about to find out just how much cash keeping them fed would take.

On the early Wednesday morning of July 30, at a seldom-used athletic lot in Kerrville, the Texans took to the practice field for the first time. Basic calisthenics and conditioning drills would be first on the agenda. There were supposed to be sixty-three players on the field, however, there were noticeably several missing. Garcia was dispatched to go find them. Maybe they were just lost?

They were indeed—but lost only in sleep. Ten were still in bed and had to be awoken to get to the field.

A winner at every prior stop, Phelan quickly observed that most of his college teams had better personnel and discipline than what he saw now. He was an affable man and knew building a team from this group of castoffs, some of whom lacked ambition, was not going to be easy. He had to wonder, "Where the hell is Gino Marchetti?" before realizing he hadn't reported yet. After one practice, it was already clear this team would stretch him to his limits.

With the assistant coaches leading drills, Mother Nature was doing her part. The heat was on, and many players had never felt anything like this. Year-round physical conditioning was not something that any of them practiced. They would need to quickly improve their stamina to survive in this Texas inferno.

From the very beginning, the Schreiner staff had warned all involved of the first opponent the Texans might face—rattlesnakes. With the make-shift practice fields surrounded by tall prairie grass and weeds, the area was a natural fit for the poisonous predators to call home. Their color also provided camouflage in the hardscrabble landscape, so they were very hard to see—unless you got close, which of course you would not want to do.

The rattlesnakes' favorite time to be out and active were the early dawn hours, just in time for the morning practices. Word did not take long to circulate among the players, or for the footballs to begin bouncing off into the heavily infested areas. The players were already not putting in a full effort. Unsurprisingly, this danger only exaggerated their shortage of enthusiasm.

On the plus side, there were no field mice to be seen.

Unbeknownst to the players, but public knowledge to the staff, was that the equipment man Garcia had a wooden prosthetic leg, usually covered up by his pants. Most of the players just thought he walked with a limp. After some quick thought, Phelan discussed the ongoing lost ball situation with Garcia. He offered what he thought was a simple solution, and Garcia agreed to the idea.

It was decided that at the end of the day, Garcia would receive twenty-five cents per football retrieved from the tall grass. Phelan's logic was that Garcia, because of his prosthetic, only had a 50 percent chance of being bitten. The solution worked; although coming close at times, Garcia was never wounded.

Safely away from the prairie grass that contained rattlesnakes, yet still in the sweltering heat, Buddy Young *(left)* and George Taliaferro *(right)* take a breather during training camp in Kerrville, Texas. Photo credit: Johnson Publishing Company Archive. Courtesy of J. Paul Getty Trust and Smithsonian National Museum of African American History and Culture. Made possible by the Ford Foundation, J. Paul Getty Trust, John D. and Catherine T. MacArthur Foundation, The Andrew W. Mellon Foundation, and Smithsonian Institution.

Already on high alert after averting the rattlesnake dangers, the attention now turned back to the daily heat. At every previous stop, halfback Buddy Young fancied himself the locker-room representative and player counselor. Prior to leaving for camp, he was told that Kerrville was one of the coolest spots in the state. Over the next six weeks, he came to find out that was absolutely false.

It never rained, aside from an overnight trace. There was a lucky break, though, as the one-hundred-plus degree temperatures only occurred on twenty-two of the forty-two days camp was held. Young kept track and found the remainder of the days were in the mid-to-high nineties, which seemed irrelevant given that, whether the temperature was one hundred two or ninety-eight degrees, it still felt blistering.

One curiosity Young and his teammates began to take notice of while walking to the dining hall for their midday lunch break involved the large anthill beds. They witnessed huge ants crawling about and working away at their empires. But when the lunch period was over, going back along the same pathway, there were no ants to be seen. They all had virtually disappeared, either retreating down into their holes or simply moving on. The players' takeaway was that the temperature was too hot even for the ants, and they were the natives. The camp heat was unbearable, but in hindsight, the situation could have been worse.

Poor Willie Garcia didn't know what he was getting himself into, as his position wasn't well defined. Not only was he the lone equipment man, his daily additional assignments were basically the things no one else wanted to do. It was beyond demanding.

When he brought out the equipment and uniforms for distribution on the first day of camp, he was introduced to a group of ill-mannered players who shoved him aside while muscling away the best available socks, shoulder pads, and other assorted necessities. Since they were all much bigger than him, Garcia learned quickly to drop the goods and flee the scene. Eventually, neatly folded sportswear was replaced with jerseys, pants, and socks all heaped together in a pile so that the players could begin the fight amongst themselves.

Once the first few days had passed, most of the players began complaining to him about the heat, many of them thinking that he had something to do with it. Garcia tried his best to brainstorm and invent ways to cool the players down, but his understanding of sports and heat was greatly limited. After a few practices, he noticed some of the players ladling water over their heads to cool off, rendering them completely wet from the head down. Seeing this, Garcia came up with the idea of soaking all of the uniforms in cold-water tubs prior to distribution. Unfortunately, he did not clear it with anyone.

Things did not work out very well when Garcia threw the heavy pile of soaked apparel in the middle of the locker-room floor. Players still fought through the wet mess, but the plan was quickly kiboshed.

Back in Dallas, the Miller brothers had to initially forgo traveling to Kerrville due to other family business. On Saturday, August 2, Giles celebrated his thirty-second birthday. The next day, after attending church services, he packed up some belongings and headed to Connell's house.

The family butler, Earl Goins, then drove them both down to the Highland Park Station where they would catch the MKT-Katy train down to San Antonio. Upon arriving there, they would travel by car to the great encampment to see their creation for the first time.

On his third day at camp, Giles Miller was mingling with some of the players in the dining hall during lunch when Maule approached him with what he called a "small" problem. Miller thought the issue might be something trivial, but it turned out to be anything but.

The trouble concerned the team's news coverage and the reporters on hand who had traveled down from Dallas to the middle of nowhere. Working to get good PR started for the Texans, Maule told Miller that the writers were not all teetotalers and asked if there was any objection to regularly serving up a few drinks as a hospitality offering. Miller replied that not only would he allow it, but he encouraged it. In fact, he would not mind one or two himself, just as long as all alcohol was kept completely away from the team.

That was not the real problem, though. Maule pointed out that there was no liquor supply on hand, being that they were on school grounds, and business manager Al Ennis was refusing to answer his long-distance request for money in order to purchase the drinks. Also, Phelan was not in favor of it.

Miller could fix the money situation with Ennis, but he sought out the old coach and inquired as to why he had a problem with the idea. Phelan tartly pointed out that this was a football training camp, and if anyone wanted to booze it up, let them head into town and do it on their own time and their own money. He admonished, almost scolded Miller that it was already hard enough to get this bunch focused as it was, and he did not need a bunch of alcoholics around influencing them.

Phelan obviously had strong feelings about this, so not wanting to meddle, Miller did not press the subject any further with him. He then went to see Dr. Andrew Eddington, president of the Shriner Institute, to inquire whether the school would have any objection to Maule keeping a *small* amount of whiskey in his room to serve as bartender to the sportswriters. The president gave a reassuring reply, saying there was absolutely

Far away from the discrimination that existed in Dallas, there was no segregation at the Texans' training camp, as Buddy Young is seen here sitting at the end of the table eating with his white teammates. Photo credit: Johnson Publishing Company Archive. Courtesy of J. Paul Getty Trust and Smithsonian National Museum of African American History and Culture. Made possible by the Ford Foundation, J. Paul Getty Trust, John D. and Catherine T. MacArthur Foundation, The Andrew W. Mellon Foundation, and Smithsonian Institution.

no problem with serving just a few drinks. Maybe he would even come around for one himself.

Leaving for a side trip back over to San Antonio, Miller and Maule gathered the needed supplies while there, ordering enough booze to accommodate the new standing cocktail hour. Miller, though, asked his mischievous accomplice to swear to only one thing: do not divulge to the coach or anyone else where he got the help or the money to get the booze into the grounds. He told Maule, "Just have it on hand. Don't let anyone know. Make them think that the bottles just magically appeared by themselves overnight."[2]

From that point on there were never any complaints or issues about the subject. The booze made the practices look better as well.

When he later turned the bill over to Ennis, Miller was unable to come up with a workable ledger reason to cover the expense, so he told him to simply put it under "contributions to another good cause." And Phelan eventually became aware of what was going on, softening his position.

Maybe because he, too, needed a drink after watching the workouts.

10

GROWING OPTIMISM

IN THE LEAGUE'S third decade, players showing up to training camp out of shape was still commonplace, as none of them had done anything physical since the end of the previous season. The primary objective of camp was to get conditioned through a series of scrimmages, games that were referred to as exhibitions, unlike today's preseason tilts.

Although the exhibitions did not count in any standings, they were more competitive than preseason football today. They were considered a big part of team building and were used to gauge talent-for-talent against competition.

Most often the games would not be played at home fields or even in the teams' home territories. Neutral locations were scheduled independently by the clubs, and some used a barnstorming travel-tour mentality. Franchises scheduled their own contests with junior colleges, military-base squads, or semipro challengers, warming up with these games before balancing out the remainder of their schedule with NFL teams. Every coach's goal was to play against amateurs early on and increase the strength of the opponents each week until the season opener.

The Texans scheduled two military-base teams to start. Of their six games total, they would play five on the road at neutral sites and host one at home in Dallas.

Attention now turned toward when they could hit someone other than themselves in practice. It would also be good for their confidence to play against a lesser team.

The first game ever for the Millers' new franchise came on Saturday night, August 16, 1952, against the Brooke Army Medical Center Comets, who were based out of Fort Sam Houston. Played at nearby Antler Stadium in Kerrville, there was no need for any travel. Antler was a makeshift high school stadium where an estimated crowd of over five thousand spectators, many of them standing due to lack of seating, jammed in to see professional athletes competing against an undermanned army-base squad of smaller two-way players. The game was never close; the final score was Texans 34, Comets 7. They had gotten off to a right start with a convincing win.

Although being there was important to him, Giles Miller was unable to go to the first game due to a previous commitment. Instead, he attended the Southern Garment Manufacturers Convention in Memphis and from there decided to visit Chicago to see the College All-Star Game.

In the days leading up to the all-star game, Miller learned that the event's organizer, Arch Ward, was holding a press party. Deciding to go, Miller was introduced to the various media outlets that had yet to cover anything regarding the Texans. But his main reason for going to Chicago was to get a good, up-close look at their prized draft pick Marchetti competing against the NFL champions.

The city had been hot and humid, but by kickoff rain was coming down heavily. Miller made attending the game a sales call by entertaining an old friend who worked for Sears Roebuck, and they planned to enjoy dinner and a show afterward. When the game ended, the two got across town as quickly as they could to meet another friend who had been holding their reservation at the famed nightclub Chez Paree. But traveling was a mess, and they winded up missing half the show due to the rainstorm.

Once the show concluded, they were invited backstage to personally meet the entertainers they had missed, the famous duo of Dean Martin and Jerry Lewis. Miller immediately hit it off with them and found they had a lot in common. The hour was late, so they exchanged contact information and promised to get back together soon.

Feeling guilty for missing his team's first game, Miller went back to his hotel where he frantically tried to find out what had happened in Kerrville earlier that night. The next morning he returned to Texas as fast as

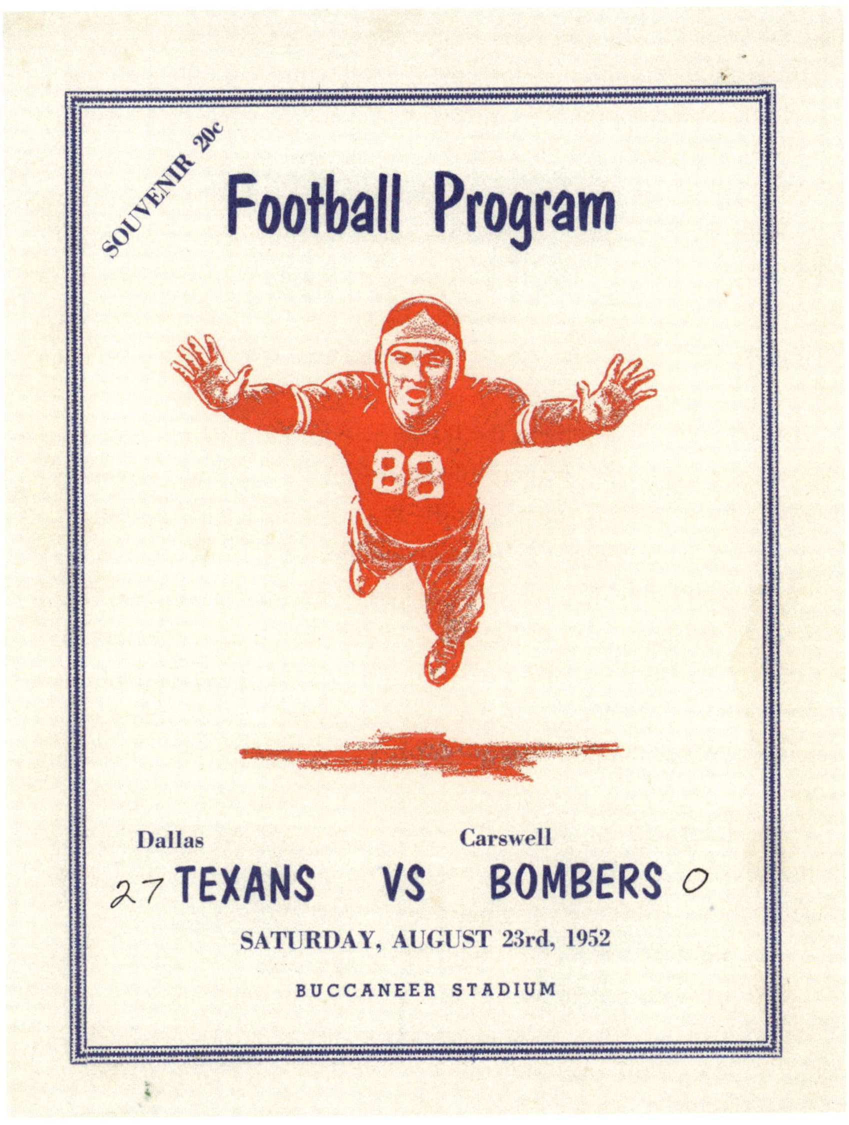

Just six thousand spectators witnessed the Texans' only shutout victory, which occurred in their second exhibition game against an undermanned Carswell Air Force Base squad. Photo courtesy of the author and the Texas Sports Hall of Fame.

he could, vowing to never miss another game. He kept that promise.

The second exhibition affair came the following Saturday night, August 23. This time the opponent was the Bombers of Carswell Air Force Base, who were stationed in Westworth Village, an area northwest of Fort Worth. Once again, the game took place at a high school venue, Buccaneer Stadium in Corpus Christi. Buccaneer was one of the largest high school facilities in the state and felt more professional. An estimated crowd of more than six thousand spectators saw the game, and for the second week the outcome was not close, the final score Texans 27, Bombers 0. Optimism was growing.

The following Friday night the team traveled to the West Texas town of Odessa. The opponent for their third game, played on August 29, would finally be a worthy NFL adversary, the Philadelphia Eagles. The Eagles were a team in decline just three seasons removed from being league champions, but they did offer to make the trip, which was a plus. The matchup was staged at W. T. Barrett Stadium, a high school facility that opened in 1948 and was home to the powerhouse Odessa football program. A decent crowd estimated at seventeen thousand area fans came to watch two teams compete that many felt were worse than their local high school.

With a final score of Texans 7, Eagles 24, it was the first loss that the team experienced on the season. Making the defeat even harder to take was that they weren't at all competitive.

Friday night, September 5, would be the fourth game of the exhibition schedule. This time the opponent was the Washington Redskins and their animated owner, George Preston Marshall. He had grown tired of his team's middle-of-the-pack play, so over the offseason Marshall brought in legendary head coach Curley Lambeau to turn the franchise's fortunes around.

Competing against an innovative league founder would prove to be a noteworthy measuring stick for the new Texans. Held under the bright lights of San Antonio's Alamo Stadium, 19,075 fans witnessed Dallas win its first game against real NFL competition. The final score was Texans 27, Redskins 14.

Winning against a Lambeau-coached team that night was a huge confidence booster. Phelan, though, was quick to remind all that the game really didn't matter.

The team was about to enter another exciting phase. After spending their last six weeks in the purgatory of Kerrville, the players and staff broke training camp and returned to Dallas to finish up locally at Burnett Field, their regular practice facility. They would still endure some of the heat, although temperatures weren't as bad, and it was getting later in the summer. The Texans were also fortunate to trade the snakes and fire ants for the rat population that claimed the Burnett locker rooms as their home.

For game five of the exhibition slate, the Miller brothers wanted to finally introduce the team to a home crowd in the Cotton Bowl. So far they had not been focused on promoting any real in-person familiarity between fans and the club, but now that they were all back in town, Maule put together some promotional player appearances across the area.

This was the first showcase moment with actual locals in the stands. With Giles having partnered with the Salesmanship Club of Dallas, a portion of the gate proceeds were set to benefit Camp Woodland Springs . . . and not the team's bottom line.

The game took place on Friday night, September 12, typically a high school football night. Still, the gate attendance was a very impressive, although inflated, estimate of thirty-two thousand fans. That total was not a paid turnout, however, since many tickets were given away as a promotional tool. An added attraction was that the Detroit Lions, their opponent, brought many area favorites to town with them, including Doak Walker, notably not a member of the Texans.

Dallas's performance that night was another confidence builder. Despite losing, they did keep the game competitive. Final score: Texans 14, Lions 21. Final publicity score: the Millers 100, Naysayers 0. By hanging in against one of the NFL's best, this upstart team was beginning to feel like a real NFL organization.

The final game would be played on the road. The brothers believed showing their club outside of the immediate area might be beneficial. Texas, after all, was massive, and they could claim the whole region. So a decision was made to go to Houston, which was even larger than Dallas.

Having put the Doak Walker acquisition to rest, the Texans were finally able to catch him on the field of the exhibition game played at the Cotton Bowl. From the collections of the Dallas History & Archive Division, Dallas Public Library.

They selected the campus of Rice University. Securing the site took some Texas arm-twisting because the college had a policy in place that did not allow any pro games to be played on its campus. But Rice Stadium, with a capacity of seventy thousand, was the second-largest stadium in the state, outside of the Cotton Bowl. The venue would be the perfect place for the Millers to stage their traveling Lone Star roadshow.

As a promotion, they billed the game as the "Shamrock Charity Bowl" with proceeds being donated to the Holly Hall Home for the Aged, the Houston Council of Church Women, and the Bayshore Home for Underprivileged Children. Their opponent was the Chicago Cardinals.

Besides of the Texans, the Cardinals were one of the worst teams in the NFL. Not many tickets were sold in advance, so the hope was that there would be a big walk-up crowd. There wasn't. On that Saturday afternoon, September 20, only an estimated 12,500 people showed up to fill the massive stadium. It looked bad. Attendees with no real knowledge of either squad were scattered throughout the stands, leaving voids that led to a dearth of motivation on both teams' parts.

Neither side was impressive, and the contest could have easily been called off due to lack of interest as well as effort. Dallas dropped the game and seemingly gained nothing of benefit to close out its exhibition season. The final score was Texans 0, Cardinals 10.

After a blistering summer and the conclusion of six games, the Texans had posted an overall record of 3–3, which sounded respectable enough. Except they were only 1–3 against established NFL teams. Yet optimism was high going into the upcoming regular season. They had taken their baby steps that summer, and the time had now arrived to play some real games.

Going unnoticed was the important fact that for the last two weeks the Millers had given away valuable gate receipts to charities. Charity begins at home; they should have realized that.

11

THE SEASON BEGINS

THE EVE of the season was upon them, which meant that final player cuts were now needed. After returning to Dallas, head coach Jimmy Phelan had to narrow down the roster and finalize the personnel. The decisions were not that difficult due to the lack of talent. It was merely picking the best of the worst. The easygoing coach was never one for long conversation. The calls were obvious to him after talking with his assistants, so he acted quickly, wanting to get the task off his plate.

Everyone gathered into the locker room at Burnett Field and experienced something they had never seen. In front of all, Phelan methodically circled the room and pointed a finger to each player, declaring, "You're gone," or "You're good."[1]

Bob Celeri, the holdover quarterback once on the bubble, heard, "You're good." Highly touted rookie Gino Marchetti and heavyweight class clowns Art Donovan and Chubby Grigg all heard, "You're good." Many others, like local SMU rookie Jack Adkisson, were given a "You're gone" to no one's real surprise. First-round pick Les Richter didn't hear anything because he wasn't in the room after being traded for those eleven players, six of whom were told "You're good." Finally, the two talented Black players, Buddy Young and George Taliaferro, also heard "You're good" and rightfully so.

By the time Phelan finished his rounds in the locker room that day, the Texans roster was set. They would soon find out how they would measure up against the rest of the league.

Off the field, the Miller brothers were getting ready for the season opener, making lavish plans for the festivities while trying to push ticket sales by word of mouth. NFL commissioner Bert Bell continued to impose a watchful eye on the books and their spending, to the point of meddling. Bell warned the brothers on multiple occasions that gate receipts were far more important than some of the extravagant ideas being considered.

Giles Miller estimated from day one that the franchise would need a minimum of twenty-five thousand paid attendees per game just to break even. Bell countered that it would require more than thirty thousand, and that he should always aim higher. After all, the Cotton Bowl held seventy-five thousand, so even at thirty thousand the stadium would still appear less than half full.

Since much of the idea to expand into Dallas was his own, and because of added travel expenses for the visiting team, Bell continued to dwell on getting more tickets sold. Conversely, Miller offered free admission to anyone donating blood toward the Korean War effort. The commissioner would shake his head and argue that the overhead, payroll, and administrative costs were too high. Further, Miller planned to have a chartered helicopter, paid for by the team, transport the newly crowned Miss Dallas Texans to the Cotton Bowl before each game, land on the 50-yard line, and then release a golden balloon shaped like a football that contained a gift certificate from a local area merchant.

To his dismay, Bell would routinely find himself preaching about excessive spending to the point of scolding Giles and Connell. He continued trying to mentor them about the game and how to run a sports organization. Usually, though, his words would only partially register. There was only so much influence Bell could have from his office in Philadelphia. Tips and suggestions on frugality were the extent of what was possible this close to the season.

On the Miller family side, game days were going to be something of a reunion outing. All participated in the fandom and attended games, even "Pop" Clarence and "Mom" Esther. Close friends and business associates also came, along with Giles's and Connell's three sons apiece.

Young boys and football in Texas were about as American as you could get in the 1950s, so the brothers decided to have the team sponsor their sons' YMCA Park Cities Pee Wee football squad. Outfitted in the same uniform color scheme, they were known as the Little Texans. Connell Jr. wore jersey number twenty-two for his favorite player, Young, while Ed wore number seventy-seven for his favorite player, Don Colo. Giles even dedicated the time needed to coach the kids. In effect, he was now running two Texans clubs. As far as anyone knows, the Little Texans may have had a better record.

For the NFL version, excitement continued to build leading up to the opening game. But outside of the organization, many area Dallasites were still not even aware that they had a local pro football team getting ready to play. Publicity had not been able to muster much interest. The college game was still king.

In the season's first weekend, area fans would be treated to two college contests at the Cotton Bowl—Friday night SMU was set to host Duke, and on Saturday Texas A&M would play Oklahoma A&M. Giles Miller believed that these would serve as a warmup act, and during both games Texans tickets were advertised for sale over the public-address system. Only a few hundred were purchased.

On Sunday morning, September 28, game day had finally arrived. A full-blown pregame party was held at Giles Miller's home on Beverly Drive. In addition to friends and family, well-known VIPs and other dignitaries were present. An early nod to modern game-day apparel, the adult board members were provided with denim Western-style team shirts, identical to what the players traveled in. Connell Miller's wife, Martha, had commissioned Ripley's of Dallas tailors to craft the shirts in team colors, which were elaborately decorated with contrasting pointed yokes, shotgun cuff sleeves, and the all-important snap buttons.

Awaiting across the street at the nearby Dallas Country Club were two large motor coach buses that had been contracted by the team. Surrounded by a police escort, they would transport everyone in the party straight to the Cotton Bowl, where they would all sit at the 50-yard line in the best seats in the house.

Young Connell Jr. and Giles's son Ed boarded the bus and found their way past the adult section in the front. They knew most of the people, as they were either family or close friends. Taking their seats in the middle of the bus, the boys noticed an older man in the row across from them. He began talking to them about current news events and made small talk about school and football. They felt like they had seen him before, although at ages eight and nine, they were understandably more preoccupied with going to the game. As it was, they were actually talking to Allan Shivers, the governor of Texas, who was attending as a guest of the family.

For fans arriving at Fair Park, game programs could be bought for fifty cents each. Inside, the opening page contained a photo and full-page letter from the same governor's office with a declaration stating:

The State of Texas
Executive Department
Allan Shivers
Austin Texas

September 12th, 1952

I am happy to join with other sports lovers in welcoming the Dallas Texans professional football team to Texas.

A new chapter in the history of Texas sports will be written this fall when the Texans take the gridiron as the first professional football team to be organized in the state. Football fans are to be congratulated that we now have the opportunity of witnessing pro football of the highest type for the Texas team on the field.

With best wishes to the Texans for a successful season, I am

Sincerely yours,
Allan Shivers

As everyone began entering the gates, it became apparent that the turnstiles would not receive much of a workout that day. After seeing what thirty-two thousand fans looked like for one of their previous exhibition games, the team saw what appeared to be substantially less.

By the 2:30 kickoff time, the Texans had drawn only 17,499 fans, far short of the 25,000 minimum needed to break even. For those who did attend, though, excitement was in the air. The Texans took the field for their pregame warmups wearing their new navy blue jerseys with white pants while their opponent, the New York Giants, sported red jerseys with gray pants and their signature blue helmet with a red stripe.

Hosting the illustrious Giants, a team full of future hall of famers and local heroes, was supposed to be a huge advantage. They had a celebrity quarterback in Charlie Conerly to match their much-heralded rookie halfback sensation Frank Gifford. Their defensive backfield was anchored by Emlen Tunnell and future Cowboys legend Tom Landry. But the day's biggest attraction was SMU's own Kyle Rote, the former backfield teammate of Doak Walker, now in his second year.

The temperature was a sunny and hot ninety degrees at game time. For the midfield coin toss, the Texans called heads, and it came up as heads. They were already winners. The opening kickoff was fielded by the home team, and they ran three unsuccessful plays before setting up for a punt.

What followed was a gift from Landry, no less, who fumbled, allowing the Texans to recover the ball. Two plays later, Taliaferro ran a halfback option pass and connected with Young on a 22-yard completion for the first touchdown in Texans history. The closest Giants defender was Landry.

Expecting a loud crowd reaction, Young looked up into the stands behind the end zone to see nothing but empty seats. The extra point was missed, but the Texans had the early 6–0 lead, and the game looked like it was going to be an easy go. Unfortunately, that would be their only lead of the day—and for a long time to come.

What followed would be 24 unanswered points posted by the Giants, the death knell coming courtesy of a 52-yard touchdown run by Rote late in the game. When the final gun sounded, the score was Texans 6, Giants 24.

The day started out with so much enthusiasm, a fact that would not be lost despite the disappointing outcome. They shouldn't have won, but surely the Texans could have been more competitive. Then again, this was the team's first regular game experience. Phelan's men would need to quickly put this behind them and prepare for their week two opponent.

When the brothers relayed to Bell how much they were impacted financially by the gate sales, the gruff commissioner responded with a terse, "Tim Mara's Giants lost $18,000 in payroll and traveling expenses just making the trip to play you."[2] Basically, his message was to get used to it.

As the second game of the season approached, so too did one of the largest and most-celebrated festivals in the world. Even today, the State Fair of Texas is held annually every fall on the grounds surrounding the Cotton Bowl, and hundreds of thousands of people attend. Football and the fair go hand in hand.

But in 1952, the fair's leadership decided that a new resident would become the official greeter for their annual event. His name was Big Tex, the world's largest talking cowboy, and he was part of the skyline during the Texans' season.

The fifty-two-foot gentle giant wasn't always Big Tex, hailing originally from Kerens, located about seventy miles southeast of Dallas. He was created in 1949 as The World's Largest Santa Claus, a chamber of commerce idea to promote and encourage holiday sales in their local shops. After one year of success, the novelty faded, so the town offered up the statue for sale after the 1951 holiday season.

Then state fair president R. L. Thornton purchased Santa for $750 and had area artist Jack Bridges transform the figure into a cowboy. With Bridges taking inspiration from Will Rogers to create the new look, Big Tex now sported a hat, plaid shirt, blue jeans with a belt buckle, and boots. But although the finished product was thought by many to be scary, Big Tex was the fixture fair officials were looking for to watch over their grounds. Too bad the team couldn't find a uniform large enough to fit; they could have used him.

The day following the introduction of Big Tex was Sunday, October 5, and the Texans would once again be playing at home, this time hosting the San Francisco 49ers for a 2:30 afternoon kickoff. The 49ers were entering their third season in the NFL after joining the league as part of the AAFC merger, and they were one of the better teams, having just finished second in their division behind the mighty Los Angeles Rams. San Francisco's head coach was Buck Shaw, who had suffered only one losing season in his six years with the club.

West Coast football was different. Like the Rams, the 49ers employed the same type of high-flying, wide-open offense that would move the ball quickly. Led at quarterback by Bay Area native Frankie Albert and rising star Y. A. Tittle, they also boasted one of the league's best backfields with Joe Perry and rookie sensation Hugh McElhenny.

A home game meant that Giles would once again host a massive pregame party with the same itinerary and shuttling of guests to the Cotton Bowl. He and Connell both fully believed that with the fair's large crowds, tickets sales and attendance for the Texans contest with San Francisco would be considerably better. This game was going to be a spectacle, maybe close to a sellout.

With Big Tex already invited, two other luminaries were also coming. One of the biggest acts in show business, and Giles's newfound friends, were at their peak—the duo of Dean Martin and Jerry Lewis. They had been booked to play a two-week period at the State Fair Music Hall, and the marquees throughout the fairgrounds billed the show as "America's funniest comedy team with their all-star international revue in person." Ever the visionaries for promotion, Giles and Connell invited the celebrities to attend the game as their guests. Unexpectedly, they accepted and welcomed the opportunity.

With the introduction of Martin and Lewis, surprise and pandemonium ensued among the fans in attendance at the Cotton Bowl; however, there were not very many of them. This week, the 12,566 attendees were even less than the season opener. Ninety-three degrees at kickoff, the weather was also hotter than the first game. The Texans took the field wearing the same uniform combination as game one, while the 49ers sported scarlet red jerseys with silver pants and helmets.

The game started with a fast San Francisco opening drive, capped off by a touchdown. Dallas failed to move the ball on its first possession, with McElhenny then breaking loose for an 89-yard touchdown on the 49ers ensuing drive, putting them up 14–0 before the Texans could catch their breath. Young ran for a score to put the home side on the board, and by halftime Dallas was down, 17–7. After a scoreless third quarter, the Texans were still only down by 10.

But in the fourth quarter, the 49ers finally woke up, and the blowout began. The Texans defense in that final frame was almost as funny as

Showing tremendous vertical leaping ability, rookie end Stan Williams's fourth-quarter efforts were too little, too late for the Texans to make a dent in the deficit they faced in the 49ers game. Note the Cotton Bowl crowd reaction, or lack of any crowd at all, in the background. From the collections of the Dallas History & Archive Division, Dallas Public Library.

Martin and Lewis. The 49ers scored three touchdowns in seven minutes before Dallas managed a meaningless scoring pass from Celeri to Gene Felker late in the fourth quarter. The final would be Texans 14, 49ers 37, and the game wasn't even that close.

The only silver lining was the crowd response, or perhaps lack thereof. Epitomizing the local fanbase, the players didn't hear many boos because there simply weren't many fans there to do so. The second game was in the books, and it was worse than week one. There had been a 30 percent drop in attendance even with Big Tex, Dean Martin, and Jerry Lewis.

To add insult to injury, the Miller brothers were hit with another snag they had overlooked. Part of their Cotton Bowl lease contained a clause that the Texans could not participate in the profit sharing from concession stand sales when the fair dates were in effect. That little detail may not have seemed monumental at the time the deal was signed, but every

Giles *(left)* and Connell *(right)* enjoying a few minutes of levity with guests Dean Martin and Jerry Lewis. Photo courtesy of Connell Miller Jr. and the Miller family.

dollar was needed. It was also a sign of what was to come.

Unaware of this clause prior to the season, Giles Miller had encouraged Bell to schedule at least two home games for the Texans during the run of the fair, shooting himself in the foot. That night, Miller could almost hear the phone at the McKinney Avenue offices ringing in his head, followed by, "Sir, Bert Bell is on line two."

The next day, upon learning the news, Bell bellowed at Miller, "Even a broken clock is right two times a day!"[3] Miller didn't understand the meaning, but game three was coming up and was on the road.

The low attendance for the first two home outings was quickly becoming an issue. Reserved tickets sold for $3.60. After federal and local taxes, the net total was $3.00. The proceeds were even less for the general admission seats. Further, though it was early in the season, the NFL's revenue sharing conditions were starting to heavily impact the Texans. The visitors made more money on these games than they did.

If the Cotton Bowl was to miraculously sell out, both teams would net six figures each. Of course, the large venue was not expected to, but the rule of thumb was that each week the Texans would owe a minimum payout to the visitors of $20,000, plus the required split of revenue for any amount exceeding that total. Having seen only 20 percent occupancy so far, that hefty payment trickled down into their parking intake. And now there was the unforeseen shortfall of concession earnings during the fair.

The conclusion was that there were expenses needing to be paid with no money coming in to pay them. Worse, the team was only two weeks into a twelve-game season.

12

FRUSTRATION SETS IN

THE THIRD week meant traveling to the Windy City to play the Chicago Bears on Sunday, October 12. Along with family, players, and staff, Giles and Connell left the Love Field airport at 2 p.m. on Saturday aboard a Braniff International Airways flight. Upon arriving, the team checked into the Hotel Windermere, a place other visiting NFL clubs also called home.

One of the league's founding franchises, the Bears were historically tough. Owner and head coach George Halas saw to that. He cast a long shadow across the NFL and had more influence than anyone, including Commissioner Bert Bell. In thirty-two seasons, Chicago had only posted a losing record twice. Since winning four championships over a seven-year period from 1940 to 1946, their "Monsters of the Midway" moniker had waned, but they were still good. When you played the Bears, your team usually felt it for an entire week after the game.

Chicagoans always supported their Bears, regardless of the opponent, and the crowd at Wrigley Field that day was near capacity at 35,429. This would prove to be the largest audience the Texans would see all season, so they would at least receive a good gate payout, despite incurring costs to travel.

The two teams took the field with the Texans wearing their white jerseys and silver pants for the first time. The Bears wore their traditional navy colors. At the 1:30 kickoff, the temperature was a pleasant sixty-eight degrees.

The game began much like the previous contest against San Francisco. Chicago took advantage of its guests, scoring twice in the first few minutes to take the lead, 14–0. After then driving the length of the field again early in the second quarter, the Bears were now ahead 21–0. Not giving up, George Taliaferro finally found a seam and ripped a 34-yard run into the end zone for the Texans. Alas, while the Dallas defense slowed Chicago down some, the home team still scored each time it had the ball. By halftime, the visitors were behind 31–7.

After a good rest, the Texans defense stiffened and showed some fight for most of the third quarter. But as was becoming their habit, they fell asleep on one play and the Bears' Babe Dimancheff found a hole, taking the ball in for a 77-yard touchdown. With a secure 38–7 lead and showing good sportsmanship, Halas inserted several second- and third-string players to finish out the game.

The Texans were also ready to call it a day. They ran the clock and the ball but did manage to add a couple of fourth-quarter touchdowns—one by Buddy Young and the other by Zollie Toth as time expired. The final was Texans 20, Bears 38.

Again, like the 49ers game before, the score was not indicative of what really happened. The opponent let up. Head coach Jimmy Phelan had nothing positive to offer the team afterward as they left the stadium and went straight to Midway Airport for the flight home. They landed back in Dallas at 10:45 p.m. with a record of 0–3.

In the week following the loss to Chicago, Bell continued to strongly express his displeasure to the brothers. He previously warned them that only four of the twelve league teams made a profit in 1951. Owners needed to be active and work, and in his estimation, the Millers weren't.

Recently, Bell had commented, "Don't let anyone get the idea that owning an NFL football franchise is a bowl of cherries; it's a rugged business."[1] He admonished Giles, "If you get into this business and don't work at it, you can lose $150,000 or $200,000 a year, and not just $25,000."[2] Bell previously disclosed on record that the cost of running a team had gone up 400 percent over the last ten years. Finally, he proclaimed, "We have given out forty-three franchises in this league. Thirty-one have been broke, forfeited, and discontinued."[3]

The Dallas franchise was beginning to take on that same look only one-third into its first season.

Week four would bring another home game, this time on Saturday night, October 18, against the beatable Green Bay Packers. Coached by third-year man Gene Ronzani, who had yet to have a winning season, Green Bay had fewer Pro Bowlers than the previous Yanks squad had fielded. The Packers were just not a very good team, which would provide the Texans with a favorable opportunity to get on the right track and win a game.

Dallas brought out its navy blue jerseys atop silver pants combination for the first time, while the Packers wore their yellow jerseys with tan pants and helmets. Kickoff was at 8 p.m., the Texans playing for the first time under the new Cotton Bowl lights.

The Packers struck first on a 28-yard pass from Tobin Rote to Bob Mann for the only score of the opening quarter, but the Texans responded with a Dick Hoerner 3-yard touchdown run early in second quarter and a 78-yard bomb from Bob Celeri to the versatile Taliaferro toward the end of the first half. The now-reliable Chubby Grigg extra point conversions were both good as well. Just like that, Dallas had the halftime lead, 14–7, marking the first time since four minutes into the season opener against the Giants that the team led an opponent.

Being on the right side of the scoreboard was short-lived, however, as Packers rookie sensation Billy Howton scored quickly in the third quarter off a 21-yard catch to tie the game. Green Bay later got a field goal before closing out the fourth quarter with another Howton touchdown, ending the night with 17 unanswered points.

After halftime, Dallas had come out satisfied, then they appeared stunned, and then just bored. The final score for this disappointment was Texans 14, Packers 24.

Dropping their first four games was bad enough, but the lack of attendance again made things worse. Only an estimated fourteen thousand fans came out for this one, which was more than the previous game but only about half of what the team needed to break even. Once again, the visitors netted more money and took home the victory. The Texans got nothing—except deeper in the hole.

No words can describe the Texans' failure better than the sight of a sparse Cotton Bowl crowd, where white fans would scatter throughout the midfield sections of the massive stadium while African American supporters sat farther away in segregated end zone areas, leaving everything in between empty. Photo courtesy of the *Fort Worth Star-Telegram* Collection, Special Collections, The University of Texas at Arlington Libraries.

With expenses continuing to snowball, coupled with the catastrophic lack of gate revenue, Giles and Connell called a special meeting at the Texas Textile offices. Their pop, C. R. Miller, attended to show support, as did all of the board members. The hope was to rethink their direction and have some form of an adjusted plan moving forward. A few in attendance, like Harlan Ray and Jack Vaughn, had ideas that were feasible, but there was no plan for how the organization could implement them.

The meeting evolved into a blame game against the city. Every board member enjoyed a cushy lifestyle, but rather than help with the team's financial burden themselves, the consensus among the group was to begin the futile effort of once again approaching Dallas area businesses to see how many ticket packages could be sold to stop the bleeding. What had not worked up until then, even when optimism was high, was foolishly thought to be a viable option now.

Board member John Coyle spoke up with the idea of creating additional funds in the form of a voting trust of capital stock. All that were present were agreeable, but none were willing to stick their own neck out.

At that moment, Phelan had heard enough. His frustration boiled over, and he asked to have the floor, serving up perhaps the most memorable tongue-lashing many of them had ever heard. And it was not so much what he said, but the way he said it.

"You and the rest of you big shots here in Dallas are quick to open your mouth, but slow as hell to open your pocketbooks," Phelan snarled. "It takes time and guts to build a pro team, and no one begins to appreciate what I have put together—not with your help, but in spite of you all."[4]

Phelan was clearly agitated, not only by what he heard that morning but also by all that he had endured since arriving in town. The Doak Walker wall, for example, stared at him every time he went to his office and festered in him like a migraine. He made use of the occasion to unload on the group that seemingly had all the ideas but none of the dedication to follow through.

By now red-faced, Phelan did not say thank you after he finally finished nor did he leave anything on the table. He simply sat down to a deadly silent room. No one had any response to offer. Reluctantly, Al Ennis then took the hushed floor, attempting to provide some form of summary and an opportunity for the group to take a break.

About half the board members got up and left. Those who remained were all in shock. Phelan's admonishment bruised feelings around the organization that would never subside. Giles and Connell, along with Pop, were in complete agreement with what Phelan had conveyed. But the board's deaf ears and the deflection of responsibility were not things the Millers were going to challenge any further. These men, of course, were all friends.

After the Texans' miserable effort in the second half against the Packers, the situation worsened by the day. The worrying was a cancer. Any optimism had disappeared. The shortage of money was taking its toll, and the team on the field was not working at all to get better.

Most of the young roster shared a lack of experience and focus, two problems that led to players becoming lazy and quickly out of shape. This

In happier and more optimistic times, Giles Miller *(facing third from left)*, along with his brother Connell Miller *(facing second from right)*, meet with local media in Giles's living room. They are joined by board members Harlan Ray *(facing left)*, Harold Byrd *(facing second from left)* and J. Curtis Sanford *(facing right)*. Photo courtesy of Ed Miller and the Miller family.

manifested itself from the top down, and Phelan became overwhelmed. He was exhausted from reasoning with the front office over solvency while battling the insurmountable burden of trying to win with nothing.

This weariness showed in his sudden disinterest in overseeing player discipline. Practices became unorganized with no more hitting. The players also invented a new game they called "football-volleyball." Using a football as a substitute, they would improvise with the goalpost serving as their net to play volleyball. The contests became competitive, and Phelan turned a blind eye, pretending not to notice. With a fondness for horse racing, the coach began taking part in extracurricular activities as well. In between what should have been team drills, he would make notes as to which thoroughbreds to bet on at the tracks.

The wheels were officially off.

13

MOUNTING DESPAIR

THE TEXANS, off to a 0–4 start, now had to reluctantly prepare for a West Coast road trip. The first stop would be against an undefeated 49ers team that had already beaten them badly. From there, the Dallas contingent would travel down to Los Angeles to play the reigning champions. Not exactly an optimistic two-week outlook.

They were not without some bright spots, though, as both rookie Gino Marchetti and big Art Donovan had played well. The duo of Buddy Young and George Taliaferro were also godsends, providing most of the team's scoring.

As they did with the Chicago trip, the Miller brothers and their spouses, excluding children, accompanied the Texans. They would stay the weekend in the Bay Area and then travel south the following week before returning home in eleven days. After boarding an American Airlines flight from Love Field on Friday at 1:25 p.m., they all arrived at San Francisco Municipal Airport later that afternoon. Their base would be the Alexander Hamilton Hotel, very luxurious accommodations for a team that was losing so much money.

On game day, the weather was typical for the time of year. Kickoff at Kezar Stadium was set for 12:30 p.m., and there was a light drizzle, fog, and a temperature of fifty-nine degrees. Both teams wore the same uniform combination as they had during their meeting in Dallas. Hopefully, the results would be different.

The game started out rough. Scoring twice in the first quarter and twice again in the second, with one extra point missed, the 49ers were up 27–0 before the Texans finally found the end zone. The touchdown came thanks to a long 45-yard pass from Bob Celeri to Young before halftime.

Their confidence destroyed again, and without any good words of encouragement from head coach Jimmy Phelan, the Texans came out in the second half completely deflated. Their defense let San Francisco score in the third quarter and two more times in the fourth. With a now 48–7 advantage, the rout was complete.

Giles painfully watched from the Kezar stands that day. Over the course of the game, he noticed a maddening, scratchy fight song being played repeatedly over the public-address system. He turned to his brother Connell sitting next to him and commented, "That cotton-pickin' song has been playing all afternoon."[1] By the third quarter, it finally hit them—the annoying music started up after every 49ers score. That, along with seagulls from the nearby bay flying overhead, made for a miserable afternoon.

The Texans went through the motions but added a couple of meaningless late touchdowns against the 49ers' third and fourth stringers. Both were scored on trick plays, with rookie halfback Hank Lauricella tossing passes to Celeri and fellow halfback Billy Baggett. The final tally read Texans 21, 49ers 48.

Once again, the scoreboard was not indicative as to what really happened over the full sixty minutes. But off the team went, returning to the posh luxury of the Alexander Hamilton for dinner and a night's rest before departing south for week six. Also going south was their record. Defeat was now routine as they dropped to 0–5.

After the massacre was over, Giles Miller was drained. He hopped on the bus going back to the hotel and sat between Chief West and Willie Garcia, making small talk. No one had much to say during the trip back.

Upon arrival at the hotel, Phelan awaited. With his face flushed, he called Miller over to one side as they departed the bus and suggested they have a beer and a talk inside. Miller was in no mood for conversation, and he did not sense the coach was in the right frame of mind either, as he was visibly agitated. Miller just wanted to go back to his suite, but the coach pressed him to stay for fifteen minutes.

Realizing his efforts were not working, Phelan suggested that they talk the next morning on the flight down to Los Angeles. Miller explained that he made different plans with his family members to take a train. The coach was insistent, so finally Miller agreed to meet him at the airport at 10 a.m. before the team left.

After midnight, when most everyone else went to bed, Miller decided to go out on a walk in San Francisco's neighborhoods. What kept running through his mind was that somehow, someway, the Texans needed to win. But how? The list of injured players coming out of the most recent loss seemed far greater than the healthy ones.

As he strolled through the streets, he found himself in front of a bar and stopped to go in. He took a seat as the bartender approached, ordering a bourbon on crushed ice with a water on the side. After finishing his drink, the bartender then gestured to see if he wanted a refill. Miller nodded yes, and without really looking up, he said of the person sitting beside him, "Why not one for him too?"[2]

The "him too" turned to thank the stranger who had bought him the drink, but interrupted himself midsentence, saying, "God almighty, I'm dead."[3] He knew that Miller was already very familiar with him. The man was his bruised and battered fullback Dick Hoerner.

Now making full eye contact, Miller responded, "Hello, Dick. Good to see you."[4]

Hoerner proclaimed that he had never broken curfew before, and now the one time he did, it was just his luck to run smack-dab into the team's owner. But on this night, Miller understood what having the weight of the world on one's shoulders was like, so he knew the right thing to say.

"Look, Dick, just skip it, will you?" Miller said. "It couldn't matter less."[5]

Hoerner's secret was safe. Miller did not subscribe to the curfew idea in the first place, and he assured him that he would not mention this to anyone, including the coach. He told Hoerner that they should just have another drink and try to relax. Miller's only insistence was that they not discuss football or the Texans.

And that is exactly what they did until arriving back to their rooms at 3 a.m. Both were pretty worn down but also feeling more at peace with the world than when they had left the hotel hours before. It was ironic that Miller got the decompression he so needed that night with a player and not Phelan.

The next morning, Miller put the family on the train and stayed behind to speak to the coach. The Texans were taking a United Airlines flight down to the Burbank Airport and would arrive shortly before noon on Monday. Phelan wanted the owner to travel along with the team, but Miller declined, preferring to hire a limousine to drive him down to Los Angeles after their meeting was over.

Clearly, the coach was extremely concerned. At the same time, Miller just wanted to be alone. He did not want to engage in long, depressing conversations. Consequently, their morning talk was quick and yielded nothing. Miller could not offer any reassurances to anyone, including himself, that things would get better.

Indeed, trouble began to come at the brothers fast after that terrible first week in California. Miller sent desperate word for his board representatives back home to request financial assistance from the Dallas Citizens Council. The first payment for the $200,000 balance toward the remainder of the Yankee Stadium lease was now due. With debt piling up by the minute, the team would not have sufficient capital to cover any of its other expenses once the stadium matter had been cleared.

The request to the council was for half the amount needed to get the Texans through this season and provide some help with next year. Before leaving for Los Angeles, knowing the weekly conversation would be forthcoming with commissioner Bert Bell, Miller decided to make the SOS call to Philadelphia and request the same relief from the league.

Several hours after everyone else got to Los Angeles, Miller finally arrived. In the meantime, Phelan's idle mind had been working. He still needed answers. Persistent, he immediately cornered Miller, wanting to talk more. The on-field frustrations, injuries, lack of backups, word on the street—all of it.

The coach needed a boss and he needed to vent. Mostly, Miller just listened. One very important point that Phelan wanted to make clear was that he was not referring to Miller during his board meeting rant the previous week. At the same time, he reconfirmed what he had said about everyone else and hoped Giles understood.

Miller let the coach know that he harbored no ill will toward him and that he did not feel the board members did either. Phelan, though, did not really care what the others felt; his concern was just with Giles and Connell. He felt they were bearing the brunt of the franchise's hardships.

Changing the subject, Phelan then insisted on going over the roster and the many injuries, hoping to cushion the blow for what he was certain would be another upcoming loss. Giles Miller listened through all the details in an attempt to appease the old coach, but it was clear that he wasn't interested.

Before they got up, Phelan once again dropped his voice and began with the inquiry as to where they were headed now financially. All Miller would offer was that frankly he currently had no idea whatsoever, but something would work out. Giles felt that his coach had enough to worry about without also carrying the team's unraveling economic disarray. Right or wrong, sometimes not knowing what you don't know is better.

After finally shaking off the coach, Giles went to Connell's room to brief him on his talk with Phelan. He also wanted to level with his brother on the state of the franchise, it seeming an eternity since the last time they spoke. Candidly, both had huge concerns and together phoned home to see if any headway had been made on the financial relief plan.

Jack Vaughn had been working the ticket drive idea but had nothing positive to report while Harlan Ray relayed that he and John Coyle had met with zero luck in drumming up any other new outside investor interest. Following the Millers' directions, Harold Byrd was set to present the financial assistance proposition to the Dallas Citizens Council, and he wanted to go through all the details to see if they would approve it.

Without even hearing Byrd's pitch, the brothers both committed to a "yes" for him to proceed. The proposal was to challenge the council to raise $125,000 in public funds to match the $125,000 they hoped would come via a loan from the other league teams.

The Millers had exhausted almost every avenue trying to raise capital and keep the team afloat. In truth, these ideas were not just the latest thing that someone came up with; they were all the Texans had left, a last gasp.

The pressure was mounting, but no one seemed interested in helping.

In Los Angeles, it was too late now to start saving money. With the accommodations already paid for, the team and staff set up at the Hotel Green in Pasadena. The property was beautiful and would prove to be yet another distraction from the season at hand, including for the now-unconfident Phelan. And the horses at the Santa Anita Park racetrack were less than ten miles away.

For Giles's drinking buddy Hoerner, the lynchpin in the Les Richter trade, returning to Southern California was personal. He expressed his desire to prove that the Rams made a mistake in letting him go. Leading up to the game, the local press was giving more attention to the Texans than any other 0–5 team warranted, all due to the big offseason swap and the players who were returning. But their primary focus was on Hoerner. In that week's Wednesday edition of the *Los Angeles Times*, Rams beat reporter Frank Finch wrote:

> *Hoerner gladly would sacrifice his right arm all the way up to the armpit to squash a few Rams and score a couple of touchdowns by way of informing the Ram high command that they were plain loco when they cut him loose. And as an added incentive to make his personal crusade, the terrible-tempered neo-Texan has all the warm affection for his old backfield coach, Hamp Pool, that a cobra has for a mongoose.*[6]

Leading up to their next outing, the Texans' workouts continued to be unorganized with little to no contact. On one afternoon, Phelan eventually made his way to the practice field only to find his squad at the goalpost engaged in another impromptu volleyball match. The coach broke up the shenanigans and gathered the team together to come up with a simple game plan of survival and run some basic plays.

The lack of effort instantly hit a new low. When practice opened, the players could not do anything right, already in surrender mode. Pushing and shoving ensued after almost every play. No one wanted to be there except for Hoerner and his grudge.

After the offense ran two successful screen passes, Phelan was satisfied. He blew his whistle, cancelling the rest of practice. Getting the team's attention, he yelled, "Save it for the Rams!" He then followed with, "Everyone on the bus."[7] The players were taken on a field trip, a thirty-minute drive to the Santa Anita racetrack.

At the end of the day, Phelan reported to the Miller brothers that he did not want to overplay his men, instead hoping to keep them fresh for what was to be an upcoming victory. Giles knew the old coach had been drinking.

Sunday, November 2 arrived, and they had to play the Rams. The day was a beautiful, sunny eighty degrees for the noon kickoff at the Memorial Coliseum. The Rams typically led the league in attendance, although there was media buildup during the week that fans might stay away from this one. A crowd of 30,702 attended, but while that was respectable for the Texans, the total marked the lowest home gate for the Los Angeles club that season.

In a rare showing of frugality, a last-minute decision was made to carry only one set of uniforms for the West Coast trip and have Willie Garcia get them cleaned in between games. With a roll of dimes in his pocket, he did his best at a local washateria.

Aside from looking better in their yellow jerseys with white pants and their distinctive blue helmets with the trademark yellow horns, the Rams were full of All-Pro-caliber players. They literally had too much talent, including two future hall of fame quarterbacks in Norm Van Brocklin and Bob Waterfield, who split duties during the season. Both were proven, but it was Waterfield who got the bonus of being married to Hollywood's leading actress, Jane Russell.

The opening drive was the same old song, as the Rams quickly moved across midfield and scored, their following possession bringing another touchdown to put them up 14–0 in the first few minutes. In the second quarter, the Texans drove the length of the field to get into scoring position. But rather than trust Young or Taliaferro to run it in, Celeri called for a pass, only to have Rams defensive back Herb Rich pick it off at the 3-yard line and return the interception 97 yards for a touchdown, the longest in the NFL that season.

Then the barrage came. Over the final few minutes of the second quarter, Los Angeles blew it open with two more trips to the end zone. Just like that, the score was 35–0, the game essentially over by halftime.

After the Rams reached the goal line again to make it 42–0 early in the third quarter, the now desperate Texans resorted to trickery and had the giant defensive lineman Marchetti play offense. Hauling in a 17-yard halfback fake option from Lauricella, the catch would be the only reception, a touchdown no less, of his illustrious career. With the game well out of reach, Los Angeles was content to let the Texans have their fun and allowed two more touchdowns in the fourth quarter. The final was Texans 20, Rams 42. Although this sounds like a broken record, the outcome was not as close as the lopsided score looked.

Each passing week was bringing a new low. At the season's halfway point, Dallas was now a winless 0–6

Upon returning to the hotel after the game, Giles Miller decided again to leave the crowded family suite and go for a walk to clear his mind, seemingly developing a new habit. The time being much earlier, he remained away from any bars. By now, his mood was too dark to even drink.

The next morning, Miller went to the airport in Burbank to see the family and the team off on their 9:15 flight back to Dallas. He was staying for a lunch that Rams owner Dan Reeves had implored he attend, and he really didn't want to get back to Dallas any sooner than he had to anyway.

At the airport, Connell reported that he had been on the telephone with the office and had approved an idea to release a statement through the newspapers. The announcement would read that all ticket prices had been cut in half for the remaining home games. General admission seats would be reduced to just sixty cents. Also, for the first time, they arranged that African American fans paying $1.80 for a reserved ticket would be able to sit near the goal line in the corners of the stadium, not in the end zones.

It was a last-ditch effort in the hopes that ticket sales would pick up. Giles could only cringe at the thought of the lambasting he would receive from Bell upon hearing the news. Giles knew that (discounting the product),

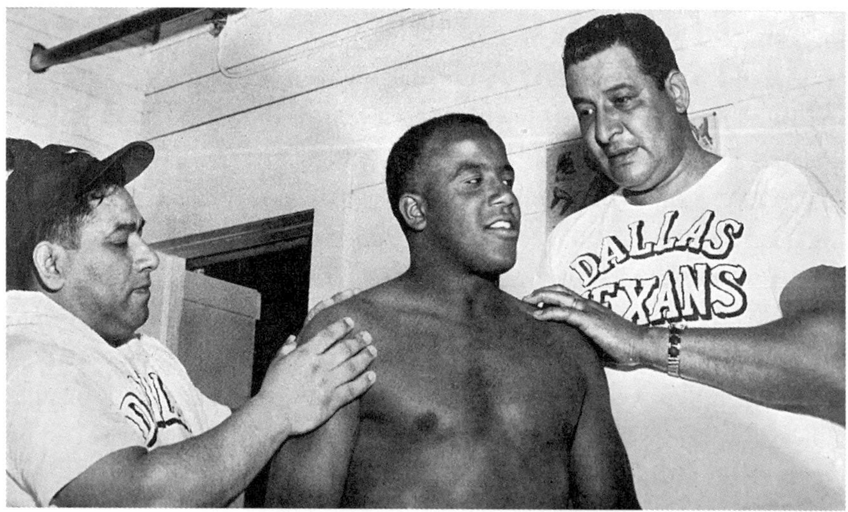

Compact and nimble, Buddy Young receives a much-needed after-game rubdown by trainer Chief West *(right)* with assistance from equipment manager Willie Garcia *(left)*. Photo credit: Johnson Publishing Company Archive. Courtesy of J. Paul Getty Trust and Smithsonian National Museum of African American History and Culture. Made possible by the Ford Foundation, J. Paul Getty Trust, John D. and Catherine T. MacArthur Foundation, The Andrew W. Mellon Foundation, and Smithsonian Institution.

it might be the last straw with the commissioner.

Returning to the hotel to meet Reeves for lunch seemed to help Giles's mood. The fellow owner genuinely wanted to know what he might be able to do to assist with whatever problems the Texans franchise was having, outside of financial assistance, which he was prohibited to do. Reeves saw Dallas as being very similar to Los Angeles in terms of economy and style. Miller agreed and explained that it took him some time to realize their problem was community acceptance of the professional game. By then, though, the fact they were a bad team did not help the matter.

Reeves let him know that he *might* have some potential ownership and investor interest that might be able to alleviate the financial pain. This, of course, was provided the team could hold on, make it through the season, and live to see another day. They would also need prior approval from Commissioner Bell before letting anyone else enter the picture.

Miller knew that it was a fairytale, unlikely to happen. Bell would never enable any sort of cash infusion at this point, as Giles began to feel the noose tightening around his neck. He believed that Bell now wanted him out of the league. Reeves could hardly dispute the claim.

They left the subject, finished lunch, and Miller then departed Los Angeles feeling that he had a good friend in his corner. The franchise was still in as much trouble as it had been when he woke up that morning, but he felt much better knowing that maybe one owner was on his side.

Returning to Love Field later that evening, Giles assumed it was time to face the music. Connell confirmed that the Dallas Citizens Council had held a meeting earlier that day at the Baker Hotel and denied any assistance to the franchise. Adopting a hands off policy, they refused any monetary relief toward the $250,000 needed. At the same time, Bell declined to provide any help whatsoever on the league's behalf.

Entering the second half of the season, the situation simply could not have been worse.

14

A MUDDY END IN DALLAS

SADLY, things got worse—and in a hurry. Upon his arrival home Monday night, Giles Miller learned that the office receptionist had rung his residence late in the day, informing that Bert Bell had called in three times. The commissioner's last message demanded that Miller be ready to talk first thing Tuesday morning, and the matter was urgent. Bell was in tune with money going out if there was sufficient money coming in. But he could smell that the Texans did not have enough funds to keep going.

Miller knew he could not avoid him and that the conversation would be unpleasant. The Dallas Citizens Council, along with the league, were not coming to the rescue. The fact that no one offered any assistance at all seemed unfair. With the bad debt load the franchise voluntarily inherited from the New York Yanks, and now officially out of money, the Texans were circling the drain. Indeed, they were in a lot of trouble. Still, Giles kept his hopes up.

Bell contacted the brothers first thing the next morning, and his tone was severe. The early days of Bell's semiconsiderate advisement were over. Chastisement was the new order of business. Giles never dreamed that the commissioner would turn on him and Connell, especially now when they needed help the most. Bell proceeded as if the end was already here, the team's failure a foregone conclusion.

"Boy, you have really loused this thing up," Bell stated to Giles.[1]

He then unloaded, telling Giles that they had failed because they did not go about things in the right manner. Bell brought up issues for the first time as if they'd been discussed on multiple occasions. He put words in the brothers' mouths, chastised Giles that his problem was that he thought this would be an exclusive club for Dallas, and contradicted what the Millers said and did on record.

In sharing what he had learned when he owned the Philadelphia Eagles, Bell would reference supposed conversations with Giles and Connell in January that never really happened. He then gave an example that the Eagles drew 60 percent of their fan base outside of Philadelphia proper.

"You should have gotten out your spurs and gone to promote in surrounding towns and regions," Bell ridiculed, reasoning that Texas is big. "Don't you think that driving five hundred miles to see a football game is something that them Texans would do?"[2] Bell was beyond frustrated. Exhausted, he hung up the phone with the brothers still on the line.

Everything aside, the next game was still on the way. Well known was the fact that Bell singlehandedly made the entire league schedule from his dining room table. He would generally consider things like travel distance, seasonal weather, baseball conflicts, and, above all, he would attempt to give each franchise attractive matchups in certain weeks. Some owners—his friends—usually received more favorable consideration. The brothers were, of course, not in that group.

Although it was not completely unheard of, the Texans' next opponent would be the same one they had faced in the prior week, the imposing Los Angeles Rams. This time at home.

As the days went on, the offices were so quiet that they became like a morgue. Employees and staff began to wonder whether they would be paid, and word didn't take long to trickle down to the men practicing at Burnett Field. The players were paid every two weeks, and the last time was during their California road trip. Despite having nothing to do with finances, in serving as general manager and head coach, Jimmy Phelan still sensed that something was coming down the line.

Being blown out the previous game, the players were less enthusiastic than ever. Once again, they were more interested in football-volleyball than anything else—except for getting paid. Prior to Wednesday's practice, which was also payday, Phelan had received inside knowledge that the player payroll would cause the team's account to be overdrawn, even before all the other bills were paid for the week. Insufficient checks were drafted and were already placed in the mail. The players were to receive their checks at the end of practice.

Phelan, wanting to be sure the players could beat the creditors to the bank, called the team to midfield, laid down the stack of checks, and blew his whistle before barking, "Everybody to the bank before it closes!"[3] Grabbing their checks and running to their cars was the most effort he had seen out of the players since they hit Kerrville. At that point, no one knew how long it would be before the official end came.

On game day, Sunday, November 9, there was a hard-driving rainstorm blanketing all of Dallas. Just like the team itself, the field was a mess. Leading up to the afternoon kickoff at 2:30, the rain continued to pour. Unsurprisingly, the deluge kept even more needed supporters away. The crowd was reported to be a generous ten thousand fans, even with the additional gate loss.

By now, Giles's pregame parties and shuttle transportations had been cancelled. He shared a ride to the game with a friend after having Earl Goins take his car down to Fair Park the day before, leaving it overnight. Miller's intentions were to not hold up the rest of the family following the contest against Los Angeles. And, admittedly, having a getaway car might be a good idea for this one.

In attendance would be the Rams' bright, young public relations assistant Tex Schramm, who in 1960 would become the Dallas Cowboys' first team president. Taking his post in the press box that afternoon, he saw a scene that looked more like a night game. The sky was dark, and the stadium appeared empty because everyone was sitting under the upper-deck overhang areas to stay out of the rain.

Leading up to game time, the ever-observant Bell had been keeping his ears open. He heard of the poor attendance and sent word to Schramm in the press box: "Don't you leave that office until you get your check."[4] Schramm then sent a message over to Texans business manager Al Ennis that he preferred to wait outside after the game for the payment.

Ennis responded that the payment probably would not happen directly afterward but would follow later, so Schramm introduced a new twist. The

Rams now demanded firm confirmation that they would receive what they were owed, and if this could not be done, they would not take the field.

Unable to accommodate the request on his own, and knowing that the team was already in the red, Ennis advised that he would reach out to minority owner Harlan Ray in order to work the problem out. Ennis knew that the team didn't have the money to cut the check unless someone stepped up.

Downstairs, just arriving at the Cotton Bowl, Giles Miller was dressed head to toe in warm-weather clothes to keep himself safe from the elements, and he quickly dropped by one of the concession stands after entering the gate to pick up a hot cup of coffee. Walking along, he suddenly became aware of his name being called over the public-address system, requesting that he come to the press box. As he headed toward the elevator, Ray spotted him, asking where in the world he had been and warning that everyone was looking for him.

They both took the elevator up, and as they stepped into the press box entryway, Ennis was anxiously waiting. Then and there, Miller was advised of the Rams' demand for payment or that they would not take the field. He questioned Ennis as to why the issue had not already been taken care of with another account, to which Miller was informed that those were without sufficient funds as well, rendering any written checks no good.

The main operating account was already overdrawn, and the secondary accounts would be by the time the checks in the mail hit. Miller was aware of this, but the team had another account of reserve monies with the Mercantile Bank of Dallas that should still have plenty of funds left to cover this crisis. With personal guarantees attached to it from the brothers and board members, the account was meant for emergency use. It would be drawn against their own individual finances.

To his surprise, Miller learned from Ennis that there were not enough funds in that account either due to the prepayments and deposits he had to make for the forthcoming two-week road trip. Ennis had been given no choice. The team needed to travel to those games, which Miller and Ray both completely understood.

Proactively, Ennis had already drafted a check for the Rams, but he could not sign off on it himself; two authorized signatures from the guarantors were required. As the discussion went on, Ennis admitted to Miller and Ray that if the gate guarantee was paid out, the account would likely be short $6,000 to $7,000.

At that point, Ray took the check from Ennis and endorsed it first. He then handed it over to Miller, telling him, "Let's you and me split the makeup money and get this game underway before the field freezes over."[5] The two shook hands in agreement. The only issue Miller had was signing off on a check that he knew was no good at the time. The transfers from their personal accounts would not follow until the next day. He told Ennis the only way that he would sign off would be for the check to be postdated. Ennis advised that the Rams would protest the stipulation, but Giles was adamant, not wanting to sign any check that appeared to be insufficient.

Overhearing this, Ray reminded Miller that this was not truly a "hot check" they were signing. They were both guaranteeing the money could be drawn out of their own accounts by their authorization signatures. Despite the argument, Miller signed as a co-guarantor and changed the date from November 9 to 12, initialing it in ink. He told Ennis to assure the Rams that the check was in his possession, was good, and that only after the game would they receive it. Ennis relayed the information, omitting the date issue, and the plan to play proceeded as scheduled. By the time the Rams found out, the game would be over.

When the teams took the wet field for warmups, both sidelines looked similar. The Texans appeared to have little energy and interest, worn out from the dramatic events of the week. The Rams could not work up much energy either—after all, they were playing a team they were expected to dominate and had already beaten handily a week earlier.

The days leading up to the game were so bad that, with no money, Willie Garcia didn't even have the uniforms laundered upon returning to Dallas. So the Texans would utilize the only clean combination they had, white jerseys with the silver pants, while Los Angeles once again wore its trademark Hollywood look. Both uniforms were about to get muddy anyway, except for the two rotating Rams quarterbacks, who would not get hit much.

The game started out slow. The Rams chose to keep the ball on the ground and stay away from their usual high-flying aerial circus. The only points in the first quarter came when Los Angeles completed a drive, eight minutes into the game, with a field goal. In the second quarter, Dallas followed suit with its rushing attack and capped off its own drive with a 4-yard touchdown run by Zollie Toth. The extra point was missed, but for only the third time in the season, the Texans were ahead in a game, 6–3.

The lead did not last long, as the Texans were their own worst enemy with multiple penalties that kept the Rams' drives alive. In the first half's final series, Los Angeles would retake the lead, 10–6. The downpour continued during the intermission, and both teams tried to find a compelling reason to finish out this soaker.

In the second half, it was penalties that suddenly rained on the Rams and turnovers that plagued the Texans; only the visitors were able to add a field goal in the third quarter. The back and forth continued into the fourth.

Quarterback Frank Tripucka, who was making his first start for the Texans after being acquired earlier that week in a trade with the Chicago Cardinals, saw that the Rams were not playing their best game and thought they could be beaten. He decided to gamble through the air and try to sneak out a win. And he did complete a pass for a touchdown, but unfortunately in the wrong direction. The interception was returned by Rams future hall of fame defensive end Andy Robustelli for a 14-yard score. It was now Los Angeles 20, Dallas 6.

Late in the game, after eight turnovers, the Texans decided to slip up again, this time on a punt. The Rams' Woodley Lewis fielded the kick and ran it back 65 yards for the final score of the day. The sloppy affair was over.

Even though they lost, Dallas equaled the Rams in rushing yards with 174, while topping them in passing yardage, 88 to 8. Los Angeles also had more penalties, twelve to four. But the Texans' turnovers and the numerous sacks of their quarterback kept them from establishing any offensive punch and killed any good they could have done. On paper, at least, the game was their best so far.

The final game played in Dallas against the Rams. Although Buddy Young had tremendous speed, the mud and the financial devastation awaiting was something he nor the organization could outrun any longer. From the collections of the Dallas History & Archive Division, Dallas Public Library.

The players ran off the field and into the tunnel. No one sat in the end zone seats to encourage them that there was always next week. Final score: Texans 6, Rams 27. They had lost to the same team two weeks in a row, and their record now was 0–7.

With the rain still coming down hard after the game, Schramm waited under the cover of the Women's Building near Fair Park's front gate entrance. Once he received the guaranteed check, he quickly hailed a cab to get across town to Union Station, where the rest of the Rams' traveling party was preparing to head to Chicago for next week's game. In a rush, Schramm never noticed that the check was postdated for Wednesday, November 12. He almost missed the train.

After the misery of the last three hours, Giles just wanted to leave the stadium as fast as he could and get home. First and foremost, he wanted to avoid the risk of pneumonia. He also had no desire to be around anyone or participate in any of his newfound neighborhood walks after the defeat. Everything seemed terrible.

But Connell dropped by his home with board member and friend J. Curtis Sanford, a gesture that seemed to help. They wanted to brighten the mood and determine if there were any brilliant thoughts as to where to go from here. Giles was emotionally spent, having no idea but very aware that they needed to do something fast.

There was, however, one task that he wanted to get off his plate. Giles told his brother that it would be very helpful if he could cover a commitment to speak at a luncheon the next day in San Antonio. Connell agreed to do it, sight unseen, so that Giles could stay in town and be free to formulate some sort of plan of action for the coming week.

Connell was not enthusiastic, but he would do anything to help get his brother out of the dumps. He asked Giles, "What in heaven's name am I going to talk about?"[6] Giles told him that he had no idea and had not planned any topic when he accepted the engagement. He then suggested Connell speak on putting together a professional football team, and that doing so is no bed of roses.

The muddy loss to the Rams that night proved to be the final appearance for the Texans in the Cotton Bowl, though that fact was unknown to the brothers. The next day would be a tough one—and the next week one for the ages.

15

FORFEITURE

MONDAY'S ARRIVAL could not be stopped. Giles Miller drove to the office to work on getting the team out of the red, his first concern making good on the check that was given to Rams public relations assistant Tex Schramm as he left Dallas.

Asking his father for a loan was not a possibility. Miller went to lunch with his pop, Clarence, seeking something positive or some words of encouragement. What he received was his father saying, "Bucky, you have managed to get completely in over your head, and it just does not look good . . . not good at all."[1]

Returning to the office, Miller learned that the drafted checks had made their way through the mail and had begun to bounce. Hopelessly, he was trying to find any solution so the Texans could live to see another day. But nothing was there.

Each hour seemed like an eternity, the possibility for miracles long passed. NFL commissioner Bert Bell phoned in several times, bellowing demands for Giles or Connell to call him back. They couldn't dodge him any longer. By Wednesday, November 12, Giles had no other options left. The time had finally come to face the music and make the lethal decision on the franchise's fate.

Earlier that morning, unaware of the forfeiture plan and having yet to hear from the Millers, Bell laid down his new edict. He left word demanding to see both brothers, or at least Giles, in his office by Friday afternoon at 1:00 or face the consequences of repossession by default.

The decision had already been made that the Dallas club could no longer support itself. The charter and the franchise's assets would be forfeited over to the league and become NFL collateral property. From there, Bell and his office would determine how the remainder of the season would be finished, and how, or even if, the players would be paid.

For the time being, Giles ignored the message.

Across town at Burnett Field, the players assembled, most of them late. They played football-volleyball until head coach Jimmy Phelan arrived. Recently, each day began with their questions. Phelan had no answers. The team was out of money. They had all just been paid. Whether they would be getting another check was uncertain. The team was due to depart Love Field at 3:00 on Friday via Braniff Airways on a flight to Detroit for a game against the Lions. This was the extent of what the coach knew, that is, until Wednesday after practice.

Summoned back to the McKinney Avenue office, Phelan was told that the Miller brothers and board of directors had decided to fold. Later that dreary afternoon, shortly after informing the old coach and the rest of the organization, Giles formulated a short and simple telegram to Bell in Philadelphia that read: "I regret that it is necessary to inform you the Dallas Texans Football Club Inc. as of today is unable to complete the current season because of lack of finances."

After sending the telegram, Miller put the word out, calling for an immediate special press meeting in his office. He planned to make the announcement to the media without any preparation. Instead of taking time to draw up a proper release, the decision was made to simply field questions.

Once the conference began, however, the atmosphere quickly disintegrated into a frenzied exchange. Several reporters bombarded the two brothers and the board members present with questions of, "Why this?", "Why not that?", "What happened?" Giles was the main target for most of the daggers, with others in attendance finding it impossible to get a word in between the questions. Connell finally took over and tried his best to deflect the heat. He shouldered the burden of interrogation for his exhausted brother.

Wanting to provide some insight, Connell made the case that the franchise did not have a chance for success. He stated that the Texans didn't get to participate in the draft, didn't receive any timely know-how from the league, and that no other NFL staff would give them any real help. Without true guidance, there was no way to expect success. Connell's explanation was a nice way of informing the press that all Commissioner Bell did was bark at the brothers instead of trying to help.

One last brash question came from *Fort Worth Star-Telegram* sports editor Flem Hall, who was waiting impatiently for Connell to wrap up his statement. He bluntly asked, "If that were the circumstance, why did you invest in it in the first place?"[2] The level-headed person he was, Connell mildly replied while scratching the back of his neck, "At the time, it seemed like a good idea."[3] With that, the meeting and the franchise were finished.

In Philadelphia, upon receiving the telegram, Bell was furious. The Millers had beat him to the punch. The decision was his and the league's to make, not the team's. He didn't like losing. Again, he called and demanded that Giles now come to his office by 1:00 the next day for what was to be a private hearing. There would be no response from Giles the rest of the day. There was really no reason for him to attend anything, or to endure any more of Bell's scolding rants.

Friday brought the original 1:00 deadline, but Bell still had not heard from anyone in Dallas. It became obvious that neither Giles nor any franchise representative was going to show up. As Bell stormed back and forth, pacing, he angrily barked out, "Get Giles Miller on the line!" The office phones in Dallas had not been answered all day, but knowing the time had arrived, Miller reluctantly picked up the call. At that moment, Bell pulled out a prewritten statement he had drafted earlier that morning. With an assembled media contingent in his office to witness, he read it to Miller over the phone and then planned to turn the announcement over to the press for release. His message proclaimed:

> *I have determined that the Dallas Texans Football Club Inc. is guilty of acts detrimental to the National Football League, namely a refusal to continue to operate the club and field a team throughout the balance of the 1952 season. The franchise is hereby canceled and forfeited*

> *and the player contracts, including the reserve player list, are hereby taken over by the National Football League on behalf of the remaining clubs in the league.*

After the reading, Bell then softened his tone, dismissed the group assembled, and showed some much-needed compassion toward Miller. He told him, "I think you were a wonderful sport," going on further to comment, "I want you to know that I will never forget that you and your brother Connell, and Harlan Ray dug into your own pockets to pay the Los Angeles Rams their $20,000 guarantee."[4] With that, the Texans were officially no more.

The franchise only lasted forty-six days into the season, not counting the optimistic early days of the January purchase, which spread into the offseason planning and then to training camp.

When all was said and done, the only thing remaining was for the team to finish out the season. The players would gather on Friday afternoon at the airport for an eerie flight to Detroit—alone with only the coaching staff. Some wondered why no one else from the organization was accompanying them.

After a grueling, pressure-filled week, Miller had dismissed football from his mind until the call from Bell. But he went to the airport to bid the team farewell, knowing it would be awkward for both him and the players. Notably for Buddy Young and George Taliaferro, parting was indeed sorrowful. Others said that they would keep in touch by letter every few days. Phelan, preoccupied with the magnitude of the recent events, merely said goodbye, nothing more.

Miller walked away feeling like he had abandoned the team. He believed that he had failed not only the city, but the players and coaches who depended on him. All that he and Connell ever wanted to do was bring pro football to Texas and be successful enough that Dallas would be considered a legitimate NFL city. Giles couldn't remember a single moment when the franchise's intentions were misplaced. There were, however, several times when everyone else failed both him and the franchise. But it wasn't in his nature to hold a grudge or blame anyone else.

Back in Philadelphia, Bell needed to put a plan together on where to go from here. He did mandate that the NFL wouldn't be returning to Dallas. The team would be nowhere near the ownership or fanbase that failed. With the league now essentially in possession of the franchise again, Bell would make it his mission to manage the operation with a shoestring budget, the players soon to see this new reality.

Around 8:00 that night, the team landed at Detroit's Willow Run Airport. Taking a bus downtown to the Sheraton Cadillac Hotel, the players knew nothing regarding their future except that there were still five games remaining on the schedule. They had made the trek up to Detroit but were unsure whether or not they would actually play and be paid for the upcoming game and beyond.

Coach Phelan didn't know any more than them at this point. When approached by a group of reporters, he mentioned, "We're still a football team, whether we have a home or not. We hope to knock somebody off before the season is over, but it sure looks like a tough assignment."[5] So the players did the only thing they could think of to do that night—they hit the bars in and around the hotel.

By early the next morning, Bell had gotten word to Phelan that the game was still on as scheduled. He also informed him that the team would play the four remaining games on the road and would not return to Dallas. And he confirmed that they would be paid, as per their individual contracts, by a league pool.

Phelan had been through so much since the New York move and knew how highly visible his mannerisms would appear to the players. His job was to be a source of stability, to minimize the disruption they now found themselves in. He called all the players into a conference meeting room at the hotel and delivered the news. It wasn't received well.

Many of the players were from Texas and, of course, did not want to be away from their families for an extended period. For the players who made the move south from New York, here was yet another change in scenery, and they didn't even know where their next destination would be. Ultimately, everyone would have to move somewhere if they decided to stay with the club.

When word broke to the Detroit media, area reporters asked Phelan what he had said to the team. His reply was straight and simple, "Their

Giles Miller at his desk. The afternoon of Wednesday, November 12, 1952, was a day of loss after no one would come forward to provide aid. Photo courtesy of Connell Miller Jr. and the Miller family.

job is to play football, and they are going to get to do that right down to the wire."[6]

Many players were still trying to process what had happened when they went to a nearby site on Saturday for a quick walk-through. Some felt things would get better; others felt worse. One thing was now for sure, though: it was hard to focus on football.

On Sunday morning, November 16, Phelan decided to get his men out of the hotel early and over to the stadium. Kickoff wouldn't be until 3:00, but anywhere was better than where they now were. Staying inside an old building gave the players a feeling of being held hostage.

Outside, the weather was unseasonably warm in Detroit for that time of year. The temperature was fifty-nine degrees, and there was little to no wind at game time. Relieved that they would play out the rest of the season and be paid, the players generally believed that this was a change for the better.

They were quickly reminded that the more things change, the more they stay the same.

The Lions started off the game with time-consuming drives that largely kept the Texans offense off the field, perhaps for their own good. Taking a 10-0 lead into the second quarter after keeping the ball on the ground, Detroit then went to the air in an attempt to finish off the Texans early. It worked, as the Lions added points on five of their possessions in the first half. Meanwhile, the Texans only found the end zone once—and it was their own, for a safety. The halftime score was all Detroit, 29-0.

To open the third quarter, the Texans finally began to show some fight. Quarterback Frank Tripucka came out throwing and connected with Ray Pelfrey for a touchdown pass that would end a scoring drought that had stretched over four quarters, going back to the previous week against the Rams. The Texans' blocking was unable to open up any holes, so Tripucka deployed Dick Hoerner to get open and completed passes to the fullback to put them in scoring range. There Zollie Toth crossed the goal line on a 4-yard run. The missed extra point made the score 29-13 going into the fourth quarter. It was the proverbial last gasp.

Over the remainder of the game, the Texans turned the ball over every time they got their hands on it. Although not their intent, the Lions had no choice but to attack from there. The final score was Texas 13, Lions 43.

The 30-point difference was the worst loss for the team so far. Detroit, which would go on to finish first in the National Division, won in every phase of the game, though the Texans outdid them in yards lost and turnovers. The defeat dropped the club to 0-8, and they didn't know where they were going next.

Back in Dallas, as the days rolled by, the brothers oversaw the orderly wind down of franchise business affairs. The league was now running the team, leaving nothing for the former, defaulted syndicate to do except pay more bills. The routine phone calls from Bell quickly ceased. The office went quiet.

16

HERSHEY

MONDAY MORNING'S original plan was to depart Detroit's Michigan Central Station on a New York Central Railroad train and arrive in Chicago by lunchtime. The team was all set to stay once again at the Hotel Windermere and then travel up to Green Bay on Saturday, the day before the next game. The players loved Chicago and were looking forward to the nightlife, but there was a change of plans. NFL commissioner Bert Bell had other ideas and advised head coach Jimmy Phelan of his intentions.

Rumor began to circulate among the players after overhearing one of the coaches whisper what he had just heard. The talk centered around them going to a different destination to dock instead. Rightfully so, the recently orphaned players assumed the new stopover would be another larger populated area with good facilities and travel lanes. None of them expected to hear the words "Hershey, Pennsylvania."

To a chorus of laughter, a couple of the players jokingly asked if that was the place where they make chocolate. As fate would have it, the town was indeed home to the manufacturing plant of the world-famous Hershey's Milk Chocolate Candy Bar.

Having experienced Hershey once, all Phelan could think about was how he was going to keep this already unmotivated group focused on football. The sweet smell permeating the entire area would itself be a distraction, especially for Art Donovan and Chubby Grigg.

Bell's decision came about because he had a lot of previous experience using Hershey as a training camp base for the Pittsburgh Steelers and Philadelphia Eagles when he was affiliated with those teams. Though none of the players remained, the New York Yanks had also held training camps there in 1948 and 1949. Moreover, the site was close enough for the commissioner to keep an imposing, watchful eye. Bell could easily look over Phelan's shoulder, whom he would leave in charge of the basic day-to-day activities. More importantly, since the remaining eleven owners were fitting the bill, it was cheap.

The players and coaches were shipped out of Detroit later that day. By a combination of train and bus, they arrived in Hershey on Tuesday. By then, word of their coming had spread through the town, and they were welcomed like royalty. Still known as the "Dallas" Texans, they were embraced as Hershey's team now.

While there, the club would utilize the Hersheypark Stadium facilities as its home base. The facility held upwards of fifteen thousand people, which based on the franchise's prior gate numbers would easily suffice. However, the Texans would finish out the rest of the season as a road-only team with no games to be played there.

By Wednesday, Phelan finally got his men out to the practice field where they tried to put together something that looked like a team still wanting to play. But the players' interest soon waned, the troops breaking off into the inevitable football-volleyball games. After seeing enough, Phelan blew the whistle and called it a day.

Instead of cleaning up, most of the players hit the road into town to find something to do. They found it in a watering hole called The Tavern, putting forth more effort getting to the legendary bar located on Chocolate Avenue in downtown Hershey than they did on the practice field. For Phelan, he simply wanted to play out the string and go home. This did not feel like long-term employment for the coach anymore.

At practices that week, the team paid even less attention to the upcoming game. More was placed on football-volleyball, beer guzzling, and a newfound recreational activity—fishing on the nearby lakes, which Phelan felt would be a better option than drinking. Practices were to be called off early from now on. But by Friday, the time had come to make the trek back to the Midwest again.

Week nine's opponent would be the Packers on Sunday, November 23, at Green Bay's City Stadium. The venue was a single-level, glorified high school field, primarily constructed out of wood. It was at the bottom of the league's facilities. Given their new conditions, the Texans would feel right at home there.

They traveled first by bus, and then took an overnight train with no sleeping areas, before reaching Chicago by late morning on Saturday. Immediately hopping onto another train, the players and staff finally arrived in Green Bay around 5:00, just in time for a team dinner and final meeting before bed.

At the Hotel Northland, word was sent to Phelan that sometime after Sunday's game, Bell would reach out and give him instructions for the following week. The scheduled site was to be a home game in Dallas on November 30 at 2:00, but of course that wouldn't be happening.

As Sunday arrived, the game-time temperature for the 1:00 kickoff was forty-two degrees, typical for Green Bay in late fall. Over a month had passed since their first meeting in Dallas—when the world was different—and the suddenly competitive Packers were entering the match with a 5–3 record.

Like the Texans' other games, their opponent started out fast. Green Bay's plan was to put the ball in the air much of the time, utilizing a rotation of Tobin Rote and rookie Babe Parilli at quarterback. On the Packers' second possession, Rote threw a touchdown pass for the game's first score. Within minutes, the Texans fought back with a drive to tie things up at 7–7.

The Packers continued their aerial assault in the second quarter, passing so often that they were intercepted a couple of times by the Texans defense. But with Dallas now not moving the ball, Green Bay was eventually able to reach the end zone twice more before the half ended. Going into the locker room, the score was Packers, 21–7.

The second half was more of the same. Green Bay drove the length of the field for scores, adding more nails to the coffin, while the Texans still couldn't move the ball for much of the third quarter. The Packers became bored and sloppy, turning the ball over seven times, but Phelan's boys could never take advantage of the gifts. The running game was unable to gain a yard. And for every turnover the Packers suffered, more often than not, they would later connect for a score.

Toward the end of the quarter, the time had come to put the game away. Rote launched an 81-yard completion to increase his side's lead, 35–7. Whether it was the Texans showing some fight, or the Packers were just getting tired, Dallas drove the ball down to the 6-yard line where fullback Dick Hoerner punched it in.

The fourth quarter was a mess on each side. Only the penalties were plentiful. Late in the game, the Dallas defense fell asleep and allowed another touchdown run, this one from 45 yards out, to wrap up the scoring. The final score was Texans 14, Packers 42.

The box score showed both teams with the same amount of first downs and penalties that day, but while the time of possession favored the Texans, the quick-strike nature of the Packers' passing attack led to Green Bay having twice the number of offensive yards.

This game felt the same as all the others—basically over by the end of the first half, as the Texans were outscored by four touchdowns for the second straight week. The good news was there were not many who saw this lopsided affair. Only 16,340 people showed up.

The Texans were now sitting at a winless 0–9 on the season and, once again, did not know where the train or bus would take them next.

17

A THANKSGIVING MIRACLE

THE NEXT MORNING, the plan was for the players and coaches to retreat frugally toward the direction from whence they came. With only one real way out of Green Bay, it would be by way of train back to Chicago.

Week ten's opponent was the Bears, in a game that was originally set to be played in Dallas the following Sunday. Since that wasn't going to happen, the meeting would need to be staged in Chicago or somewhere else. Very quickly, the decision was made that the matchup could not take place in Chicago, as the crosstown Cardinals were already playing at Comiskey Park. There was a standing agreement in place that the two Chicago teams would alternate home games and never compete for gate receipts on the same day.

As the Texans departed for Chicago, there had still been no word yet from Commissioner Bert Bell on where they would go. The players and staff logically assumed that meant they'd be staying in Chicago for the week. But maybe another train and then finally a bus back to Hershey?

Upon the team's arrival in Chicago, Bell had left word at the station for head coach Jimmy Phelan. The team would continue east but stop at a point exactly halfway back to Hershey. Accommodations were already in place.

The site would be Akron, Ohio, and the Sunday game had been moved up to Thursday, which was Thanksgiving Day. Bell arranged with the local school district there to stage the Bears game as the second half of what was billed as a "doubleheader day" for football. This was a new low.

The state of Ohio was a hotbed for high school football, and the Akron Public Schools were having their championship game, referred to as the Turkey Day Game, that morning at 10:45. Featuring the Akron South Cavaliers versus the Akron East Fighting Orientals, the title tilt would be held at the Rubber Bowl, a twelve-year-old stadium that was home to the University of Akron Zips. The venue could accommodate up to thirty-five thousand fans, and the high school championship game was said to be close to a sellout. With a built-in audience already in place, what could possibly go wrong?

By midday Wednesday, the team had arrived in Akron. There wasn't any time to get in a practice walk-through, so Phelan decided to arrive at the stadium early on Thanksgiving morning and prepare there before the high school game. The players were amazed as they witnessed the droves of people coming through the gate before the first game was to be played. They thought the buildup was all for them, and the fanfare filled the team with so much excitement and emotion that they couldn't wait to play their showcase against the Bears.

By the time the high school championship game started, it was clear the estimated crowd of more than thirty thousand fans had been over-reported. In reality, there were only 14,213 on hand, the stadium about half full. In other words, the crowd was of average size for a Texans' home contest, despite being almost twelve hundred miles from Dallas. But the team believed more would show up for the second game, making this by far the largest "home crowd" of the year for the team.

Phelan's men scattered to an adjacent area during the high school affair to practice and prepare a little more. This was to be their day. Even though a local newspaper wrote headlines that week of "Mighty Chicago Bears" and "Texans Burial Due," this just felt different. There was no temptation to play football-volleyball, drink beer, or mess around. This was the most focused they had been since opening day.

Reentering the stadium, the Texans contingent saw the completion of the first game where Akron East defeated Akron South by a score of 26–19. Then they saw something that utterly shocked them.

Most all of the game's spectators stood up en masse and left, never having any intention of staying. It was as if they were unaware there was even a pro game about to begin. The weather was beginning to turn cold, so the school supporters went home to eat and celebrate Thanksgiving. Or most of them did. Only 2,208 people stayed, according to the local *Akron Beacon Journal*. The fan exodus was one of the craziest things the players had ever seen.

The Bears were coming off a last-minute victory over their rivals, the Detroit Lions. Chicago's owner and head coach George Halas was so thrilled with his players' efforts in their Sunday win that afterward he promised and delivered bonus checks to the entire team. Now going into the game against the Texans, Halas knew the state of his deflated opponent and pondered how much preparation and motivation would really be needed.

The temperature had been thirty-six degrees during the first game, but as the teams came out for their pregame warmups, the mercury was beginning to drop and would dip into the twenties by the 2:45 kickoff time. The Bears took the field in their traditional navy jerseys and white pants, looking more like the home team, while for the first and only time all season, the Texans wore a combination of all white, both jerseys and pants. Perhaps indicative of waving a white flag over the season.

The horseshoe-shaped Rubber Bowl now appeared completely barren, as those remaining were scattered around. The Texans, who had been so excited during the morning hours, were now completely distraught. After warmups, the players retreated to the locker room where they were to receive their customary pep talk.

Dead silence permeated throughout the room, enough that you could hear the players breathing. A hollow metal door opened with a creaking noise, turning into a vibrating slam as it shut. In walked their leader.

Phelan entered the locker room smoking a cigar. Taking a puff and then talking out of the side of his mouth, he began his short pregame speech to the players with these powerful words: "Gentlemen, this has not been the best of seasons, but it is Thanksgiving Day, and you do have a lot to be thankful for. Oh, we were put out of Dallas, and now we are wards of the league. But of all those clubs that have won before, you have never had the experience that you're going to have today."[1]

All around the room, the players gazed at each other, then looked at him for much-needed emotional mentoring. He responded further: "The big responsibility that you have in the National Football League, and no other club has had this, that the crowd is so small, rather than introduce you as a team, you all can go up in the stands and meet the crowd individually."[2]

Minutes later, while walking onto the field, Bears coach Halas noticed the homeless and hopeless Texans wandering about the grandstands, shaking hands. Across the way, he saw a vulnerable team that was so cold that its players constructed trashcan fires at both ends of the bench just to try to stay warm. He thought they looked like a bunch of street bums.

It was at that point when he decided to give most of his starters, and their backups, the day off. With quarterback Bob Williams being the lone exception, Halas started almost everyone at the end of the bench, using third-string and even some fourth-string options. Just so long as they had a uniform.

Halas's plan did not take long to backfire. After seeing Williams throw interceptions on each of his team's first three possessions, the coach benched him and put in backup George Blanda. The Bears' reserves had not practiced together, and it showed. They were badly out of rhythm, turning the ball over and missing field goal attempts.

Chicago's struggles provided the Texans two sensations they had not experienced during the season: confidence and hope. They also felt insulted that Halas put backups in to face them. Still, the Texans were unable to capitalize on all of the early turnovers.

After the mistake-filled first quarter, Bears defensive leader Don Kindt was frustrated with his team's performance and went too far with an aggressive tackle on little Buddy Young for a safety. The hit was more than just unnecessary roughness, though, and the Texans took issue with him picking on Young because he was Black.

He and George Taliaferro had put up with so much discrimination since day one, so the rest of the team had seen enough and responded with new momentum. Something had suddenly changed in them; their blood was boiling. The homeless castoffs took the fight to their overconfident counterparts.

After the safety, the Bears fumbled the free kick, and the Texans recovered. Just four plays later, fullback Zollie Toth uncharacteristically jumped from the 2-yard line over three Chicago defenders to put the Texans ahead for what was only the third time of the season. Toward the end of the first half, the team again moved into scoring range, where Taliaferro completed a 20-yard halfback-option pass to Dick Wilkins for a touchdown. The score after two quarters was a surprising 13–2, Texans leading.

At the beginning of the second half, the Texans came out fighting with pride. Rather than staring at the empty seats, they stared down an opportunity to finally win a game. During the third quarter, with the ball at the Chicago 30-yard line, Frank Tripucka completed a pass to newcomer Ray Pelfrey at the 1-yard line. Two plays later, the quarterback reached the ball over the goal line to make it a 20–2 Texans advantage. The small crowd sounded like someone had turned the volume up to fifty thousand strong. These fans were witnessing an impossible underdog-blowout in the making and now began to chant, "Go Texans! Go Texans!"

Halas was furious. With the Bears down by 18 points, he sent in all of his starters, most of whom were not ready to play. He also let it be known that it was not too late to cancel those bonus checks they had received four days earlier. Hearing the threat, the fresh starters immediately responded with a fury that was typically reserved for their fiercest rivals, not the lowly Texans. They were scared to come back to the bench and face Halas if they failed.

To begin the fourth quarter, the Bears defense forced a fumble deep in Dallas territory and drove to the goal line, scoring on a 1-yard run to make it Texans 20, Chicago 9. Then on their next possession, the Texans moved only a few yards and had to punt. Despite their hard work, the opportunity for victory appeared to be unraveling. Chicago took over, driving past midfield before firing a 41-yard touchdown pass to narrow the lead. The better team was awake and closing in, down by only 4 points.

On the ensuing kickoff, the nervous Texans became desperate. With less than eight minutes left in the game, running the ball would have made sense, which would also have run down the clock. Whether the rusher was Young, Taliaferro, Hoerner, or Toth, any ball carrier would be a good option to keep the Bears' hot offense off the field.

Foolishly, they decided to pass instead, and Tripucka threw an interception. The Bears took over. The time had come to stop playing around, and Blanda soon connected with George Schroeder on a 35-yard missile that landed right in the heart of the Texans' end zone. Chicago had finally taken the lead, 23–20. Their work appeared done for the day; they had surely overcome what would have been a near disaster.

The clock was ticking fast on the Cinderella Texans. They took over the ball for what would likely be the last possession of the game. Starting at their own 25-yard line, it was now or never.

And then, amazingly, Tripucka picked apart the Bears secondary, completing five passes on the drive to move the Texans down to Chicago's 20-yard line. At the very least, they could try a last-minute field goal to tie. But with the clock continuing to run, the old gambler Phelan decided that a tie just would not do. He wanted the win, by hook or by crook.

Noticing that the Bears were double-covering the smaller Young, Phelan inserted his tall defensive back, Tom Keane, who had good hands and was a part of the eleven-man trade with the Rams before the season. Noticing the substitution and fresh out of timeouts, the Bears' captain, Kindt, frantically sprinted toward the bench to notify Halas that they should rotate their coverage. However, the notoriously stubborn coach angrily waved off his player, telling him to stay in formation. With Keane now in the huddle, Tripucka decided to take advantage of the double-coverage on Young and use Keane's height to throw a jump ball into the end zone.

Tripucka dropped back, planted his feet in the soft ground, and threw a high-arching pass toward Keane with just enough touch to get the ball over the cover man Kindt. Both players collided near the goal line and wrestled for possession, but amidst all the chaos, no one had a good view of who made the catch. Then Keane rose up with the ball in his hands after winning the fight.

While the trickery worked, the completion brought only a 17-yard gain, coming up short of the end zone. But just two snaps later, with the clock still running and now down to thirty-four seconds, Tripucka ran a quarterback draw and lunged the ball over the goal line. Unbelievably, it was touchdown Texans. Both the crowd and the team's bench erupted.

A newspaper announcement that appeared in *The Evening Independent* (Massillon, Ohio) on November 24, 1952. Advertisement courtesy of the author.

Reliable Pat Cannamela trotted onto the field to boot the extra point, and the game was over.

Meanwhile on the Bears bench, there was also an eruption—Halas was livid. He knew that what had transpired was a debacle of biblical proportions and was heard yelling, "Getting beat is bad enough, but getting beat by these bums, well, it's just terrible!"[3]

As the Chicago defense made its way to the sidelines, Halas took out his anger on them physically. He began to kick several of his players and most notably went after Kindt. They had argued throughout the second half, and this exchange served as the breaking point. When Halas finally connected with Kindt's back side, the player had endured enough and kicked the coach back. Teammates and coaches quickly broke up the melee and rushed the coach to safety.

Statistically, the game was not a thing of beauty, featuring twelve combined turnovers. But the damage was done; Halas had been defeated. The final score was Texans 27, Bears 23. At last, a win for the nomads of pro football.

Afterward, in the Bears' locker room, things only got worse, and the uproar continued during their trip back to Chicago. The team had already arranged the serving of a Thanksgiving meal on the plane, but Halas was not in the holiday spirit and still not done with his tirade. He marched up and down the aisle, slapping plates off the players' trays.

On the other hand, the Texans' celebrated their Thanksgiving miracle in true style. They never went to bed, fearing if they fell asleep they might awake to find the victory was just a dream.

The day following the game, the *Chicago Tribune* called it "one of the greatest upsets in National Football League history," with the *Chicago Sun-Times* writing, "Texans could not be stopped." Most would translate the win as being more of a Bears' failure than a Texans' success. Locally, the *Akron Beacon Journal* was the only outlet able to speak with Phelan after the game. They wrote: "For a man with so little recent practice at it, Jimmy Phelan bore up well today as the coach of a winning team."

Phelan would go on to say, "Unaccustomed as I am to winning, I feel all right.... It's remarkable the kids were able to keep their morale up, considering they have no home ties, nobody to root for them, and nobody to play for except Bert Bell."[4]

Holidays are a time when miracles happen. Thanksgiving is a day to reflect on being fortunate. On this cold November afternoon in Akron, the Texans certainly had a miracle to be thankful for. Whatever was written, and however the game was defined, these wards of the league were no longer winless.

18

A MERCIFUL END

WITH THE TEXANS out of the mind of most back at the old homestead in Dallas, Giles Miller felt that two games away from his former team was like an eternity. In a very short time, he had become a forgotten man. He wanted to make the trip to Akron but did not. After seeing the team get dismantled by the Detroit Lions and then at the Green Bay Packers, he made a decision that he would forever regret.

Disheartened by how the team continued to play, he decided instead to travel down to Austin on Thanksgiving Day to watch the University of Texas take on rival Texas A&M. He had no knowledge of what was going on at the same time in Akron, Ohio. Once back home, he picked up a delayed rebroadcast of the game and was overjoyed to hear his Texans had finally won, especially over the Bears.

He made calls throughout the evening in an effort to track down the team and was finally able to talk to some of the players. Miller excitedly asked them to pass along his congratulations and let everyone know that he was counting on seeing them all in person at the next game in ten days. He no longer owned the franchise or made decisions, but he was still their biggest fan.

Now entering December and the final two weeks of the schedule, the team was sitting at 1–9. But playing on Thursday meant having extra time before the next game.

From Akron, the Texans made the short trip back to Hershey, feeling a sense of accomplishment that unfortunately allowed them to let their guards down and revert to the undisciplined habits they had displayed all season long. The following Friday, they left on a quick bus ride to Philadelphia, and arriving midday, checked into the Bellevue-Stratford Hotel.

True to his word, Miller made his plans, coordinating his itinerary with another business trip. Still having debts due, and no longer traveling by plane, he left on a train Tuesday night, arriving in New York on Thursday. From there, he spent two full, unproductive days on business calls. His heart just was not into it; he really came to see the Texans.

Taking a midafternoon train down to Philadelphia on Saturday, Miller went to the team hotel and was able to talk the staff into putting him in the same block of rooms where the players were staying. He had not spoken to Jimmy Phelan in a real conversation since the Texans left Dallas.

Once settled in, Miller rang up the coach's room, and the two had a very good talk. Phelan kept things strictly business, lamenting about all the injuries the team had going into the game. Understandably, because of their short history together, the exchange was like one between strangers rather than the companions they once were.

Philadelphia was Bert Bell's hometown, so Miller reached out and the two agreed to meet for breakfast on the morning of the game. Arriving at the hotel, the commissioner seemed surprised that Miller would make the trip all the way up to the Northeast. He wondered why he would want to reopen any wounds.

Feeling compassion, and whether he intended to honor his invite or not, Bell suggested that maybe they could meet up sometime after the game, too. Miller declined due to his travel schedule. For all the two had gone through that year, it was an awkward morning.

On Sunday, December 7, the temperature for the 3:00 kickoff was forty-four degrees with gusty winds and gray, gloomy skies—typical for Philly that time of year. Aside from the first week against the New York Giants, the Eagles represented the only other nonconference opponent the Texans would face during the season. Coming into the week, Philadelphia had a 6–4 record, led by first-year head coach Jim Tremble.

Both teams arrived at Shibe Park right after lunchtime. The Texans, eager to continue their winning ways, took the field first for warmups. Conversely, the Eagles took their time, perhaps signifying the level of importance they placed on their opponent.

Shibe Park was a turn-of-the-century baseball stadium. The Eagles routinely got around twenty-five thousand fans into the thirty-eight-thousand-capacity building. On this day, with it being the Texans, they would only draw 18,367.

Both sides started out slow, with the visitors playing competitive while the home side racked up penalties. As the first quarter wore on, the Eagles ground game took hold and drove down to the 5-yard line, where fullback John Huzvar punched in the game's first score. After stopping the Texans, Philadelphia's next drive found the squad near midfield when quarterback Bobby Thomason connected on a 41-yard pass to future Minnesota Vikings hall of fame head coach Bud Grant. And before the end of the first quarter, the Texans committed their second turnover, allowing the Eagles to kick a 29-yard field goal for another 3 points.

Already down 17–0 as the second frame began, the Texans found themselves pinned deep near their own goal line. When they proceeded to fumble the ball in the end zone, the prize was recovered by the Eagles for their third touchdown of the half. Near the end of the quarter, the Texans benefitted from some Eagles penalties and drove down to the 1-yard line. There Buddy Young put them on the scoreboard with a plunge over the goal line. Still, at halftime Philadelphia had a comfortable advantage, 24–7.

The Texans' motivation was now nonexistent at the start of the second half. After both teams traded possessions, another fumble gave the Eagles the ball deep in enemy territory. And for the second time of the day, Thomason connected with Grant for a touchdown, this one from 23 yards out.

Later, toward the end of the third quarter, with their hopes now completely fractured, the Texans were at their own 9-yard line when quarterback Bob Celeri threw an interception that was returned 24 yards for a touchdown. Eagles 38–7.

By the fourth quarter, the Philadelphia backups came in and were cold. On a special teams play, Texans receiver Stan Williams picked up an Eagles fumble and returned it 24 yards for the team's second touchdown of the day. Phelan had been rotating quarterbacks throughout the game in attempt to make the score look more respectable, and so with time running out, and the Eagles just going through the motions, Frank Tripucka connected on a 42-yard pass to Dick Wilkins for the team's third trip to the end zone.

The final whistle blew, and it was the same old, sad story. The opponent quickly blew things wide open, the game was essentially over by halftime, and against uninterested backups, the Texans were able to make the scoreboard look not quite as bad as the competition level really was. Texans 21, Eagles 38.

Back on the bus to Hershey, the 1–10 team would now prepare for the finale. It seemed as if the Thanksgiving win never happened. This season could not end fast enough.

Traveling back through the Pennsylvania countryside, Phelan knew beyond a shadow of a doubt that he was likely out of a job once the schedule ended. His relationship with Bell was no relationship at all. It consisted primarily of the commissioner barking orders at a man whom he had no real respect for, all due to the team's performance. The franchise's failure was not Phelan's fault, but to Bell, the on-field results were a different story.

After the Texans' traveling party returned for what was to be their last week in Hershey, the coach basically let the players conduct their own practices and workouts. He had nothing else to offer them. No hope, no future, and no idea as to where they would be located next season. The only real thing he could provide at this point was leniency.

The players took his act of mercy and drank their way through the week. Chubby Grigg was the group's champion chugger. He could hold a lot. The equally large Barney Poole, Art Donovan, and others managed to hold their own, but no one could top Grigg. He would drink to the point where his overindulgence involved others. There would be nightly uproars and arguments at The Tavern, all due to him.

Early in the week, Grigg got into it with another bar patron over the music playing, and Young, likeable but small, unfortunately tried to play peacemaker. Grigg picked him up and threw him into the jukebox, breaking it in the process. No more music.

A few days later, Grigg set up an end-of-season drinking contest with

Poole. Seventeen glasses of grasshopper shots were lined up—eight on each side with one in the middle. The first one to get nine down, including the deciding middle one, was the champ. Grigg, of course, won.

After a few minutes, he told teammate Tom Keane that he didn't feel so well and promptly upchucked all over the both of them. He then passed out and couldn't be woken. Closing time at the bar soon came and Grigg was still unresponsive. Outside, the fresh snow was almost three feet deep. Needing to get him back home, Keane spotted two Flexible Flyer sleds on a home porch across the street. He borrowed them, and with seven teammates, lifted the massive 340-pound Grigg onto both sleds. The four men on each side made pushing him home look much like a funeral procession.

Maybe the snow set the mood, as halfway there the players began singing Christmas carols, and when they reached their destination, a light came on from Phelan's upstairs room. He yelled down at the players, "All right, boys, feeding time at the zoo is over. Now get to bed!"[1] And they did, except for Keane, who had to return the sleds.

The time had come for the final game of the season, the team once again matched against the Lions. The affair was originally set to take place on Sunday, December 14, at 2:00 in the Cotton Bowl, but it would now be played in Detroit. Kickoff was also moved to 1:30 on Saturday afternoon.

The Texans would be the home team, but they were returning to Briggs Stadium, where just a month earlier the players had first learned they would be homeless. They had also suffered their worst defeat of the season there.

The team left Hershey for good on Thursday morning. They took the same transportation back through Ohio, pausing along the way in Akron to reminisce before eventually reaching the Sheraton Cadillac Hotel in Detroit. Miller quietly decided it was time to stay home and not attend.

When Saturday morning rolled around, the players just wanted to finish out the nightmare that was their 1952 season. The high temperature for the day was expected to be thirty-one degrees at game time with a strong wind but at least no precipitation. The Texans arrived at the stadium around 11:00 and suited up with some extra cold-weather protection borrowed from the Lions.

The earlier visit in November drew over thirty-three thousand fans, the second-largest crowd they would play for during that season. On this day, though, the turnstiles only counted 12,252. Although the Lions came in with the league's best record and would be NFL champions that year, no one really wanted to brave the cold and see what was a foregone conclusion. Both teams wore the same uniforms as they had donned in the previous meeting, the Texans in their combination of white jerseys and sliver pants. Someone started the rumor that the blue jerseys had been sold for travel money.

From the game's start, Lions head coach Buddy Parker was determined to run the ball and the clock quickly to get this one over with by dinner. After a scoreless first quarter, and a little perturbed that the visitors had decided to put up a fight, Parker let Texas legend Bobby Layne go to the air. The quarterback quickly completed a pair of touchdown passes, and the Lions were up 14–0 at the half. Although going into the third quarter down by two scores, the Texans had experienced much worse in recent games.

Parker wanted to rest Layne for the upcoming playoffs and replaced him with Jim Hardy, who soon drove Detroit to within field goal range, the 24-yard kick adding another 3 points. Shortly thereafter, the Texans turned the ball over, and Hardy threw a 40-yard touchdown pass to make the score 24–0 as the quarter ended.

The routine numbness of defeat engulfed the Texans bench, and having mentally beaten them down, the Lions could go back to simply running out the clock. They moved the ball down the field and kicked a 31-yard field goal, with another Texans turnover then yielding a 41-yard touchdown throw for Detroit. The scoreboard read Lions 34–0 with two minutes left to play.

As bad as they were, Phelan hadn't experienced a complete shutout yet and didn't want this one to be his first. Catching the Lions sleeping, Tripucka first connected with George Taliaferro on a trick play and then found Stan Williams open to put the Texans within scoring range. Now at the Lions' 7-yard line, Tripucka capped off the drive by hitting Ray Pelfrey with a pass in the end zone. They were finally on the board, better late than never. Fittingly, the extra point was missed.

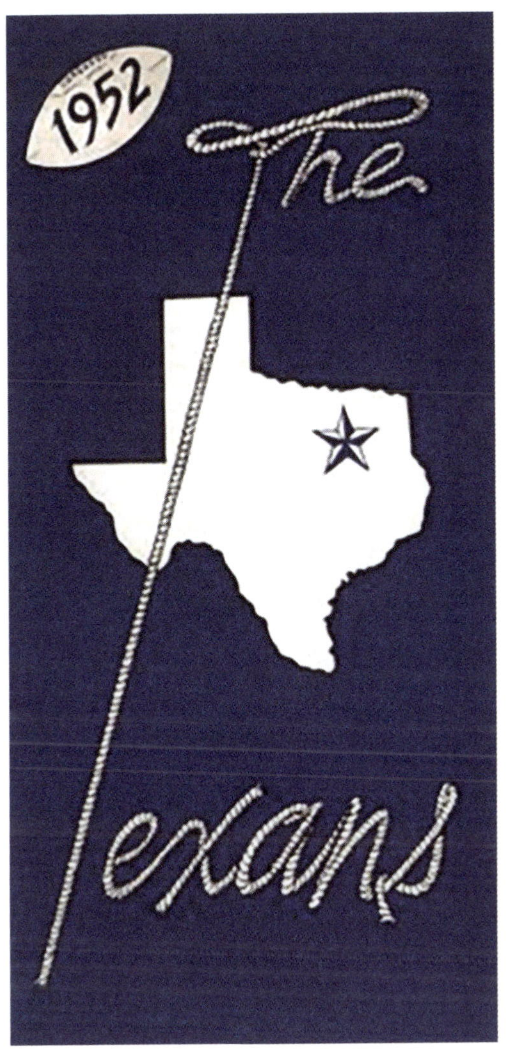

With the season finally concluding, rest in peace
1952 Dallas Texans. Media Guide courtesy of the author.

After scoring, an animated Phelan bounced about the sidelines while laughing and yelling, "We got 'em now, boys! Go for the jugular!"[2] No one saw the flask in his coat.

The ensuing kickoff was sent out of bounds, and the ball was placed on the 35-yard line. With less than a minute left, the Lions put in future hall of fame defensive back Jack Christiansen to play offense, and he immediately ripped off a 65-yard untouched run for a touchdown as time ran out. The final score was Texans 6, Lions 41, Flask Contents 0.

The season-ending game at Briggs Stadium would prove to be the team's wake. Up until the final gun, the wards were still known as the Dallas Texans. No longer. Many decisions regarding their future lay ahead.

None of the players or remaining staff in the locker room that day would have anything to say about the matter. One man, though, did depart with an everlasting remark—head coach Jimmy Phelan. And he perhaps put it best: "We got all the breaks, and they were all bad."[3]

19

DEAD LAST

BERT BELL was once famously quoted as saying, "On any given Sunday, any team can beat any other team."[1] The commissioner must have originated the belief after he saw the Texans' Thanksgiving victory over the Chicago Bears.

By January 1953, one of the worst NFL franchises ever had mercifully come to an end. The experiment of Dallas supporting a professional sports team had clearly flopped. And the Texans needed only one season to prove it.

They finished with a woeful 1–11 record that made them sound better than they really were, though this stigma was forgotten and buried over time. The endeavor started out with eagerness, optimism, and high hopes, but those feelings were quickly dashed.

Evidenced by the public's response, the NFL in Dallas never had a chance. Not then, in 1952. The college game was still king, which was not unique to Texas.

If the team had been any good, the story certainly would have been different. They could have struggled for survival in lieu of simply being obliterated. Once the Texans' attempt to procure Doak Walker from the Detroit Lions failed, they had no marquis celebrity, no face of the franchise. So what small fanbase they did establish rapidly lost interest and eroded after the team immediately showed no signs of being competitive. They perhaps benefited in one aspect, however, in that the local and national newspapers did not cover the team much.

There were no home victory celebrations. No All-Pros. They never even had a team picture taken. And there were certainly no sellouts either. Not surprisingly, the Texans had the league's lowest total for attendance, drawing only 54,065 fans to the Cotton Bowl over four games. That average of just 13,516 per contest was barely half of what was required to hit their ledger's break-even mark.

Even before the seventh game of the season, the home loss to the Los Angeles Rams, everyone could see that the franchise was bleeding to death. During that week from hell, fellow board member Harold "Dry Hole" Byrd, in his local vernacular, advised Giles Miller, "It's time to call in the dogs, piss on the fire, and go home."[2]

With their final appeals to city leaders and the league falling on deaf ears, the white flag was raised, and the team was relinquished back to the league. There was no regard given to Dallas keeping the franchise or finding a new owner in town. The Miller brothers and syndicate partners did the only thing they could do—give up. The amount of money lost was never documented.

Sadly, the "road home" nomads earned their lone victory of the season in Akron, Ohio. Played in front of no one. Since Giles did not attend, whether any real Texans fans traveled to see the game is unknown. Aside from the asterisk of the 2020 COVID restrictions, the 2,208 fans who attended that Thanksgiving Day matchup is believed to be the lowest attendance for an NFL game since 1940.

The actions of Bears coach George Halas that day also spoke volumes. He conveyed the message universally felt around the league: that they all had absolutely no respect for the Texans. The NFL operated with twelve teams in 1952, and eleven of them were better than the Texans. In fact, all of them had second and third strings that could likely have beaten the Dallas starters on any given afternoon.

To put their résumé into context, they were near the bottom or dead last in most statistical categories on both sides of the ball. The team set the permanent standard for how not to do things, a proper adjective having never been invented that would describe just how bad the Texans were.

The offense was clumsy, ranking no higher than tenth in passing yards, rushing yards, touchdowns, first downs, and nearly every other measure that was counted. The Texans scored only 182 points on the season, an average of just more than 15 per outing, and in seven games they failed to mount more than 14 points.

For its part, the defense was equally bad, giving up forty-eight touchdowns with the team surrendering a total of 427 points on the season. That was 101 points more than the second-place club on the list, the Bears totaling 326. By allowing their opponents to put up an average of nearly 36 points every week, the Texans were routinely outscored by at least three touchdowns per game. Just like their offensive counterparts, when all the statistical areas were combined, Dallas ranked dead last in overall team defense.

Not to be outdone was the special teams play, which was not so special, at least in the kicking game. To say the Texans' aim was off would be an understatement, as staggeringly they missed every single field goal they attempted. And they did not fare any better at short-distance kicking, splitting the uprights on only 74 percent of their extra point conversions. That total, too, was by far the worst in the league that season.

During one game, a backup quarterback named Don Klosterman was sent in for a field goal attempt and missed. This prompted head coach Jimmy Phelan to cut him the following day. Upon hearing the news, Klosterman was livid. Having joined the team to get a fair shot at the starting quarterback job, the rookie was by no means a kicking specialist, and so he directed a few terse words at the coach for all to hear.

Later, when reviewing the game film with the team, Phelan stopped the tape at the point when the field goal attempt came up and ran it back again, jokingly telling his players, "There, who says I didn't give him a second chance?"[3]

The roster consisted primarily of well-intentioned journeymen who tried but failed, doing the best they could with the talent and motivation they had. Aside from a few players including Art Donovan, Gino Marchetti, Dick Hoerner, Buddy Young, George Taliaferro, and John Wozniak, very few could have made another NFL squad, and the average talent of the team reflected what their record said they were: terrible.

The young linemen Gino Marchetti and Art Donovan would both later blossom and were future hall of fame players. Marchetti was a promising rookie, while the jovial Donovan had played for three different teams in his first three seasons, with all of them going out of business. Marchetti's best virtues were his strength and quickness, while Donovan's were his massive frame and perhaps his thick skin.

The NFL sent sixty-four players to the Pro Bowl in 1952. The Texans had just two earn invites, the fewest representatives of any team in the league: versatile halfback George Taliaferro and veteran guard John Wozniak.

But after twelve grueling games were played, along with six exhibitions and the oven training camp in Kerrville, Texas, the final whistle blew, and the season was thankfully over. Nonetheless, the team had still been a family. A family true to themselves and undivided along racial lines. While the city of Dallas enforced segregated seating at the Cotton Bowl, the team itself followed the same balanced, loyal, and nondiscriminatory-based principles that the Miller brothers learned early and practiced in real life.

Still, one obligation remained: they needed a going away party, so the franchise held a final event after the blowout loss to the Detroit Lions. Originally, the game was supposed to be played on a Sunday afternoon in the Cotton Bowl with a prescheduled team banquet on Monday night, hosted by Giles and Connell Miller. Of course, the team corporation was now insolvent. But the Millers were able to pull off the event because the hosting deposit had been prepaid prior to the season. The "celebration" was held at the upscale Hotel Adolphus, a lavish property where the rich and famous stayed. It would now play host to a disbanded football team.

The brothers, still highly regarded around town and able to wield influence, went to the Adolphus management and made arrangements to move the Monday date to later in the week so that the players and coaches had adequate time to travel to Dallas. Unable to get all of their money back, the Millers could not merely cancel the party, nor did they want to. The event was to serve as a reunion and fond farewell, a sendoff to everyone in the organization.

Not all the coaching staff chose to make the trip back down, knowing that they were likely already out of work. Several of the players forewent

A cartoon that ran nationally in 1991 by the syndicated team of Bruce Nash and Allan Zullo. The comic illustrator was Bill Maul. Reprinted with permission granted by Allan Zullo of Nash & Zullo Productions, Inc.

the gala as well. With the constant strain of being on the road, most went directly home to be with their families for the holidays and to begin their offseason lives. In fact, many would give up the game and never play football again. Of the ones who remained, some just could not find any good reason in their minds to ever return to Dallas. Surprisingly, though, two of the players in attendance were the very men who were made to feel the least welcomed in town.

Taliaferro and Buddy Young were among the first to arrive at the Adolphus. On and off the field, they were bright spots on a terrible team, never giving up during the season while also rising above the prejudices they faced. Unfortunately, in 1952, local and state segregation laws were still in place, which made socializing with the rest of the players outside of football impossible. If anyone had a good reason to skip this event, they did. Certainly, no one would have blamed them.

But that night at the Adolphus, something unexpected happened. Without notice or attention, Young and Taliaferro were seated with their teammates and served dinner. Two Black players, regular men, ate a meal with their white peers. This was a seminal moment, marking what may have been the first known occurrence of such an act taking place at a hotel facility in Dallas. A defunct football team that no one had paid much notice to over the last twelve months had finally done something right by circumventing the Jim Crow laws.

Ranking ahead of the Thanksgiving miracle, this was the singular most important achievement in the Texans' lifespan and the only positive incident, in terms of civil rights, that either man would experience in Dallas that year. No one could deny the significance of the gesture, not only to these two but to their teammates and the city's local sports history—all from the simple treatment of Young and Taliaferro like the rest of the team. The ending was the best anyone could have written to an otherwise very bad year.

The NFL has seen its share of terrible teams. The expansion 1976 Tampa Bay Buccaneers went a winless 0–14 in their first season. Thirty-two years later, the 2008 Detroit Lions would finish even worse at 0–16, as the league schedule had expanded by two games. Nine years after that, the 2017 Cleveland Browns would be the next club to go without a victory. Almost as bad as losing every outing, the Baltimore Colts posted a 0–8–1 record in the strike-shortened 1982 season, and even the Dallas Cowboys went winless in their first campaign, going 0–11–1 after tying the New York Giants to avoid defeat. Not to be outdone, there have been several other teams that have been remembered as winning just a single game over the span of a season. Both the Buffalo Bills and Houston Oilers have turned the trick more than once.

Whether any of these teams were as bad as the Texans is debatable, as the times, their opponents, and the circumstances were different. Nevertheless, the first chapter of the NFL in Dallas will forever hold an unfortunate distinction. But as bad as the Texans were, the true indignity is that their story has been ignored and forgotten.

Although if he were here today, Coach Phelan might say, "Well son, maybe that's not such a bad thing."

20

FAMILY LOSSES

THE DECEMBER DAYS of 1952 were winding down. No longer carrying the weight of the disbanded franchise, Giles Miller was now preparing for the upcoming departure of a close family friend, Lance Webb, who would soon be leaving town. Pastor Webb was exiting his post at the University Park Methodist Church to lead the North Broadway Methodist Church in Columbus, Ohio, and Miller was honored to serve as one of the committee members who would select the man to replace him.

Webb gave his final regular sermon at University Park on December 21. He was then set to leave Dallas on Christmas Day, but a sudden event would dictate that he delay his departure. He needed to deliver a eulogy. He needed to help the Millers deal with another, more important loss.

The midmonth death of the Texans franchise would pale in comparison to the heartbreak the family would experience just eleven days after the season was over.

Across town, on Christmas Eve, Connell and Martha Miller had taken Connell Jr. to see a matinee movie at the Inwood Village Theater to kick off the holidays. As they were watching the movie, Connell was paged to come to the theater office where he received the news that his pop was on his way to the hospital. Clarence Miller had suffered from a condition known as thrombosis, a clotting of the blood vessels.

Wearing a look of distress, he came back to the auditorium to retrieve his wife and son. They immediately left, dropping Connell Jr. off at home in the care of Earl Goins and then rushing to the hospital. Once there, both brothers received news that Pop had been found unresponsive after suffering a coronary occlusion. An existing blood clot broke free in his leg and had traveled to his heart, causing it to stop beating. According to his wife, Esther, Pop had been upstairs lying on his bed when she heard him call out, "Mother, come here. I need you."[1] Those were the last words he spoke before passing out, never awakening from his sleep.

The sting of losing a sports team was one thing, but this was a real loss for the brothers. Both returned home to share the news with their boys. Connell Jr. would remember it as the first day he saw his dad cry. Giles would later reflect on the irony of his death happening on Christmas Eve. Needless to say, the holiday never regained its former meaning. The Miller family lost their patriarch that day as Clarence Ransom Miller passed away at the age of only sixty-eight years old.

Less than two years removed from the passing of Clarence, the family endured another sudden, catastrophic loss. The day before Thanksgiving, November 24, 1954, started out like any other. Eleven-year-old Connell Jr. had been invited to the birthday party of a distant relative whom he barely knew. He was not thrilled with the idea and really didn't want to go. There would be a lot of other kids there whom he did not know, but since they were "kinfolk" and so close in age, his mother insisted he attend.

The party was being held at a landmark spot known as the Deuback Skating Rink in the Lake Highlands area of Dallas. Connell had roller-skated there a few times before and always had fun. The biggest thrill of the day, though, would come later when his dad was to pick him up afterward in his new Jaguar XK-120M sports roadster.

As the party ended, Connell was surprised to see his Aunt Betty arrive at Deuback's to pick him up instead. Being a kid, and not knowing any better, he got in the car without an ounce of suspicion, and they were off. Once on the road, she told him that they were going back to her and Uncle Giles's house in Highland Park. After playing and visiting with his cousins for a couple of hours, Connell was finally taken home, unaware that anything might be wrong.

When they drove up, several people came outside to greet the car. Notably, his mother and family friend, Gordon McLendon, were the first ones to approach. Connell went into the house with his mother, where he would hear the grave news that no eleven-year-old boy should ever have to endure.

As his dad was making his way to pick him up from the party, he had been involved in an automobile accident around Walnut Hill Lane and Central Expressway, less than two miles away from the skating rink. Back then, the auto industry manufactured cars with different safety standards than those of today, and his Jaguar, being of European origin, was dramatically different—it was not fitted with seat belts. An erratic driver caused Connell Sr. to swerve in order to miss another vehicle. When he did, his car hit a median at full speed and rolled several times, throwing him from his seat.

Arriving at the hospital by ambulance, he clang to life for about thirty minutes before ultimately succumbing due to head injuries. Connell Ransom Miller died at the young age of thirty-six and left behind Martha and their three boys: Connell Jr; Alex, age seven; and Burnes, age three. Miller was laid to rest next to his father in the Hillcrest Mausoleum at Sparkman-Hillcrest Memorial Park.

The world would not be the same. Dallas had lost one of its two sports pioneers. In the years that followed, Martha would never speak about that day or the events surrounding it.

After Connell's passing, Martha stayed in Dallas and continued to raise their three boys. She involved herself in various garden and women's clubs, becoming president of one of them. She later met Horace Chilton Boren, a Braniff International Airways executive who also owned several radio stations, and they married in 1957. The family moved from Dallas to Muskogee, Oklahoma, in 1959, and their marriage produced two more sons.

In 1974, tragedy struck the family again. Connell and Martha's middle child, Alex, suffered a broken neck in a boating accident and was left a quadriplegic for a short time until he passed away at the age of only twenty-seven.

After thirty-one years of marriage, Horace, who suffered from Alzheimer's, passed away in 1988. After his death, Martha rekindled her passion for collectibles and lived a long and fruitful life. She always carried a deep sense of pride in the fact that she and her sister-in-law, Betty, were the

Connell's 1953 Jaguar XK-120M parked in front of his house on Wenonah Drive.
Photo courtesy of Connell Miller Jr. and the Miller family.

first two females who had ownership in and sat on the board of an NFL team. Over the years, she made it her goal to compensate the members of the Texans syndicate for every dollar they invested and lost. Martha passed away on December 11, 2007, at the age of eighty-six.

In 1976, almost twenty-four years to the day after her husband's passing, the Miller family lost its matriarch. Queen Esther Connell Miller, who spent the rest of her life residing in the family mansion, fell into bad health and eventually needed a caretaker. Living well into her eighties, she was beginning to have memory issues—likely due to Alzheimer's, although she was never officially diagnosed—and by the end did not recognize any family members. Esther passed away comfortably at her Swiss Avenue home of fifty years on December 23. The mansion, however, was not just any old asset. The treasure remained in the family as Giles moved in shortly thereafter. Esther's passing marked the end of an era for the Miller family. Giles would now be the only one left of the four family members.

Throughout his lifetime, Giles Miller always wanted to be someone who would take the family money he inherited and parlay that wealth into something bigger. Something that would turn the world on its ear. He fanaticized about living in Hollywood and producing films. On occasion, some even noted that he resembled a movie star. Regardless, showing everyone that he could do something new was important to him, rather than just following along with the textile business that was theoretically running itself.

Financial and personal loss changed his plans, though. Still only thirty-four years of age in 1954, Giles was in his mind just getting started. He had big dreams to explore. But after Connell's passing, Miller no longer had the same motivation.

Following the death of his father and brother, Giles out of necessity again became active in the dealings of Texas Textile Mills. But the family losses took all the wind out of his sails. Miller was left adrift without his two primary sources of inspiration, those whose steps he had followed in. The family nest egg had been built on the industry, and times were changing. Since the end of World War II, cheaper imported materials from countries like China and Japan had wrecked the US textile business by the mid-1950s. Unfortunately, under his leadership, all of the family-owned mills in Dallas, McKinney, Waco, and South Texas would become obsolete and ultimately shutter. Appearance-wise, he was no longer seen as a socially prominent citizen.

Having grown tired of being in the news, Miller instead decided to report it. So in the late 1950s, he established and was the publisher of the *Park Cities-North Dallas News*, a weekly newspaper that served the wealthy Highland Park and University Park communities. The paper was a partnership effort with his wife, Betty, who was originally the editor and grew up in the newspaper business herself.

Giles later entered radio by launching GEMCO Broadcasting. He had witnessed firsthand his friend, McLendon, as well as Connell's widow, Martha, acquire radio stations, and now he too wanted to be a part of the action. He quickly set up KPCN, which was carried across North Texas and southern Oklahoma.

After that, Miller expanded into four more markets across the state: KSEL in Lubbock, KBUY in Amarillo, KOKE in Austin, and KELP in El Paso. All operated under the GEMCO umbrella. Just as she did with the newspaper, his loyal wife joined him in running the radio venture and was there every step of the way.

As the calendar turned to 1960, Miller felt empty. He was no longer satisfied with the day-to-day. Now entering his forties, he continued to live in the family mansion on Swiss Avenue, smoke heavily, and drink more while looking for his next big thing.

During this same period, he dropped a major bombshell on his family. One evening, he brought Betty and their three sons together to deliver life-changing news: "Just so you all know, I have a mistress on the other side of town. We have a kid together, and she's pregnant with our second kid."[2] Miller also revealed that the woman was his secretary who worked for him at the newspaper. The message was blunt. He now had what he referred to as his *primary* family and a *secondary* family.

At home, the primary family was not terribly close to begin with, as the boys had seen more of their nannies growing up than they had of Giles. Shortly after hearing this news, Betty divorced him, leaving him free to marry the other woman.

Years after leaving Giles, Betty remained proud of the work she had done as a woman in sports and media. In addition to her pioneering role in football, she was the first woman to serve on the board of directors for a Texas radio station.

Betty eventually moved on and remarried to Guion McCaleb. They settled down near Austin, where she operated her own antique and gift shop, Bettiques. She lived to the age of seventy-eight, passing away in 1999 due to complications after her lung was punctured during surgery to install a pacemaker. She gave Giles many of the best years of her life.

Now living with his secondary family, Giles thought the time had come for another start. He still had both money and an interest in politics, so he became a donor and supporter of local and state politicians. There was even an urge to hold a role in office himself; in 1962 he ran a statewide campaign for the at-large congressional seat that the census had opened two years before. He lost to a career politician named Joe Pool.

Miller stayed in the radio business until the late 1960s, but even that became unsustainable for him, and he had to sell off his stations. Once out of radio, he fell back on the law school education that he had received earlier in life, becoming a civil investigator for the Dallas County District Attorney's office. He started to work for other people, instead of people working for him.

The experience was humbling—how the mighty had indeed fallen. Miller could no longer afford to keep the mansion on Swiss Avenue, so the home was sold and the proceeds used to live on.

A decade later, Miller was now a full-time attorney. He set up his own private practice, working in Dallas for several years before moving his secondary family south to Fredericksburg, Texas. But the small town was an area primarily built by German settlers, and the locals soon perceived him as a big-city guy who spelled his name incorrectly, instead of the German "Mueller." Of course, he never claimed to be of German descent.

Even though he did not fit in right away, he still tried running for election, this time as the judge for Gillespie County. Once more, he failed to win. At this stage of his life, Miller was the epitome of going from the penthouse to the outhouse.

His final retreat was to Corpus Christi, Texas, where he continued his private law practice for several years as he slowly faded away. Late in his life, people would often walk by, not knowing that the man they had just passed was once a pioneer of pro football in Texas—a forerunner before the Dallas Cowboys.

Miller exhausted his family's fortune with one failed business dealing after another. Since his ten-month association with the NFL in 1952, he had been abandoned by friends, family, and the city of Dallas. Losing his social standing early on, he spent the rest of his life trying to earn his relevance back.

By the late 1980s, Miller was running on empty. With no prospects for a new business or career, he maintained his small law practice on a very limited level until his death. On Sunday, April 2, 1989, Giles Miller passed away at the Spohn Hospital in Corpus Christi. He was sixty-eight. His cause of death was lung cancer due to a lifetime of heavy smoking. He was brought back to Dallas and laid to rest next to his father and brother at Sparkman-Hillcrest Memorial Park.

Because of the life he'd built outside of his marriage and the time spent away from his boys as they grew up, he left his primary family with a

With better days far behind, Giles Miller lived out the rest of his life both unrecognized and fortuneless. Photo courtesy of Connell Miller Jr. and the Miller family.

broken relationship that would never heal. The connection was beyond strained.

Ed, his oldest, worked in operations for various radio stations before moving on to journalism. His middle and youngest sons, Randy and Donny, respectively, followed somewhat in their father's footsteps by attending law school. Randy was a real estate attorney while Donny practiced tax law and eventually became a CPA.

Giles squandered away the family fortunes that his grandparents had so dutifully secured and never had a successful company or a story of his own. Ed perhaps harbored the most resentment toward him, once saying, "In less than twenty years, he went through all the money. And the bottom line is he inherited three fortunes, but he pissed it all away."[3]

Over the years, Giles attempted to make amends, but his efforts did not work out. At one point, he sent Randy a remorseful, handwritten letter, a very long and arduous attempt to apologize for everything he had done and for all the mistakes he had made. He vented his feelings about how hard it was to be a father, and how hard it was to be a good man. He tried to explain his transgressions, saying that he had done the best he could.

The gesture backfired. Randy, skillful with a red pen and still angry, proceeded to circle and correct all the punctuation and spelling errors. He then sent the note back to him. After that, the two did not speak for a long time. Later, Randy regretted his response, but Giles never mentioned it, and no word was ever spoken about the incident.

After his death, it became clearer that the complicated bond the father had with his sons always revolved around football. After all, he was their coach, and those relationships were at their best when they were on a football field. The game was all they had in common, although ironically it was also synonymous with the beginning of his business failures.

Sometime after his death, Giles's three sons went down to Corpus Christi to help clean out some of his belongings. Fittingly, now that he was gone, the lifelong love of sports was the only real personal connection they all enjoyed together. Among their findings was envelope after envelope filled with unsold Dallas Texans game tickets—a final, chilling reminder of Giles's legacy.

21

NEW LIFE IN BALTIMORE

WITH THE ARRIVAL of 1953, figuring out what to do with the remnants of the Texans franchise would be the first thing on Commissioner Bert Bell's to-do list. He and the NFL were right back where they had started the year before—they needed a replacement ownership group and ultimate landing spot. Otherwise, the league would have a lopsided eleven teams.

Bell wanted a solution and plan in place before the predictable question "What are we going to do now?" was asked. He knew that talk around some of the usual location possibilities would inevitably be brought up, but there was one city, still in limbo, that stood out. Bell wanted to act quickly and keep the twelfth team close to the league office in the Northeast. More importantly, he needed owners in place he could trust. Ones who would stay the course and not run for the hills when things went wrong, which they no doubt would at some point.

The city of Baltimore had a professional football franchise at one time—or two, depending on how you look at it, having fielded teams in a couple of different leagues. The first was established with roots in the All-America Football Conference, playing in the upstart circuit from 1947 to 1949. The second appeared when that same squad was part of the 1950 merger with the NFL.

Declaring bankruptcy after the inaugural 1946 AAFC season, the Miami Seahawks' franchise assets had been bundled together and acquired by the league, who later resold them to a group of five businessmen led by Washington, DC attorney Robert Rodenburg. The team was relocated to Baltimore where they were nicknamed the Colts, a nod to the thoroughbreds that raced in the annual Preakness Stakes, an event that has been held at the city's Pimlico Race Course since 1873.

Struggles soon followed the franchise to its new town, though, and the group walked away after only one season. Ultimately, with new ownership needed once again, the help of Abraham Watner would arrive. But the financial issues continued, and with the on-field product inherently short of talent, the team regressed every year. The Colts finally bottomed out with a record of only 1–11 to finish the 1949 season as the league's worst.

Just a few days later, the AAFC announced a pending merger with the NFL. The Baltimore club's future was at risk and likely finished, as the NFL had decided to end the football war and make peace, primarily because of the powerhouse Cleveland Browns. They would accept Cleveland and two other AAFC teams into the league in time for the start of the next season.

That the AAFC's two strongest franchises were the obvious choices to join the NFL was no big secret, but a third team was part of the agreement as well. The dominant Browns were the main motivation for the merger to begin with, and their recent championship game opponent was a part of the plan. To strengthen the West Coast market and give the Los Angeles Rams a geographic rival, the AAFC's San Francisco 49ers were granted a coveted slot.

The league's intent for the third franchise was to enter a new market, so the consideration was between either the Buffalo Bills or Baltimore. The Bills petitioned hard for admission, and they had better attendance and a wealthier owner. However, the city would be the second-smallest market in the league, just ahead of Green Bay. Bell also felt Buffalo was too close to Canada. The Baltimore advantage was based on the region's potential, not so much because of the squad they had. Thus, the choice was clear: the Colts were the final team added, by a vote of nine to one.

The dissenter was Redskins owner George Preston Marshall, who had voiced objections to the forty-mile distance between Baltimore and Washington, DC. He ultimately changed his vote after accepting a payment of $150,000 to waive his self-proclaimed territorial rights. The payout would put the financially strapped Baltimore franchise into a further hole.

Because the 1950 Colts then had to face better NFL talent each week, they were even worse than the year before, posting another 1–11 record. All parties involved had seen enough. The awful franchise was dissolved by the league at the end of the season, having won only eleven games over its four years.

Despite this, Baltimore embraced the Colts. The team's rabid fans revolted, and the city threatened a lawsuit against the NFL and Bell. For the time being, the legal threat remained pending.

The dilemma of what to do with the Dallas Texans' spot returned to Bell's desk, but there was an elephant in the NFL room—the ongoing problem of Baltimore's threat of a lawsuit. With a painless settlement not imminent, the sharp-witted commissioner recognized that he could kill two birds with one stone, resolving the Baltimore threat while purging the Dallas issue at the same time—in other words, assigning Baltimore the Dallas franchise after the dissolving of their own.

Baltimore had one thing that Dallas did not, fan support. As a tease, he floated the possibility that the city *could* be in consideration for relocation if they sold fifteen thousand season tickets over the next seven weeks. He also gave the stipulation that unanimous approval would be needed in a league vote. That would not occur until the season-ticket initiative was met first. At the very least, if the ticket drive was not successful, that might provide the league a perfect defense against the lawsuit.

City leadership immediately launched its fundraising efforts and yielded 15,755 season tickets in less than half the time. Reports came back to Bell that Baltimore now had $300,000 in the bank and was ready to go. They had the necessary seed money.

Bell was not a superstitious person, but he also knew that the lineage of the franchise revealed a three-time loser across three different cities. He did not want Baltimore to continue that history, so the commissioner was very deliberate in portraying this as a new franchise with no connection to the failed Dallas club or the teams that came before it. This newly placed franchise would simply inherit the Texans' existing player pool in lieu of completely starting over with an expansion draft.

Baltimore's city leaders had done everything they needed to do. They just needed an owner. That ball was now in Bell's court, and one person in particular immediately came to mind—Carroll Rosenbloom, his summer neighbor in Margate City, New Jersey.

Rosenbloom was a successful millionaire businessman and longtime acquaintance of Bell. Growing up a sportsman who not only played football and baseball but also boxed, he came to know Bell in 1927 when he attended the University of Pennsylvania, lettering as a halfback with Bell as his backfield coach.

Ironically, he, too, built his fortune in the textile industry. Like the Miller brothers, Rosenbloom went to work at his father's clothing company, Blue Ridge Overalls, and landed exclusive, lucrative deals that put his products into Sears and J.C. Penney outlets across the nation.

The company profits exploded. So much so that Rosenbloom retired for the first time at the age of only thirty-two. But following the death of his father in 1942, he was named executor of the estate. With that inheritance, and needing to manage the many business issues associated with it, he chose to return to an active working life. Through the restructuring and sale of his family's assets, he became a millionaire several times over.

When Bell initially contacted his friend, Rosenbloom insisted that he was not interested whatsoever, jokingly saying, "I ain't buying that damn bunch of hillbillies."[1] He thought his answer would suffice, as he was too busy with his other interests. But Bell was persistent and leaned on his neighbor, insisting Rosenbloom was the only man who could give the franchise the stability that the city deserved.

Not making any headway, Bell continued to press harder and told him that he could get the transaction done with very little upfront financial risk. Rosenbloom put off the commissioner with the hesitant excuse, "I'll think about it."

Within days, typical of Bell, he finally interrupted the silence with his usual mixture of decisiveness and gruff charm. He called Rosenbloom late one night to tell him, "Carroll, you're the new owner of the franchise. I just announced it."[2]

At that point, Rosenbloom relented, although he still maintained that he did not want to be the sole owner. This request was not due to money; he simply did not want to singlehandedly take on all the time and responsibility demands that would be required.

The terms Bell laid out for the purchase were much more accommodating than those the Miller syndicate had to meet in Dallas. All of the old New York Yanks' debt had been wiped clean, and there was already $300,000 waiting in the bank. For Rosenbloom, the price tag was only $200,000, and the payment would not all be required upfront. Only $25,000 was needed initially. After that, the balance would be paid out, with interest, over an eight-year period. Rosenbloom's majority share cost him only $13,000.

To help him out, a five-man syndicate group would be assembled. Automobile dealer and thoroughbred horse breeder Bruce Livie was the largest investor. Making up the rest of the minority founders were Thomas McMullan, a building contractor, Zanvyl Krieger, a businessman and philanthropist, and William F. Hilgenberg, a banker. Rosenblum assumed 51 percent of the ownership.

Baltimore was back in pro football.

After passing a special league vote, the NFL announced that Baltimore would be the new location for the Texans. That the team would be adopting the cherished nickname of its previous incarnation, the Colts, was already a given. However, the silver and green the Colts had once donned were out. The new team would be blue and white, holdover colors from the Texans.

By doing this, the new Baltimore club would be able to utilize the remaining leftover equipment, a luxury the Texans did not enjoy. Among the salvaged items to be refurbished were the sideline hooded parkas. With clever patchwork, the same capes worn by the players in 1952 were given a new life and identity, covering up any sign of the words "Dallas Texans."

Rosenbloom asked fans to give him five years to create a winning team, but setting up in Baltimore was a very different experience than the process a year earlier in Dallas. This time success would not be insurmountable. Bell did not interfere or meddle either, since he had his man in place. And with the fanbase already built in, marketing the new team was not as strongly needed as it had been for the Millers.

Baltimore's new lease on football life would begin with former Naval Academy man Keith Molesworth as the team's first head coach. The line of applicants was not very long, so he was hurriedly hired. Alex Agase would be the only assistant from Jimmy Phelan's Texans staff to make the move, but not as a coach. Having retired as a player to work the sideline in Dallas, he decided to come back and take the field for one more year with Baltimore.

Not surprisingly, the list of talent on hand was short. There were twelve carryover Texans players on the Colts' opening-day roster, eleven of them starters. Aside from Agase, leaders Gino Marchetti, Art Donovan, Buddy Young, George Taliaferro, and Barney Poole were all retained. Others remaining were Sisto Averno, Joe Campanella, Brad Ecklund, Dan Edwards, Ken Jackson, and finally Tom Keane. Sadly, Keane was the only man remaining from the eleven-player swap with the Rams just one year earlier.

Just as Rosenblum predicted, the team's work paid off five seasons later; in 1957 the Colts went on a historic run by avoiding a losing campaign for the next fifteen years. The stretch started with back-to-back NFL Championships in 1957 and 1958, their epic clash with the New York Giants in the 1958 title game at Yankee Stadium becoming known as the "Greatest Game Ever Played."

Nationally televised by NBC, the classic marked the beginning of the NFL's surge in popularity, eventually replacing baseball as America's number one sport. Watched by over forty-five million viewers that day, a small detail on the Colts' sideline was overlooked by most. Over their first few seasons, the Colts had played in their share of inclement weather, and the equipment staff was always on alert to bring out whatever was required in wet and cold conditions. On this gray and gloomy day, the old, hooded parkas were needed.

As the nation watched the game's final moments, NBC cameras panned behind the Baltimore bench, showing the players as they stood in their repurposed capes featuring the Colts logo. When the light hit their backs that day, if looking hard enough, underneath the embroidered needlework one could faintly read the word "Texans."

In only six years, what was one of the worst franchises on record had

Along with twelve players, the Texans parkas also made the move to Baltimore where they were repurposed. Just six years later, when the Colts defeated the New York Giants in the NFL's "Greatest Game Ever Played," these patchwork coverings, along with Gino Marchetti and Art Donovan, were the only remnants from the franchise's days in Dallas. Photo taken, and used with permission, from NFL Films, Mt. Laurel, NJ.

ascended to the top of the sports world. The Texans' new life in Baltimore, however, ultimately came to an end, resulting in the death of the successful Colts. The team played there for thirty-one seasons before Robert Irsay, who took over ownership in 1972, moved the team to Indianapolis in 1984 under much controversy.

All the success—nine hall of fame players, two hall of fame coaches, two NFL Championships, and one Super Bowl title—came under Carroll Rosenbloom's watch. The franchise also retired seven uniform numbers from that era, three of them former Dallas Texans: Gino Marchetti, Art Donovan, and Buddy Young.

Today, the name "Baltimore Colts" still exudes football. They became one of the most recognized and cherished teams in professional sports. And it all happened because the Dallas Texans . . . were the Dallas Texans.

22

A HUNT FOR PERMISSION

TEXAS OIL TYCOON H. L. Hunt was one of the world's wealthiest men. He had fifteen children, but there was one son, sharp as a tack, who had quite an imagination. He was a dreamer.

By the late 1950s, upon graduating from SMU, and on the strength of the family's massive oil wealth, this twenty-six-year-old heir named Lamar had his heart and mind set on owning a professional football team. He would soon change the world of sports.

Lamar Hunt had been an avid sports enthusiast since his childhood. He had played youth football and joined his college team as a walk-on. His family's status virtually guaranteed him a spot on the roster, but he rode the bench. What position he played wasn't a concern; he was a football player. That is all that mattered to him.

He wanted to be involved in sports wherever he was in life. The young man was wise beyond his years, which could have benefited the family business, but that was not the career about which he dreamed. Although he was smart, his only flaw was that he believed professional football could someday succeed in Dallas.

Hunt wasn't oblivious to the fact that someone had already tried and failed. To the contrary, he was one of the very few fans who attended the NFL games in 1952, and he had the same conviction of others before him. The difference was that Hunt's was stronger, stronger than anyone else's. And he was about to prove it.

With rose-colored glasses and blind faith, and without the pedigree, résumé, or his father's blessing, Hunt approached the NFL in 1959 about an expansion franchise. He was turned down flat. No one among the league's brass knew who he was. From the outside, he appeared to be a spoiled rich kid. The NFL made it clear: they did not want to oversaturate their suddenly hot commodity by moving into new markets. Even if they did, Dallas would never be on the list after what the league had lived through seven years earlier.

Bert Bell was still commissioner, and his opinion was that young Hunt was cut out of the same expensive cloth he had seen with the Millers. At the same time, Chicago Bears owner and head coach George Halas was the self-appointed and unofficial head of the NFL's expansion committee. Not only that, he *was* the expansion committee. Though the league had already decreed its firm stance that no growth would be taking place, there was still a committee of him and Bell. So Hunt would need to go through both.

Undeterred by rejection, Hunt learned that Halas usually spent his winter months away from the frigid Chicago winds, living at the Biltmore Hotel in Phoenix, Arizona. He boldly made a phone call to "Papa Bear" Halas, asking if he could come out and discuss his expansion plan. Hunt was instantly cut off and discouraged to make the trip. Halas told him that doing so would be a complete waste of time for both of them. Perhaps the old coach still harbored resentment toward anything to do with Dallas after the epic embarrassment on that Thanksgiving Day in 1952.

Having failed with Halas, Hunt once again reached out to Commissioner Bell and this time was told, "Call the Wolfners," who owned the crosstown Chicago Cardinals franchise that long been a thorn in the side of Halas.[1]

Quickly processing what he'd heard, Hunt thought, "Wait, did Bell just say that an existing team might be on the market for sale?"

Immediately, Hunt decided that this opportunity was his best and only option. He beat a path to Chicago and requested a meeting with the Cardinals ownership. He told them by phone that he would be there all week and could adjust his schedule accordingly. But the truth was that gaining an audience with them was his only reason for coming, and he would meet at three o'clock in the morning if that was what it took.

At the time, the team was owned by Charley Bidwell's widow, Violet, and her husband, Walter Wolfner. The Cardinals were a downtrodden, losing organization that was finding it hard to operate on the South Side of Chicago while always playing second fiddle to the Bears. Halas was now looking over their shoulder, his quest being to force them out of town, leaving the city solely to his Bears.

Hunt was granted a meeting, and he laid his intentions out clearly to Mr. and Mrs. Wolfner, revealing that his hope was to purchase the team and relocate it down to Dallas. His plan was not exactly what the couple had in mind. They were looking only for cash investors to buy a stake in the franchise and become minority owners, while they still held controlling interest.

Hunt pivoted and quickly revised his approach, proposing the couple retain a large portion of ownership with Hunt owning the controlling and managing interest. Still, this wasn't what the Wolfners wanted. In the end, there was never going to be a workable situation. They simply were not going to allow the team to leave Chicago, with or without them. The mild-mannered Hunt became flustered that the two sides were coming at this with completely opposite agendas. This wasn't what he was led to believe by Bell.

But just as he ended the conversation, thanking the couple for their hospitality and for taking the time to hear him out, something occurred. Standing up as the meeting was concluding, Wolfner asked the disappointed Hunt, "Do you know a Bud Adams?"[2] After Hunt said that he did not, Wolfner then explained that Adams was also a Texas oilman who had recently approached them with the same intent of buying the team outright and relocating the franchise to Houston. Wolfner told him that he turned down that offer as well.

Hunt's mind began to oscillate, feeling better that he was not the only crazy one. Wolfner then disclosed that other potential ownership groups from Minneapolis and Denver had approached him, but he wasn't budging, and "the team would stay in Chicago, he vowed, and would be controlled by the Wolfners."[3]

Hunt left Chicago that day empty-handed, but not empty-minded.

Purchasing the Cardinals and bringing them to Dallas was a long shot to begin with, but he found out that he was not alone in his quest and that three others had tried to accomplish the same. Unintentionally, the end of the discussion had planted a seed in his mind and would lead to a monumental idea.

Boarding a plane back to Dallas, the thought hit him: if Minneapolis, Denver, and Houston all wanted to buy into the NFL and relocate the franchise to a new city, just to be rebuffed by the only team in the league, Chicago, that shared its fan base, then there must be a greater national demand for the sport. If the old establishment would not let them in, then why not partner up with these same men and start a new league?

In order to accomplish this, a few things would need to happen. Hunt's first task was to find these investors, as well as any additional cities that might be interested. He had to bring together a group of committed owners, enough to form a league, and name this foolish boys' club. Only then could he accomplish his dream of bringing professional football back to Dallas.

This in turn meant figuring out what to call the upstart team that would eventually come. And to satisfy what he had in mind required tracking someone down. A person he did not know, a forgotten man. Once all the details were sorted out, the new league would take an old namesake, and a failed one at that.

On a gloomy autumn day in 1959, Giles Miller was at his downtown GEMCO office conducting routine business. His secretary stepped into the doorway, letting him know that a caller was holding on the phone. The person was requesting to speak directly to him.

Waiting on the other end of the line was Sidney Latham, a name that sounded vaguely familiar to Miller, who quickly identified him as the former Texas Secretary of State. Latham now held the role of general counsel for the Hunt Oil Company, and he advised that he was calling on behalf of Lamar Hunt regarding the availability of the copyright ownership for the name Texans.

The purpose of the call was to propose a modest sum of money in order to obtain Miller's verbal acceptance. If approved, he would follow up with a written release for the property rights to any party that might want to use the name in the future. Inquiring as to why Latham wanted the name in the first place, Miller was told that Hunt requested this as identification for a football team in a new pro league.

Until then, Miller had no prior knowledge that Hunt was working to form what would become the American Football League, or that he was setting up a team in Dallas for the upcoming inaugural season. Latham barely got his words out before Miller stopped him midsentence.

His response was abrupt. He did not mean to be rude or curt, but Miller wanted to be very clear. He avowed that he not only had no claim to the name whatsoever, but he would just as soon never be reminded of it again. Additionally, he added that he did not want anything resurfacing in the news that would ever link him or his family to the team again. Disappointed, Latham asked if Miller would entertain a call from Hunt himself about the issue, to which Giles gladly said that he would.

Later that same week, Hunt made direct contact with Miller, and he quickly explained his thoughts on the new league and his intentions of setting up Dallas as a founding franchise member. Miller thought the voice on the other end of the line was crazy but patiently heard him out. He could feel the enthusiasm from Hunt coming through the phone. The young man had already accomplished so much in such little time, which reminded Miller somewhat of himself when he had the same appetite.

At the moment, Hunt's main priority was settling on a proper team name. He told Miller that he was considering a couple of other possibilities, but was really hoping to use Texans. All Miller could think about was why in the world anyone would want to call their new franchise the same name as one that had failed. To do so was bad luck.

Hunt explained that he really loved the title because it was indicative of where the team would be based. Not to mention that there was also some football history attached to it, which Hunt viewed as being positive. He was excited, or maybe naïve, to think football fans would recollect and gravitate toward the name. Even if it was associated with the previous team, good or bad, that they remembered would be all that counts. His view was that once his Texans became competitive, and in his heart he knew they would, Hunt believed the name would become associated with winners.

Hunt sensed this was not about money and cut to the chase, simply asking Miller if he had any objections from a personal standpoint. Miller responded, "Heck, no! I've been having nightmares about that name for seven years, and I'd be happy to get it off my back."[4]

With that, working out an agreement was not so much a domain issue. Still, Hunt knew Miller and the former organization were in fact there first, and he felt they owned the rights and use of the name. He pressed the more formal point, if Miller had any legal objections to his using the name. Miller had already emphatically said no; for Hunt, there remained a "but."

From his point of view, Miller didn't believe that he could give legal permission for something he didn't claim to possess in the first place. He felt that the word Texans was a title that no one really owned. All he would commit to was, "Gosh, you're welcome to it."[5] As far as he was concerned, he had no say-so or interest in the matter.

Because he did not fully give a formal release, Giles Miller would not accept any form of payment from Hunt for the name. He knew from his own experience that any man taking on a pro football team would have enough financial woes to worry about. He wished Hunt the best and said that it was his decision to use whatever name he chose. With that, the new AFL Dallas franchise was born. Hunt had the name he wanted. Whether it was cursed would remain to be seen.

After the announcement of the AFL's formation, the NFL quickly shifted its position concerning the new league's legitimacy and now considered them a real threat. As a peace offering, it offered the Dallas franchise territory to Hunt and allowed his ally, Bud Adams, the Houston market. However, no other accommodations would be made for the remaining six franchises in the AFL.

Hunt thought the proposal over but not for long. He decided against joining the NFL and took the high ground of staying with the other owners who had committed to the new league. Hunt's resolve was the ultimate example of moral responsibility, arguably the last time that any major sports decision was made ethically.

The bigger league now wanted to take Dallas before Hunt did. The NFL then quickly debuted the Cowboys just in time to compete head-to-head with the startup AFL in its first season of 1960.

The NFL decided to not play nice, and Hunt made his feelings known. In a statement, he declared that his league attempted to keep the relationship with the NFL harmonious, on a high level, and would work amicably on all matters. He then added that the NFL had shown no interest in having this type of a relationship and kept pro football out of markets that the AFL had currently set up as founding cities. The NFL—Bell and Halas—had now done something that was pretty hard to do—make Lamar Hunt firing mad.

Hunt's Texans took to the gridiron for the inaugural AFL campaign and would call the city home for three seasons. On the field, they fared much better in the win-loss column than not only their 1952 NFL counterpart but the Cowboys as well. In 1962, with a record of 11–3, the Texans won the AFL title, the city's first major professional league championship.

Without question, Hunt's Texans did much better at the gate than the Miller brothers'. And they did so while having to share the city with the Cowboys. The AFL Texans' paid attendance figures were widely considered exaggerated due to the team employing gimmicky tools, discounted prices, and free ticket giveaways. However, one of those backers notably in the stands was Giles Miller. He paid full price and attended most of the Texans' home matchups.

After playing forty-three games over a three-season span including the playoffs, and winning most of them, Hunt decided to call it a day in Dallas and move the team north to Kansas City in time for the 1963 season. He had come to grips that North Texas was just not big enough for both his Texans and the Cowboys, and he had the foresight to see that long-term success would not come for either franchise if both were to stay in the city and fight for supremacy.

Hunt left town knowing that his team was better on the field than his crosstown NFL rival. But had he stayed, the long, drawn-out battle would have resulted in both sides losing money. Hunt did not blink when it came to ending the AFL-NFL territorial war in Dallas. The decision to relocate was also in the best interest of his fellow AFL owners who trusted him.

The team settled in Kansas City and was rebranded the Chiefs, who went on to build not only a winning tradition but also a diehard fanbase that few teams can match. After establishing themselves in the Midwest, Hunt's Chiefs would advance to the first championship ever played between the two leagues, losing to the Green Bay Packers in the 1966 season. However, they later won Super Bowl IV over the Minnesota Vikings to capture the 1969 title. Success came to Hunt before the Cowboys.

Strangely, one of the best gifts that Dallas and pro football ever received was the decision made by Hunt to move his team. Moving his team in 1963 was not a surrender. The relocation was a selfless act that benefited all parties in both leagues. Hunt was the definition of class and set an example that the Texans name was proud to be associated with, the type of owner that Dallas deserved, a custodian for the sport and the league. Much of the popularity that later came the Cowboys way, along with their very entry into the NFL via expansion, came in part because Hunt did what he did when he did it.

While the first version of the Dallas Texans ended in failure and forfeiture, in stark contrast, the second incarnation became winners and champions. The Dallas Texans sequel was indeed a very good one.

23

LIFE AFTER 1952

LEGENDARY Pittsburgh Steelers head coach Chuck Noll often referred to a player's career after football as "your life's work," meaning that it was more important than the actual game.[1] The sport prepares and conditions men for their subsequent years.

For those connected with the first iteration of the Dallas Texans, pretty much everything that happened to them after 1952 was an improvement. Without proof, most people would never have believed the comedy of errors ever really happened. And it's too bad the team didn't have Noll; they could have used his advice.

For the players, leaving Dallas was akin to making parole, with everyone ultimately dispersing in different directions. A few stayed together and found a football life elsewhere, but most gave up the profession. Of all the men who were a part of training camp and the regular-season roster, over half of them were out of the league before the 1953 season began. Just fifteen remained active. While every man would have his own "life after" accounts and experiences, here is what became of some of the characters in the Texans' story:

Joe Reid, a twenty-three-year-old linebacker from LSU, was about to enter his second and what was to be his last season in the NFL. He was just a backup guy with the Texans in 1952, but he suited up in all but one game for the team. He lived to be ninety years old and passed away in March of 2020, just six days before COVID-19's impact would begin to ravage the nation. Up until then, Reid was the last remaining player or staff member of the franchise.

Ted Collins deserves to be near the top of the list. Without him, there would be no team. Immediately after purging himself from the NFL, he went back to managing his moneymaker, Kate Smith, who would continue to be a staple of American entertainment. And she remained fiercely loyal to the man who made her.

In 1956, Smith was set to perform on *The Ed Sullivan Show* when Collins suffered a heart attack. She refused to appear without him. He recovered over time; however, in 1964 she drove him to a routine doctor's appointment and dropped him off at the front door. While she was parking the car, Collins had another heart attack and died inside the office at the age of sixty-three.

Earl Goins's loyal service and friendship to the family continued until the day he died. His contributions to the Miller family were without equal, and because of this, the brothers wanted to help him find a greater purpose. They set him up for what would become his lasting legacy.

Together, the Millers and Goins established The Goins Foundation, a nonprofit charity that helped underprivileged kids, its mission being to provide local youth with a nice, safe place to play. With Goins often boasting, "Only one of my boys has ever gone bad," the foundation's work became well-respected throughout the city for many years. Toward the end of his life, he also became a pastor at the South Dallas Methodist Church.

Any story about the Millers' history would not be complete without the mention of Goins. In the end, no one on record ever had anything bad to say about him. He died on August 14, 1963. Funeral services were held at the church where he preached, and there was said to be more than a thousand people in attendance—close to half of whom were white, despite segregation's ubiquity in Dallas.

Tex Maule thought he had seen it all after his time with the Texans. Once the season concluded, he left the front office world of football and took a seat on the other side of the desk, becoming one of country's premier sportswriters. He was hired by *Sports Illustrated* and covered the NFL for almost twenty years, eventually working his way up to the position of editor at the magazine.

Earl and Rosie Goins shown here holding two-year-old Connell Jr., along with his dog. Photo courtesy of Connell Miller Jr. and the Miller family.

Maule's pro football coverage was brilliant, although his talents as a writer and editor were greatly underappreciated due to his distain of the AFL. He was widely credited with being the first to proclaim the 1958 Baltimore Colts championship win over the New York Giants as "The Greatest Game Ever Played." Among his broader writing works, he also became a respected author, penning thirty-one bestselling books, most of which were about pro football.

After working three decades in the national sports media, he returned to Dallas where he served as a columnist with *The Dallas Morning News* from 1976 through 1979. Finally, at the age of retirement, he moved to New York to finish out life as a freelance writer until his death in 1981.

Forrest "Chubby" Grigg's season with the Texans would be his last. His career lasted seventy-eight games, although he only started nineteen of those due to his weight.

The Arkansas native settled in Ore City, Texas, two hours east of Dallas after his playing career ended. He owned a successful catfish restaurant there for eighteen years before finally selling it and giving way to retirement because of his declining health. Toward the end, he told his customers that he was "suffering from sugar diabetes and a few other things that go with it," the constant yo-yoing of his weight from his past playing days being the cause.[2]

By the mid-1970s, things were looking dark for Grigg. He watched his only son, a much-troubled youth, become a victim of drug abuse. Despite several attempts to help his son get sober, Grigg could no longer tolerate his addiction, which was somewhat ironic since years earlier he almost singlehandedly drank Hershey, Pennsylvania, out of alcohol.

After enduring the situation for almost three years, Grigg finally snapped. On the morning of October 31, 1976, the twenty-year-old son, still living under his parents' roof, was sleeping in his bed when Grigg came into his room and shot him in the head. Police arrived shortly thereafter, and Grigg was arrested for the murder. He was tried the following year.

His attorney initially entered a plea of not guilty by reason of insanity. In his testimony, Grigg's defense was that he was a man tortured by witnessing his son, who like himself was a high school athlete, be consumed by drugs and unable to hold a job. It was argued that, following repeated attempts to get him clean, Grigg decided he had no choice but to kill his son out of love.

Under the advice of his attorney, Grigg eventually pled guilty to a lesser charge of voluntary manslaughter and was sentenced to only five years probation. Grigg lived out the rest of his life mentally at peace with what he had done but was physically tortured by his own health. He died at home in Ore City on October 10, 1983.

Jack Adkisson was an insignificant rookie offensive lineman out of Southern Methodist University during his time with the Texans. He went to Kerrville with the team, played sparingly in the preseason, and was cut before the end of training camp. Still wanting to pursue his dream, he traveled to Canada for a tryout with the Edmonton Eskimos of the Canadian Football League. He didn't make it there either.

But while north of the border, Adkisson met former wrestler Stu Hart, and under his tutelage, he began to train for a career on the professional wrestling circuit. Paired with a fictious brother named "Waldo Von Erich,"

Adkisson took on the identity of "Fritz Von Erich," and together they were marketed as evil German brothers and Nazi sympathizers.

Adkisson originated one of the best finishing moves in the business, "The Iron Claw," and his character quickly became one of the greatest villains ever. Patriarch of the popular Von Erich wrestling family, his career began in 1953 and remained active for five decades, leaving a legacy in the sport that will never be forgotten. In 1997, he was diagnosed with lung cancer that quickly spread to his brain and adrenal glands. He died at the age of sixty-eight in his home in Lake Dallas.

Adkisson was posthumously inducted into the WWE Hall of Fame in 2009 and the Professional Wrestling Hall of Fame in 2012. He might have had a short career in football, but he became the most notable local sports figure to emerge from the Texans.

Don Colo fell into the category of players who don't always develop right away. Some need the right situation to realize their potential. In his first three NFL seasons, spent with the Colts, Yanks, and Texans, he was a largely unknown and hidden asset, having played on the worst team in the league each year.

After Dallas, Colo was one of the dispersed players who found himself back in Baltimore by the end of January. Fortunately, this time his stay was even shorter than before, as he never played a down there, becoming part of one of the largest trades in NFL history.

Ever the shrewd opportunist, Cleveland Browns head coach Paul Brown packaged ten players together and traded them for Colo and four others. In hindsight, Brown fleeced a team that didn't know what they had. And the chance to finally be a part of a winning club would prove to be just the move Colo needed. He played six years in Cleveland and flourished, becoming an ironman.

After his third Pro Bowl season, Colo stepped away from the game in 1958. Upon his retirement, Brown stated, "His play has been important to us, and we'll miss him."[3] Simple words from a coach who wasn't prone to giving out compliments.

He was particularly remembered by Giles Miller's eight-year-old son, Ed, who considered him his favorite player. Colo lived out a long and happy life after retirement, dying peacefully in Phoenix, Arizona, in 2019 at the ripe old age of ninety-four.

George Taliaferro made the move with the franchise north, but after suffering racial indignities in Dallas, he endured the same treatment in Baltimore. If anything, this time it felt even worse because he thought the social climate would be different. In Taliaferro's first season, he overhead Washington Redskins owner George Preston Marshall loudly say during pregame warmups, "[Racial slur] should never be allowed to do anything but push wheelbarrows."[4] Taliaferro then proceeded to score two touchdowns on Marshall's Redskins that day.

Still highly productive, he was again named to the Pro Bowl his first year in Baltimore, but by year two, Taliaferro was beset by a series of injuries that plagued him throughout the season and greatly affected his mobility. After having offseason surgery, the Colts decided not to bring him back for the 1955 campaign and traded him to the Philadelphia Eagles. But his comeback didn't go well; it was time for him to retire from football.

After hanging up his cleats, Taliaferro's wish was to become a high school football coach, and with his degree in hand and background as a player, his chances seemed rightfully good. But he quickly learned that his skin color would compromise his dream, as the Baltimore public school system would only hire African American staff for its two segregated schools. With no positions open in either one, he was turned down.

Taliaferro sold cars for a time, tried substitute teaching, and at one point even turned to a group of gangsters for work—and was thankfully turned down—before deciding to pursue his master's degree in social work. By 1970, having served with the Lafayette Square Community Center and the Prisoner Aid Association in Baltimore, he became the dean of students at Morgan State University. Two years later, Taliaferro was asked to return to Indiana University to serve as a special assistant to the president. Thirty years after experiencing segregation at the school, he now occupied the office directly across from its leader. His career had come full circle, and his résumé was complete.

Inducted into the College Football Hall of Fame in 1981, Taliaferro's accomplishments were many, but being the first Black player ever drafted was the most important to him. After his career ended, he reflected on the fact that he never played on a winning team but boasted, "I'm the one person in the history of the NFL to play seven positions. When I went on the field, the game was over when I came off."[5]

Taliaferro passed away from heart failure at his home on October 8, 2018, living to the age of ninety-one. One year later, Indiana University held a posthumous dedication ceremony outside of Memorial Stadium where a bronze statue of Taliaferro was unveiled. Anyone passing through the plaza—which also bears his name—is now reminded of the enormous contributions he made as an athlete, friend, and mentor to many. Taliaferro's legacy lives on through the commitment he made toward breaking racial barriers, both on and off the field.

Toward the end of his life, he once said, "I get a warm feeling when I watch football because I and people like me paid the price for them to have that opportunity."[6]

Buddy Young also made the list of Texans players moved to Baltimore. His journey, though, was very different from Taliaferro's, as he played three more seasons for the Colts and continued to be a threat at several positions.

The thing most impressive about Young was his speed. He ran with a bouncing style, and no player in the league could catch him in the open field, although some thought perhaps a horse could. In a publicity stunt staged by the team, a 40-yard dash was set up prior to a 1955 summer intersquad scrimmage at Baltimore's Memorial Stadium. It matched Young against the Colts' mascot. On the word "Go," Young gained 10 yards on the horse before it could even get going. From there, he outsprinted the animal while the crowd cheered loudly. Young was a fan favorite and a well-respected leader among both teammates and livestock, his going along with the stunt the best example of this.

When he retired from football after the 1955 season, he joined the Colts' front office in an administrative position, and the next year he became the first player in team history to have his jersey number retired, which spoke volumes about how much the franchise and surrounding community thought of him. His happy disposition was simply contagious. Whether right or wrong, Young simply had a better go of it in Baltimore than his teammate Taliaferro.

In 1966 he was hired by the league to become the NFL's director of player relations, the ultimate tribute to his career. With the appointment, Young became the first African American executive in any major professional sport. He continued to serve in his league capacity over the years that followed, while being a prime example of what it was to be a great humanitarian.

Young never seemed hardened by the negative racial experiences he endured. Instead of becoming bitter or distrustful, he dedicated the rest of his life to helping others less fortunate than him. He quietly worked with the Colts organization to make it possible for the underprivileged African American community to receive free tickets so they too could watch the games in any area of the stadium. When local schools and businesses would request that he come out for speaking engagements, he never accepted any money to do so. Young never sought, nor wanted, publicity for any good deed that he did.

Over his lifetime, he made his mark with people through the respectable way he treated them. For example, his interactions with a nine-year-old boy in Dallas who used to toss the ball and run with him after practices—a memory Connell Miller Jr. reflects fondly on to this day.

Claude Henry K. "Buddy" Young, who was everyone's buddy, passed away on September 4, 1983, after crashing his car on his way home from attending NFL player Joe Delaney's funeral. If there were men any better, there certainly weren't many of them.

Art Donovan was an entertaining character, to say the very least. When it comes to describing life in football, calling him one of the best storytellers ever would be an understatement. If you were around him, you became a big part of his future tales. And if what happened to the Texans in 1952 was not humorous enough on its own, Donovan could make the experience even more so.

Having survived three NFL seasons of futility with teams that would go out of business at the end of each campaign, Donovan was due for some good fortune after the Texans folded. Moving back to Baltimore, the change of scenery would be just what he needed, and he was no longer merely a jovial fat guy. In short order, he became one of the best defensive tackles in the NFL and went on to make the Pro Bowl in five straight seasons while being named First Team All-Pro four times and Second Team twice.

Although he had started every game in his last five seasons, he was cut during the 1962 training camp. At that point, he decided to retire from the game at the age of thirty-eight. Later that year, his number 70 would be the second that the Colts franchise would retire, and in 1968, he became the first for the franchise ever to be elected to the Pro Football Hall of Fame.

The game primed Donovan for a lifetime of comedy, which came naturally to him. In 1987, he cowrote an autobiography of his playing days with New York writer Bob Drury called *Fatso: Football When Men Were Really Men*. Obviously, the title fit. The book introduced him to a new audience, catapulting him into speaking engagements and greater popularity.

He went on to become a frequent guest on *The Tonight Show Starring Johnny Carson* and also appeared regularly on *Late Night with David Letterman*. Talk show banter suited him, and watchers never knew if Donovan was embellishing a true story or fabricating an anecdote altogether.

On one occasion, Carson brought up modern-day player injuries, to which Donovan recollected a memory of once breaking his leg. He related to the host that after two weeks, head coach Jimmy Phelan told him that he needed to play through the pain. When Donovan replied that he could barely walk, let alone play, Phelan answered, "It doesn't matter. You've got to play. You're all we've got. When they snap the ball, just fall down in front of them and maybe they'll trip over your big ass." He carried out the coach's order, and after a game the opposing offensive lineman across from Donovan came up and shook hands, telling him, "That's a hell of a move you put on me. No one has ever done anything like that before."[7]

In 2002, a most unusual tribute came when Donovan was placed in the Baltimore Ravens' Ring of Honor. Not many can say they've been so recognized by a team that they were never associated with. The gesture seemed thoughtful to him as well as to the other former Colts players who had nowhere else to call home once the team left for Indianapolis in 1984. Donovan's final tribute came in 2004 when he was notified that he was to be inducted into the US Marine Corps Sports Hall of Fame. He simply replied, "I hope they serve Schlitz."[8]

Wherever life took Donovan, people around him always laughed, although it is a pity that many remember him more as a jokester than the great player he was. As one of the most highly spirited sports celebrities ever, Donovan eventually had to face his own mortality. All good things come to an end, and for him the cause would be a respiratory ailment in August of 2013. Surrounded by his wife of fifty-seven years, Dorothy, and their five children and seven grandchildren, he passed away at the age of eighty-nine.

Art Donovan indelibly described himself once by saying, "Take me for what I am. I'm a nobody, like you or anyone else. I was lucky enough to play football, and everyone liked me. That's it."[9]

Gino Marchetti was the preeminent piece of the franchise that left en route to Baltimore. But once he arrived, first-year head coach Keith Molesworth unwisely moved him to offensive tackle. The following season, new head coach Weeb Ewbank was brought in and instantly knew Marchetti's value was on defense. By moving him back, Marchetti flourished, becoming known to all as Gino the Giant. When the Colts' 1958 title season arrived, he was clearly the defense's quintessential leader.

The NFL Championship game itself would mark the first time his parents ever got to watch him on television. In the final two minutes of the game, the New York Giants had the lead and were driving. Near midfield and needing 4 yards on a crucial third-down play, halfback Frank Gifford was stopped by Marchetti, preventing the first down. In the process, Marchetti's teammate, 285-pound Gene "Big Daddy" Lipscomb, landed on Marchetti's leg, breaking his ankle.

After the play was over, for the first time ever, Marchetti couldn't get up on a football field. He said later that he never hurt so bad in his life, and he knew instantly that his ankle was broken. Six men were needed to cart him off the field and carry him into the locker room on a stretcher for a medical evaluation while the Colts offense moved into field goal range to tie the score.

With the character of a never-say-die leader, he ignored the pain and demanded the trainers take him back to the field so that he could watch what was to be the NFL's first sudden-death ending. The trainers honored his wishes and returned him in time to witness a methodical drive of 80 yards on thirteen plays. The Colts moved the ball to the 1-yard line, where they would punch it into the end zone, resulting in their first championship.

Four months later in 1959, with his ankle now fully healed, Marchetti became a successful restauranter. He was encouraged by Colts owner Carroll Rosenbloom, so he joined two teammates to open a fast-food restaurant and drive-in just outside of Baltimore in Dundalk, Maryland. The establishment was named what else but Gino's Hamburgers.

They were so successful that the original eatery grew into a 313-unit regional chain in the mid-Atlantic states. And because he was also the franchisee in the same footprint area for Kentucky Fried Chicken, many of the Gino's were cobranded with KFC and would operate side-by-side in the same building. The chain had a great run, with Marchetti eventually selling it to the Marriott Corporation in 1982. Marriott basically bought the chain for the units' performance and sadly discontinued the Gino's brand, converting them all over to their Roy Rogers Restaurants.

Of all the recognition Marchetti ever received, being a clean player meant the most to him. He once said, "I never got hit with a fifteen-yard penalty, no late hits, no clipping, no hitting out of bounds. I didn't make stupid mistakes or put the team in trouble."[10] Playing much longer than most of the greats do, he finally retired following the 1965 season at the age of thirty-nine. Fittingly, after a very short waiting period, Marchetti was named to the Pro Football Hall of Fame's Class of 1972.

The game has never seen anyone more credited with redefining a position. Marchetti earned All-Pro honors in ten consecutive years, seven times to the First Team and three as a Second Teamer. When the league named its all-time anniversary teams for its fiftieth, seventy-fifth, and one hundredth seasons, Marchetti was included on all of them. In 2010, the NFL announced the top one hundred player rankings in its history, and Marchetti was placed at number thirty-nine. Unmentioned in any of his accomplishments, however, was that the only touchdown he ever scored during his illustrious career was with the Texans in his rookie year.

While a heart attacked he suffered in 1981 didn't seem to slow him down much—though it did prompt him to lose eighty-five pounds—he contracted pneumonia at the age of ninety-three, and the short, courageous battle would be lost on April 29, 2019, with his wife Joan of forty-one years by his side.

He casted a *long* shadow, the last starting player on the Texans squad to die. There have been giants in the NFL, and then there was Gino Marchetti.

Jimmy Phelan made it known that he wanted to stick around and continue coaching, but he never did so again. Phelan couldn't get past Bert Bell, and for the time being the commissioner controlled the franchise's future employment plan. Bell wanted a new organization, from top to bottom, and unfairly he put some of the blame for the Texans' business failure on Phelan.

For the last two years, Phelan had seen plenty of craziness from two different ownership groups. Losing was new, and it changed him, as witnessed by his lackadaisical approach on the field. Once things started to go sideways, he simply lost his motivation and energy, opting to use humor to balance the embarrassment. He had officially become an old dog.

Even so, he welcomed taking over the relocated group for one more go in Baltimore, but he was too set in his ways, and Bell saw that. Phelan decided that if the NFL didn't want him, then he didn't want them either. With that, he was out of coaching. Accustomed to longer tenures, and after living like a nomad, Phelan retreated to his California hometown of Sacramento, where he began selling real estate for a living.

Most players had humorous recollections of their experiences around the silver-haired old coot. Phelan was of devout faith, and many remembered how he encouraged his players to attend daily communion with him, once driving them all in a dump truck he borrowed. The account of him tossing down paychecks while advising the players to run to the bank would grow legs over time, but the extent of his interaction with his men was largely vague, not lending itself to a closeness with any of them.

Donovan was never at a loss for stories about Phelan, once saying, "I'll never forget that man. He was a real pisser."[11] His last memory of the coach was after the first season back in Baltimore. Donovan garnered enough respect to be named to his first Pro Bowl, and the accommodations for the event were at the Ambassador Hotel in Los Angeles. A large party was thrown in one of the suites by Doak Walker and Bobby Layne, and Donovan described the scene as degenerating into an all-night drinking contest where several of the invitees proceeded to throw up all over the carpet.

Phelan had been out of coaching for the last year, and Donovan hadn't seen him since Dallas, but living in California, the coach was also invited and showed up with his wife for what he thought was a meet and greet function. Phelan surveyed the room upon arriving, gestured, and then blamed his old player by saying, "Well, Donovan, you've certainly got a lot of fine athletes gathered here tonight, don't you?" But then he quickly recovered with, "Mind if a broken-down old coach and his missus join 'em?"[12]

Like a parent, he always knew what his men were doing when out of his sight. All who formed an opinion about the old man, whether good or bad, agreed that Phelan always put the players first, ahead of management, which was really the issue Bell had with him in the first place.

Being away from the locker room camaraderie mellowed Phelan. He became a very private person, spending most of his spare time following his love of horseracing. The racetrack became his new office.

As the 1960s arrived, he got involved in politics and served three terms on the board of commissioners for Sacramento County. He worked in the state capitol and struck up a friendship with then governor Ronald Reagan.

Fortunately, he lived long enough to finally receive the much-deserved respect he earned. In 1973, he was inducted into the College Football Hall of Fame, attending the ceremony for a sport from which he had long since divorced himself. He died less than a year later, on November 14, 1974, in Honolulu at the age of eighty.

If anyone today were to ask the question, "Who was the first professional head football coach in Dallas?", most would say the Cowboys' Tom Landry. Some might even guess Hank Stram of the AFL's Texans, both of whom are in the Hall of Fame and have won championships. But neither they nor anyone who followed them would have the same disposition and wry wit as Jimmy Phelan.

24

A FINAL LOSS

TODAY there is no Dallas Texans epitaph on display anywhere to celebrate or acknowledge that the team ever existed. Although there was one once . . . almost.

On a summer day in 1982, Giles Miller was packing to leave the Dallas area and relocate to the Central Texas town of Fredericksburg. While doing so, he came across a box containing four old mementoes. Instead of moving past the treasures and going about his business, he gave some thought as to what to do with them and decided to make a call on August 11 to a man named Bob Brooks, who was with the Texas Sports Hall of Fame.

Miller told Brooks what he had found and then asked if the museum had any interest in the four items. Of course, Brooks said they did, so Miller gifted the hall with a 1952 newspaper announcing the franchise's formation, a photo of the ownership group, and his personal copy of the book he had written in 1972 about his experience with the Texans.

There was one last incidental yet important item: the framed Certificate of Membership, issued by the NFL in 1952, that hung in the team's offices. Had Miller not picked up the phone that day, this small bit of history could have very well been buried in a closet forever, never to be seen again.

Yet regrettably, that's exactly what happened.

More than forty-two years after its donation, the priceless, one-of-a-kind credential has gone missing. The Texas Sports Hall of Fame's records indicate that the certificate was indeed received and inventoried. However, its whereabouts, as well as that of the other three items from the box, remain a mystery. They are nowhere to be found.

At the time of Miller's donation, the hall was based in the Dallas suburb of Grand Prairie, Texas. The location was closed in 1986, and the museum and its contents remained dormant. However, a 1990 revitalization effort began, which led to the hall reopening three years later in Waco, Texas. Somewhere in that time period, the valuable document vanished.

The hall's standard policy has always been to return items to the original donor or that person's appointee as needed. But there is no confirmed record of the artifact being given back to Miller or of someone else outside of the family taking possession of it. He passed away in 1989 and left no other authorized representative on file with the museum. To some, this misplacement may not seem significant, but much like the story of the franchise itself, the official certificate has been lost and forgotten.

Unfortunately, the passing decades did not treat the tale of the 1952 Dallas Texans kindly. There simply was not enough recorded about the first attempt at pro football in Dallas, and thus we will never have a perfectly clear reason why the franchise failed. Throughout the research compiled for this book, there was no single definitive root cause that pointed toward the Texans' rapid demise. On the contrary, there were many reasons. The collapse occurred after a collection of missteps, mistakes, and poor management developed into a perfect storm, one that came and went in less than ten months. Sadly, Miller's 1972 writings give no complete picture either—obviously because he himself did not really know.

Equally disappointing to never solving the secret of the team's collapse was my dismay at not hearing a single elderly person say, when asked about the team, "Hey, I remember those Dallas Texans, and I followed that team and went to their games." With the exception of my dear friend, Connell Miller Jr.

That this came about at all seems unreal. Today we know a series of events like those that played out in 1952 could not happen again. The NFL brand would never let a franchise spiral out of control the way the Texans did.

And the league never shared any ownership in the blame, leaving the

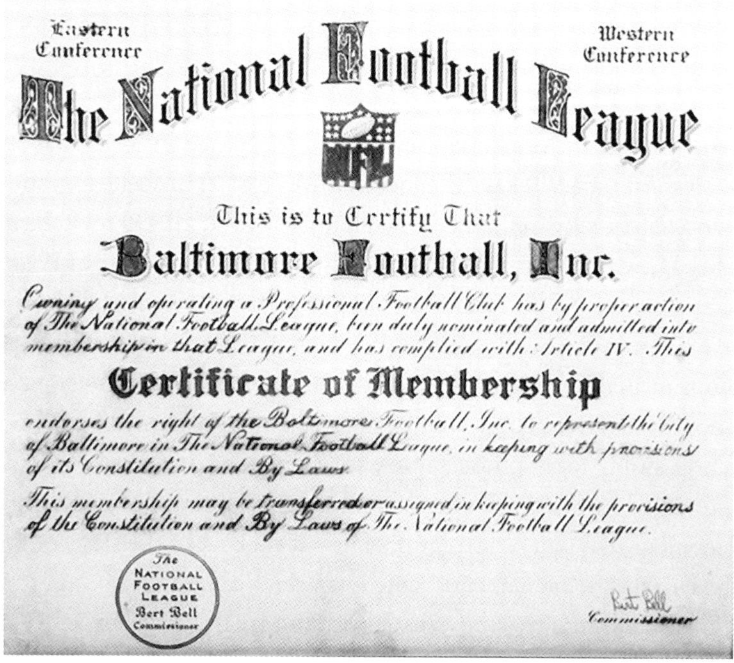

Eastern Conference

Western Conference

The National Football League

NFL

This is to Certify That

Baltimore Football, Inc.

Owning and operating a Professional Football Club has by proper action of The National Football League, been duly nominated and admitted into membership in that League, and has complied with Article IV. This

Certificate of Membership

endorses the right of the Baltimore Football, Inc. to represent the City of Baltimore in The National Football League, in keeping with provisions of its Constitution and By Laws.

This membership may be transferred or assigned in keeping with the provisions of the Constitution and By Laws of The National Football League.

The National Football League Bert Bell Commissioner

Bert Bell
Commissioner

Giles Miller's Dallas Texans Certificate of Membership was never found. The replacement shown here, which was issued to the Baltimore Colts in 1953, hasn't been lost, but it did find its way onto the auction block in February 2020. Image used in cooperation with the National Football League and its representative NFL Properties LLC.

Miller brothers to carry the entire burden themselves. The club's failure marked the last time any team would forfeit itself back over to the NFL, and astonishingly, this final occurrence happened in Dallas, now home of the world's most valuable sports franchise.

As Connell once wrote, if there really is only one reason, the simple answer might just be, "right place, wrong time."

25

IF ONLY...?

IF ONLY it had all worked out. Had the Dallas Texans survived after 1952, the NFL would not look the same—history, as we know it, would have been totally altered.

What if the Texans pulled off the Doak Walker trade? Or if they had actually won games, would that have translated into tickets sold? What if the initial franchise entry fee stayed at the $100,000 price tag that had been agreed upon for league admittance? The last-minute surprise of an additional $200,000 required for settling the Yankee Stadium lease would have gone a long way toward the new franchise's financial upkeep.

Another survival scenario could have taken place in which the Texans received a bailout by someone answering their SOS call. There is an old saying that there is a sucker born every minute. What if one of those minutes saw the formation of an altogether new ownership group, a sucker willing to step in for the brothers? Or if the Dallas Citizens Council came through with a loan after all, thus saving the team? Or if the other NFL owners offered the loan assistance that was requested? Today, the league of course would offer this help if the need arose.

Imagine that the team's recorded lack of cash flow was not an issue. That ticket sales and support equated to dollars in the bank. Any of these possibilities would have helped make the Texans solvent. They would not have gone away and been forgotten, to be reincarnated as another franchise.

Ponder the notion that the team continued on—this perhaps makes an even more interesting story. The Texans' survival would have had a ripple effect, impacting more than just one or two later teams along its path.

The 1953 season would have forged ahead as planned, with the Texans entering year two. From that point on, it stands to reason that the franchise would likely have prospered throughout the 1950s, into the 1960s, and all the way to the present day.

If so, what bearing would that have? Who would be affected?

Since there would have never been the necessity to establish a survivor franchise elsewhere, the most obvious development would be that the Baltimore Colts would not have been born in 1953. This proud franchise has a rich history that includes multiple championships and several hall of famers. However, none of that would have happened in Baltimore because the team would have still been playing in Dallas.

The city of Baltimore had the Colts for thirty-one years before losing the same franchise, as it later moved to Indianapolis where the team enjoyed continued success. However, that move to Indianapolis also wouldn't have happened. This counts one franchise, two cities, and the Mayflower Moving Company already shaken up.

Another future NFL fixture would face elimination, this one perhaps the most dramatic. With the Texans firmly embedded in Dallas, there would have never been the need or demand for the NFL to place another expansion team there before the 1960 season. The Cowboys, a sports franchise now worth $9 billion, would have never come into existence, while the Texans would enter into their eighth season. There would be no "America's Team," with all its love and hate, legendary history of players and coaches, and unparalleled success. This would not have influenced another city, per se, but it certainly would have caused a seismic shift, removing one of the most storied franchises that sports has ever known. A notion that is simply unimaginable.

Another monumental shift would have occurred around the same time. In 1959, before the American Football League came to be, neither of the Dallas pro teams, Hunt's Texans or the Cowboys, were a part of the football landscape. Lamar Hunt, along with seven others, quickly organized and founded a new league, a creation that only took place because Dallas had a vacancy and the NFL would not let Hunt in.

Had the 1952 Texans' failure not occurred, this league would not have formed, marking the single most important ramification of them all. Since there were a total of eight franchises, the impact would have been extensive.

Fittingly, the original eight AFL franchise owners, including Hunt, were called the "Foolish Club." The league's locations were Boston (Patriots), Buffalo (Bills), Denver (Broncos), Houston (Oilers), Los Angeles (Chargers), New York (Titans), and a final one in Minneapolis (Vikings). Coming from different business industries and walks of life, none of the members would have ever collectively joined together, although some were passing acquaintances with each other and Hunt.

Before the eight new franchises took the field for the first season, the Minneapolis owners withdrew from the AFL. The Minnesota group received a counterpunch offer to join the senior league as part of the NFL's plan to expand by two teams, along with the Cowboys. Minneapolis opted to jump over to the establishment as an expansion team, which made Dallas a battleground zone. With that, the Minnesota spot opened up for Oakland (Raiders) to join.

Of the eight founding AFL cities, four would eventually relocate elsewhere at some point during their football lifetime. But the formation and ten-year run of the underdog AFL defined success in the sports industry. Their goal was to compete with the NFL for equality, and they did. By the late 1960s, the AFL had forced a merger with the NFL. However, the success story would have never occurred had the NFL 1952 Texans not done their part in failing.

During and after the lifespan of the AFL, Hunt's Texans moved to Kansas City following three seasons in Dallas. The Los Angeles Chargers moved to San Diego, then back to Los Angeles again while the Houston Oilers relocated to Tennessee to become the Titans. The Oakland Raiders became a traveling show, shifting to Los Angeles, then back to Oakland, then finally settling in Las Vegas.

In the AFL's decade of existence, the list of cities grew as the league added Miami (Dolphins) and Cincinnati (Bengals), which wouldn't have taken place had there been no creation of the league to begin with. The demise of the Texans in 1952 basically set into motion what is now most of the American Football Conference of the NFL.

In 1960, the NFL was not looking to expand. But once the AFL started, they noticed and reacted. Things took off from there. In the following decades, future expansion would take place in other areas around the country.

Would any of those expansion targets, including those of the AFL member cities, have been admitted into the NFL later as a franchise? With the game's massive growth and popularity, the safe bet is yes. Had the Texans stayed afloat, by no means would they alone have locked these cities out for good. But at the same time, their success would have changed everything.

The collapse of 1952 was the catalyst for the future growth and expansion of the game. The Texans cleaned the slate.

In the end, here is the complete group of franchises that will be forever linked in some way to the Texans' life story:

- Baltimore Colts—Indianapolis Colts
- Boston Patriots—New England Patriots
- Buffalo Bills
- Dallas Cowboys
- Dallas Texans—Kansas City Chiefs
- Denver Broncos
- Houston Oilers—Tennessee Titans
- Los Angeles Chargers—San Diego Chargers—Los Angeles Chargers
- Minnesota Vikings
- New York Titans—New York Jets
- Oakland Raiders—Los Angeles Raiders—Las Vegas Raiders
- Miami Dolphins
- Cincinnati Bengals
- Houston Texans (Use of Texans name but different team)

The final tally makes up an impressive list. The repercussions impacted sixteen league cities involving fourteen franchises, which is nearly half of today's NFL.

The what-if scenarios around the plight of what was one of the worst franchises in NFL annals might be the most interesting contribution that the Texans legacy left us to think about. At its core, the conversation raises the question of how such a horrible franchise had so much influence on the game's history.

The beneficiaries began with the Colts, then the Cowboys, and then moved on to the entire AFL, growing from there. And with that, Dallas became the epicenter of pro football's popularity explosion. The Texans' 1952 downfall helped pave the way.

Once the NFL world was finished with the Texans, football started rolling into its golden age with the league's popularity becoming global. Currently, the Cowboys organization can't sneeze without making national front-page news. During the NFL's offseason, whether the other North Texas teams are in a championship run or not, they take a backseat to anything the Cowboys are doing. There is no comparison anywhere to the level of attention and saturation that the club now receives. And they, but for the grace of God, could have been the Texans.

Would anyone today like to have seen an alternative NFL? Fans of the original Texans might say yes, if there were any to count. However, fourteen other teams and the events of history would tell us no—and to leave well enough alone. Had things not happened the way they did, the league would have perhaps fared worse. What occurred is probably a much better ending to the story.

In other words, thank goodness the Dallas Texans failed!

ACKNOWLEDGMENTS

It was hot on Saturday morning, July 11, 2020, when I sat down at my desk and started to write this book. Like so many during the COVID-19 year, I had a lot of time on my hands to think, and writing a book on a forgotten NFL franchise seemed like a no-brainer that would keep me busy as the world stopped for lockdown.

That day, as she so often does, my wife sent me a nice note, commemorating what I was about to start. This gesture was not unusual for her as she has always been in my corner. With that said, I want to first acknowledge Deb. For all the times she walked by and smiled, brought coffee or something to snack on, or just listened to my boring stories about researching the Dallas Texans, I thank her in more ways than I can ever express. I'm both blessed and grateful to her for patiently waiting and putting up with me through this journey.

The next two men I must mention gladly donated their time and untold stories to what was documented in this book. I can't convey enough thanks to Connell Miller Jr. and Ed Miller, without whom this project would have never been completed. I am deeply indebted to them and the entire Miller family for trusting in me to tell their story. My payment for all their efforts is that I can call them enduring friends.

An essential contributor to this project is the very first person who ever read the manuscript. Kurt Daniels was an acquaintance whom I had known for years. He knew of the storyline and served as my editor, having to endure the constant questions and stupid ideas that I came up with. Kurt wasn't just a partner; he remains a good friend. Kurt also later introduced me to Michael Villareal, who worked through the photo restorations and issues that come with material that is over seventy-two years old. I thank Michael for making the time while tending to a newborn.

I also want to thank the team at TCU Press for all they have done throughout this process in bringing this story to fruition. Thanks go to Abigail Jennings, James Lehr, Alex Gergely, and Dan Williams.

Through the years of research and all the fact findings, there were many others who greatly helped along the way. The following people, in no order of importance other than alphabetical, I would like to thank:

Jay Black, Gil Brandt, Sara Brandt, Mike Buckner, Karen Campbell, Rand Clark, Lisa Heckman, Michael Hoerner, Steve Howen, Carol Jones, Dawn Knight, Ron Linger, Verne Lundquist, Michael MacCambridge, Kerri McLeroy, Jackson Michael, Donny Miller, Rhett Miller, John Parry, Sara Pezzoni, Richard T. Pierce, Michael Powers, William Harlon Ray, Doug Remley, Jodi Rhinehart-Doty, James Curtis Sanford Jr., Steve Schwartz, Aries Tabigue, Joseph Vassalotti, Danny Williams, Curtis Worrell, and Allan Zullo.

Finally, I want to acknowledge you the reader for the time and attention you gave this story. Hopefully now you have a new story to share at your next party. One about a forgotten football team that had a more far-reaching impact than most people know.

I thank you all.

THE PLAYERS

Through extensive research, the following is determined to be the complete roster of all Dallas Texans players who were a part of the team during the 1952 season.

PLAYER	AGE	POS	G	HT	WT	COLLEGE	YRS
Abbey, Joe	25	E	TC	6-1	198	North Texas State	2
Adkisson, Jack	23	G	TC	6-3	240	SMU	R
Aldridge, Bennie	26	DB	1	6-0	195	Oklahoma A&M	2
Alford, Bruce	30	E	2	6-0	190	TCU	7
Anderson, David	21	QB	TC	6-0	178	Arkansas A&M	R
Averno, Sisto	27	LB	12	5-11	235	Muhlenberg	2
Baggett, Billy	23	HB	11	5-11	175	LSU	R
Bonner, Dee	23	E	TC	6-4	200	Arkansas State	R
Campanella, Joe	22	DT	12	6-2	242	Ohio State	R
Cannamela, Pat	23	LB	12	6-0	195	USC	R
Celeri, Bob	25	QB	8	5-10	180	California	1
Champion, Jim	25	G	TC	6-0	245	Mississippi State	3
Clark, Bert	22	G	TC	6-0	210	Oklahoma	R
Clowes, John	30	G	TC	6-1	245	William & Mary	3
Colo, Don	27	DT	4	6-3	252	Brown	2
Davis, Jerry	28	DB	7	5-10	178	Southeastern Louisiana	4
Donovan, Art	28	DT	6	6-2	263	Boston College	2
DuBois, Howard	24	G	TC	6-1	210	Nebraska Wesleyan	R
Ecklund, Brad	30	C	12	6-3	215	Oregon	3
Edwards, Dan	26	E	1	6-1	197	Georgia	4
Felker, Gene	23	E	6	6-1	198	Wisconsin	R
Finnell, Bob	26	HB	TC	5-9	185	Xavier	R
Flowers, Keith	22	LB	6	6-0	211	TCU	R
Fray, Bill	25	OT	TC	6-3	245	Idaho	R
Gandee, Sonny	23	DE	2	6-1	216	Ohio State	R
Grigg, Chubby	26	DT	10	6-2	294	Tulsa	6
Hall, Sid	26	G	TC	5-10	210	College of Pacific	R
Halliday, Jack	24	OT	TC	6-3	238	SMU	1
Hammond, Jim	22	HB	TC	6-1	195	Wisconsin	R

PLAYER	AGE	POS	G	HT	WT	COLLEGE	YRS
Herron, Jack	24	QB	TC	5-9	180	Southwest Louisiana	R
Hoerner, Dick	30	FB	11	6-4	220	Iowa	5
Humble, Weldon	31	G	11	6-1	221	Rice	5
Jackson, Ken	23	OT	12	6-2	236	Texas	R
Jankovich, Keever	24	LB	10	6-0	215	Pacific	R
Keane, Tom	26	DB	12	6-1	192	West Virginia	4
Klosterman, Don	22	QB	1	5-10	180	Loyola Marymount	R
Lansford, Jim	22	OT	12	6-3	235	Texas	R
Lauricella, Hank	22	HB	11	5-11	175	Tennessee	R
Levermann, Gerald	27	HB	TC	6-1	205	Trinity	R
Long, Bill	25	E	TC	6-1	195	Oklahoma A&M	1
Marchetti, Gino	25	DE	12	6-4	244	San Francisco	R
McCormack, Mike	25	OT	TC	6-3	230	Kansas	1
McKissack, Dick	26	DB	1	6-2	208	SMU	R
Meisenheimer, Darrell	26	HB	TC	5-10	195	Oklahoma A&M	2
Molnar, Leslie	26	G	TC	6-0	240	Buffalo	R
Nagel, Ross	29	OT	TC	6-4	243	St. Louis University	2
Nokley, Jim	23	FB	TC	6-2	220	St. Louis University	R
O'Connor, Bill	26	E	TC	6-4	220	Notre Dame	1
Ortmann, Chuck	23	QB	3	6-1	190	Michigan	1
Pelfrey, Ray	24	E	6	6-0	190	Eastern Kentucky	1
Perry, Charles	23	OT	TC	6-2	210	SMU	R
Petitbon, Johnny	21	DB	11	5-11	186	Notre Dame	R
Poole, Barney	29	DE	12	6-2	231	Mississippi	3
Reddell, Billy	22	HB	TC	6-0	180	Florida	R
Reid, Joe	23	LB	11	6-3	225	LSU	1
Roberson, Billy Jack	28	OT	TC	6-2	235	Stephen F. Austin	R
Robison, George	21	G	4	6-2	215	Virginia Military Institute	R
Sherman, Will	25	DB	2	6-2	190	St. Mary's (CA)	R
Sinquefield, Melvin	24	C	TC	6-3	225	Mississippi	R
Soboleski, Joe	26	G	1	6-0	213	Michigan	3
Strehlow, Roland	22	HB	TC	6-0	195	Wisconsin	R
Tait, Art	23	DE	8	5-11	205	Mississippi State	1
Taliaferro, George	25	HB	12	5-11	196	Indiana	3

PLAYER	AGE	POS	G	HT	WT	COLLEGE	YRS
Tanner, Hamp	25	OT	10	6-2	280	Georgia	1
Toth, Zollie	28	FB	12	6-2	219	LSU	2
Tripucka, Frank	25	QB	6	6-2	192	Notre Dame	3
Weiner, Art	26	E	TC	6-3	212	North Carolina	1
Wilkins, Dick	27	E	12	6-2	194	Oregon	3
Williams, Stan	23	DB	12	6-2	195	Baylor	R
Witry, Jerry	23	E	TC	6-1	205	Loras College	R
Wozniak, John	31	G	12	6-0	218	Alabama	4
Young, Buddy	26	HB	12	5-4	175	Illinois	5
Young, George	22	OT	TC	6-2	252	Bucknell	R
Zalejski, Ernie	27	HB	TC	5-11	187	Notre Dame	1

Glossary

POS: Position

G: Games Played

HT: Height

WT: Weight

YRS: Years of Experience

C: Center

DB: Defensive Back

DE: Defensive End

DT: Defensive Tackle

E: End

FB: Fullback

HB: Halfback

G: Guard

LB: Linebacker

OT: Offensive Tackle

QB: Quarterback

R: Rookie

TC: Only with team at Training Camp

All player photos on pp. 227-230 given under the permission of Squire Haskins, Inc. Photography.

Sisto Averno

Billy Baggett

Pat Cannamela

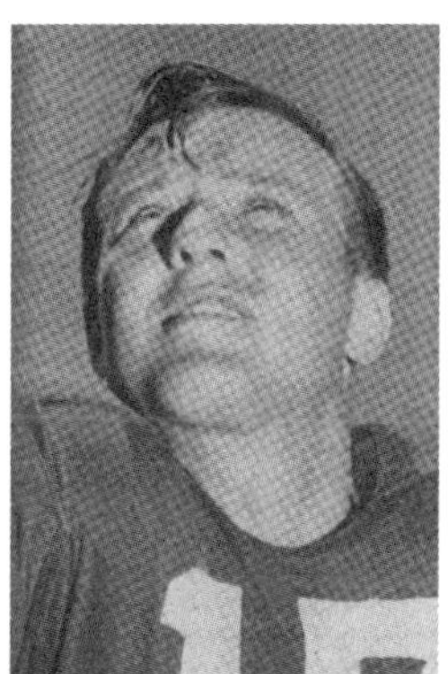
Bob Celeri

Jim Champion

John Clowes

Don Colo

Jerry Davis

Art Donovan

Brad Ecklund

Dan Edwards

Chubby Grigg

Jack Halliday

Jim Hammond

Dick Hoerner

Weldon Humble

Ken Jackson

Tom Keane

Jim Lansford

Gino Marchetti

Mike McCormack

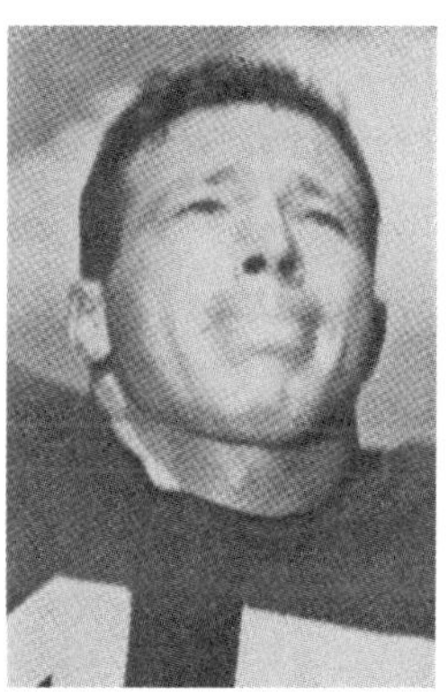
Darrell Meisenheimer

Ross Nagel

Bill O'Connor

John Petitbon

Barney Poole

Joe Reid

Joe Soboleski

Art Tait

George Taliaferro

Zollie Toth

Dick Wilkins

Stan Williams

Jerry Witry

John Wozniak

Buddy Young

FAILED FRANCHISES

Through extensive research, the following is determined to be the complete listing of all forty-nine failed franchises that have participated in the National Football League since its 1920 inception.

Detroit Heralds
Detroit, Michigan
Established and folded 1920
1 Season

Chicago Tigers
Chicago, Illinois
Established and folded 1920
1 Season

Cleveland Tigers (1920) - Cleveland Indians (1921)
Cleveland, Ohio
Established 1920 – folded 1921
2 Seasons

Muncie Flyers
Muncie, Indiana
Established 1920 – folded 1921
2 Seasons

Rochester Jeffersons
Rochester, New York
Established 1920 folded 1925
6 Seasons

Rock Island Independents
Rock Island, Illinois
Established 1920 – folded 1925
6 Seasons

Akron Pros (1920-25) - Akron Indians (1926)
Akron, Ohio
Established 1920 – folded 1926
7 Seasons

Columbus Panhandles (1920-22) - Columbus Tigers (1923-26)
Columbus, Ohio
Established 1920 – folded 1926
7 Seasons

Hammond Pros
Hammond, Indiana
Established 1920 – folded 1926
7 Seasons

Canton Bulldogs
Canton, Ohio
Established 1920 – folded 1926
7 Seasons

Buffalo All-Americans (1920-1923) - Buffalo Bisons (1924-1925) - Buffalo Rangers (1926-29)
Buffalo, New York
Established 1920 – folded 1929
10 Seasons

Dayton Triangles
Dayton, Ohio
Established 1920 – folded 1929
10 Seasons

Cincinnati Celts
Cincinnati, Ohio
Established and folded 1921
1 Season

Detroit Tigers
Detroit, Michigan
Established and folded 1921
1 Season

New York Giants
New York, New York
Established and folded 1921
1 Season

Tonawanda Kardex
Tonawanda, New York
Established and folded 1921
1 Season

Washington Senators
Washington, DC
Established and folded 1921
1 Season

Evansville Crimson Giants
Evansville, Indiana
Established 1921 – folded 1922
2 Seasons

Louisville Brecks (1921-25) - Louisville Colonels (1926)
Louisville, Kentucky
Established 1921 – folded 1926
7 Seasons

Minneapolis Marines (1921-24) - Minneapolis Red Jackets (1929-30)
Minneapolis, Minnesota
Established 1921/1929 – folded 1930
6 Seasons

Oorang Indians
LaRue, Ohio
Established 1922 – folded 1923
2 Seasons

Toledo Maroons
Toledo, Ohio
Established 1922 – folded 1923
2 Seasons

Milwaukee Badgers
Milwaukee, Wisconsin
Established 1922 – folded 1926
5 Seasons

Racine Legion (1922-25) - Racine Tornadoes (1926)
Racine, Wisconsin
Established 1922 – folded 1926
5 Seasons

St. Louis All-Stars
St. Louis, Missouri
Established and folded 1923
1 Season

Cleveland Indians (1923) - Cleveland Bulldogs (1924-27)
Cleveland, Ohio
Established 1923 – folded 1927
5 Seasons

Duluth Kelleys (1923-25) - Duluth Eskimos (1926-27)
Duluth, Minnesota
Established 1923 – folded 1927
3 Seasons

Kenosha Maroons
Kenosha, Wisconsin
Established and folded 1924
1 Season

Kansas City Blues (1924) - Kansas City Cowboys (1925-26)
Kansas City, Missouri
Established 1924 – folded 1926
3 Seasons

Frankford Yellow Jackets
Frankford, Philadelphia
Established 1924 – folded 1931
7 Seasons

Detroit Panthers
Detroit, Michigan
Established 1925 – folded 1926
2 Seasons

Pottsville Maroons
Pottsville, Pennsylvania
Established 1925 – folded 1928
4 Seasons

Providence Steam Roller
Providence, Rhode Island
Established 1925 – folded 1931
7 Seasons

Brooklyn Lions
Brooklyn, New York
Established and folded 1926
1 Season

Hartford Blues
Hartford, Connecticut
Established and folded 1926
1 Season

Los Angeles Buccaneers
Los Angeles, California
Established and folded 1926
1 Season

New York Yankees
New York, New York
Established 1927 – folded 1928
2 Seasons

Detroit Wolverines
Detroit, Michigan
Established and folded 1928
1 Season

Boston Bulldogs
Boston, Massachusetts
Established and folded 1929
1 Season

Orange Tornados (1929) – Newark Tornadoes (1930)
Orange and Newark, New Jersey
Established 1929 – folded 1930
2 Seasons

Staten Island Stapletons
Staten Island, New York
Established 1929 – folded 1932
4 Seasons

Brooklyn Dodgers (1930–43) – Brooklyn Tigers (1944)
Brooklyn, New York
Established 1930 – folded 1944
15 Seasons

Cleveland Indians
Cleveland, Ohio
Established and folded 1931
1 Season

Cincinnati Reds
Cincinnati, Ohio
Established 1933 – folded 1934
2 Seasons

St. Louis Gunners
St. Louis, Missouri
Established and folded 1934
1 Season

Boston Yanks
Boston, Massachusetts
Established 1944 – folded 1948
5 Seasons

Baltimore Colts
Baltimore, Maryland
Established and folded 1950
1 Season

New York Bulldogs (1949) – New York Yanks (1950–51)
New York, New York
Established 1949 – folded 1951
3 Seasons

Dallas Texans
Dallas, Texas
Established and folded 1952
1 Season

NOTES

Introduction

[1]Rhett Miller, "We Could Have Been Cowboys," *Sports Illustrated*, January 12, 2015, https://vault.si.com/vault/2015/01/12/we-could-have-been-cowboys.

[2]Connell Ransom Miller Jr., personal interview with author.

[3]Giles Edwin Miller Jr. (Ed), (son of Giles Edwin Miller Sr.), written exchange with author.

[4]Rhett Miller and Jasmine Belcher Morris, producer, "The Texans," 2016, Los Angeles, CA, Midroll Media, Howl FM Premium Audio, original audio documentary, 27:00.

Prologue

[1]Brad Schultz, *The NFL, Year One: The 1970 Season and the Dawn of Modern Football* (Washington, DC: Potomac Books, 2013), 2.

Chapter 2

[1]Pro Football Hall of Fame, "Bert Bell," accessed April 1, 2024, https://www.profootballhof.com/players/bert-bell/.

Chapter 3

[1]Frank Tolbert, "Can He Revive Pro Football's Sad Sacks?" *Saturday Evening Post*, September 27, 1952.

[2]Tolbert, "Can He Revive Pro Football's Sad Sacks?"

Chapter 4

[1]Dallas Public Library, "Dallas Bonehead Club Records," accessed March 31, 2024, https://dallaslibrary2.org/dallashistory/archives/08301.php.

[2]Robert S. Lyons, *On Any Given Sunday: A Life of Bert Bell* (Philadelphia: Temple University Press, 2010), 181.

[3]Lyons, *On Any Given Sunday*, 182.

[4]Lyons, *On Any Given Sunday*, 182.

[5]Louis Cox, "Halas Expects Interesting Rivalry Between Bears Texans," *The Daily Times Herald*, May 2, 1952, Heralding Sports section, 24.

[6]Cox, "Halas Expects Interesting Rivalry Between Bears Texans," 24.

[7]Bill Rives, "Pro Football Comes to Texas," *The Dallas News*, September 15, 1952, Sports section, 12.

[8]Joe Horrigan, Joe, *NFL Century: The One-Hundred Year Rise of America's Greatest Sports League* (New York: Crown, 2019), 107.

[9]Tolbert, "Can He Revive Pro Football's Sad Sacks?"

Chapter 5

[1]Tolbert, "Can He Revive Pro Football's Sad Sacks?"

[2]Paula Bosse, "The 1952 Dallas Texans: Definitely NOT America's Team," FLASHBACK: Dallas, published February 7, 2016, https://flashbackdallas.com/2016/02/07/the-1952-dallas-texans-definitely-not-americas-team/.

[3]Giles E. Miller, *The Dallas Texans Saga – or at the Time the New York Yanks Became the Baltimore Colts.* (Dallas: Gemco, 1972), 126.

[4]Miller, *Dallas Texans Saga*, 96. 5Miller, *Dallas Texans Saga*, 97. 6Miller, *Dallas Texans Saga*, 101.

[7]Bill Rives, "Make Way for the Dallas Texans," *Sport Magazine*, September 1952.

[8]Gene Gregston, "Consider Eight for Ranger Post - Wilkinson, Bryant, Todd, Cherry among Coaches Mentioned," *Fort Worth Star Telegram*, January 24, 1952, Sports section, 11.

Chapter 6

[1]Miller, *Dallas Texans Saga*, 95.

[2]Bill Fay, "It's Hard-Ridin', Two-Gun Football, Partner!" *Collier's Magazine*, September 13, 1952.

[3]Bill Fay, "It's Hard-Ridin', Two-Gun Football, Partner!"

[4]Bill Fay, "It's Hard-Ridin', Two-Gun Football, Partner!"

[5]Bill Fay, "It's Hard-Ridin', Two-Gun Football, Partner!"

Chapter 7

[1]Arthur J. Donovan and Bob Drury, *Fatso: Football When Men Were Really Men* (New York: William Morrow, 1987), 124.

[2]Wikipedia, s.v. "George Preston Marshall," last modified March 11, 2024, en.wikipedia.org/wiki/George_Preston_Marshall.

[3]Gregston, "Consider Eight for Ranger Post," 11.

[4]Rives, "Pro Football Comes to Texas," 12.

[5]Dawn Knight, *Taliaferro: Breaking Barriers from the NFL Draft to the Ivory Tower* (Bloomington: Indiana University Press, 2007), 104.

[6]Knight, *Taliaferro*, 102.

[7]Avery Yang, "George Taliaferro Made NFL Draft History," *Sports Illustrated*, February 26, 2020, si.com/nfl/2020/02/26/black-history-month-george-taliaferro.

Chapter 8

[1]Frank Finch, "Rams Trade Hoerner, 10 Other for Les Richter," *Los Angeles Times*, June 13, 1952.

[2]Pro Football Hall of Fame, "Richter Traded for 11 Players," posted August 26, 2010, https://www.profootballhof.com/news/2010/08/news-richter-traded-for-11-players/.

Chapter 9

[1]Tolbert, "Can He Revive Pro Football's Sad Sacks?"

[2]Miller, *Dallas Texans Saga*, 141.

Chapter 11

[1]Dave Fleming, "Meet the Miraculous, Disastrous 1952 Dallas Texans," ESPN, posted November 22, 2018, https://www.espn.com/nfl/story/_/id/25339283/how-1952-dallas-texans-became-nfl-laughing-stock-pulled-thanksgiving-miracle-chicago-bears.

[2]Lyons, *On Any Given Sunday*, 185.

[3]Miller, *Dallas Texans Saga*, 181.

Chapter 12

[1]Lyons, *On Any Given Sunday*, 184.

[2]Lyons, *On Any Given Sunday*, 184.

[3]Lyons, *On Any Given Sunday*, 184.

[4]Miller, *Dallas Texans Saga*, 203.

Chapter 13

[1]Miller, *Dallas Texans Saga*, 206.

[2]Miller, *Dallas Texans Saga*, 210.

[3]Miller, *Dallas Texans Saga*, 210.

[4]Miller, *Dallas Texans Saga*, 211.

[5]Miller, *Dallas Texans Saga*, 211.

[6]Frank Finch, "Dick Hoerner back to Vex Ex-mates," *Los Angeles Times*, October 29, 1952.

[7]Fleming, "Meet the Miraculous, Disastrous 1952 Dallas Texans."

Chapter 14

[1]Miller, *Dallas Texans Saga*, 229.

[2]Lyons, *On Any Given Sunday*, 185.

[3]NFL Films, *The Fabulous 50's*, volume 2, "The Dallas Texans (1952) Highlight Film," 7:00 (Mount Laurel, NJ: NFL Films Archives, 1987).

[4]Michael MacCambridge, *America's Game: The Epic Story of How Pro Football Captured a Nation*

(New York: Anchor Books, 2005), 78.

[5]Miller, *Dallas Texans Saga*, 225.

[6]Miller, *Dallas Texans Saga*, 228.

Chapter 15

[1]Miller, *Dallas Texans Saga*, 230.

[2]Miller, *Dallas Texans Saga*, 9.

[3]Miller, *Dallas Texans Saga*, 9.

[4]Lyons, *On Any Given Sunday*, 188.

[5]Neal Goulet, "The Year Hershey Joined the NFL," Goulet Communications, posted October 15, 2016, https://gouletcommunications.com/the-year-hershey-joined-the-nfl/#:~:text=When%20the%20league%20took%20control,the%20remainder%20of%20the%20season.

[6]Goulet, "Year Hershey Joined the NFL."

Chapter 17

[1]NFL Films, "Dallas Texans (1952) Highlight Film."

[2]NFL Films, "Dallas Texans (1952) Highlight Film."

[3]NFL Films, "Dallas Texans (1952) Highlight Film."

[4]Associated Press, "Only 3,000 Watch 'Dallas' Beat Bears," *The Detroit News*, November 28, 1952, Sports section.

Chapter 18

[1]NFL Films, "Dallas Texans (1952) Highlight Film."

[2]Fleming, "Meet the Miraculous, Disastrous 1952 Dallas Texans."

[3]Pro Football Hall of Fame, "The Last NFL Team to Go Belly Up," accessed April 1, 2024, profootballhof.com/football-history/the-dallas-texans/.

Chapter 19

[1]Lyons, *On Any Given Sunday*, x.

[2]Connell R. Miller Jr., "Right Place – Wrong Time: How the 1952 Dallas Texans Flamed Out after One Lackluster Season of Football," *Texas Monthly*, March 2019, https://www.texasmonthly.com/arts-entertainment/1952-dallas-texans/.

[3]Allan Zullo and Bruce Nash, *The Sports Hall of Shame*, illustrated by Bill Maul (New York: Pocket Books, 1987; reprinted by Tribune Media Services, 1991).

Chapter 20

[1]Connell Miller Jr. and Ed Miller, personal interviews with author, February 2022.

[2]Miller and Morris, "Texans."

[3]Miller and Morris, "Texans."

Chapter 21

[1]Fleming, "Meet the Miraculous, Disastrous 1952 Dallas Texans."

[2]MacCambridge, *America's Game*, 79.

Chapter 22

[1]MacCambridge, *America's Game*, 118.

[2]David A. F. Swift, *Lamar Hunt: The Gentle Giant Who Revolutionized Professional Sports* (Chicago: Triumph Books, 2010), 30.

[3]MacCambridge, *America's Game*, 120.

[4]Miller, *Dallas Texans Saga*, 267.

[5]Miller, *Dallas Texans Saga*, 267.

Chapter 23

[1]Gary Pomerantz, *Their Life's Work* (New York: Simon and Schuster, 2013), 14.

[2]Wikipedia, s.v. "Chubby Grigg," last modified January 22, 2024, en.wikipedia.org/wiki/ Chubby_Grigg.

[3]Cleveland Browns, "2015 Browns Legends: Don Colo was one of NFL's best D-tackles," September 25, 2015, clevelandbrowns.com/news/2015-browns-legends-don-colo-was-one-of-nfl-s-best-d-tackles-15944759.

[4]Knight, *Taliaferro*, 130.

[5]Timothy Rapp, "George Taliaferro, 1st African American NFL Draft Pick, Dies at Age 91," Bleacher Report, posted October 9, 2018, https://bleacherreport.com/articles/2799908-george-taliaferro-1st-african-american-nfl-draft-pick-dies-at-age-91.

[6]"The B1G Story: George Taliaferro | Trailer," Big Ten Network, September 3, 2021, Youtube video, 1:52, youtube.com/watch?v=dYzMtcJAn10.

[7]"Art Donovan on The Tonight Show," Mike Webb, August 15, 2010, Youtube video, 6:28, youtube. com/ watch?v=7HDRLnoAY9E.

[8]Michael Klingaman, "Donovan a Good Fit for Marine Sports Hall," *The Baltimore Sun*, posted August 6, 2004, https://www.baltimoresun.com/2004/08/06/donovan-good-fit-for-marine-sports-hall/.

[9]Douglas Martin, "Art Donovan, a Behemoth of Modesty, Dies at 89," *New York Times*, posted August 5, 2013, https://www.nytimes.com/2013/08/06/sports/football/art-donovan-a-behemoth-of-modesty-dies-at-89.html.

[10]*Sports Illustrated*, "Gino Marchetti," posted July 4, 2016, https://vault.si.com/vault/2016/07/04/gino-marchetti.

[11]David Eskenazi and Steve Rudman, "Wayback Machine: James Merlin Phelan," Sportspress Northwest, posted October 30, 2012, https://www.sportspressnw.com/2140649/2012/wayback-machine-james-merlin-phelan.

[12]Eskenazi and Rudman, "Wayback Machine."

BIBLIOGRAPHY

BOOKS

Brown, Paul, with Jack Clary. *PB: The Paul Brown Story*. New York: Antheneum Books, 1979. Callahan, Tom. *Johnny U*. New York: Crown, 2006.

Creative Services Division of NFL Properties. *75 Seasons: The Complete Story of the National Football League, 1920–1995*. Atlanta: Turner, 1994.

Creative Staff of NFL Properties, and Creative Director David Boss. *The First Fifty Years: A Celebration of the National Football League in its Fiftieth Season*. New York: Simon and Schuster, 1969.

Daly, Dan. *The National Forgotten League*. Lincoln: University of Nebraska Press, 2012.

Davis, Jeff. *Rozelle Czar of the NFL*. New York: McGraw-Hill, 2008.

Donovan, Arthur J., and Bob Drury. *Fatso: Football When Men Were Really Men*. New York: William Morrow, 1987.

Eisenberg, John. *Cotton Bowl Days*. New York: Simon and Schuster, 1997.

Eisenberg, John. *The League*. New York: Basic Books, 2018.

Eisenberg, John. *Ten-Gallon War*. New York: Houghton Mifflin Harcourt, 2012.

Horrigan, Joe. *NFL Century: The One-Hundred Year Rise of America's Greatest Sports League*. New York: Crown, 2019.

Knight, Dawn. *Taliaferro: Breaking Barriers from the NFL Draft to the Ivory Tower*. Bloomington: Indiana University Press, 2007.

Lyons, Robert S. *On Any Given Sunday: A Life of Bert Bell*. Philadelphia: Temple University Press, 2010.

MacCambridge, Michael. *America's Game: The Epic Story of How Pro Football Captured a Nation*. New York: Anchor Books, 2005.

MacCambridge, Michael. *Chuck Noll: His Life's Work*. Pittsburgh: University of Pittsburgh Press, 2016.

MacCambridge, Michael. *Lamar Hunt: A Life in Sports*. Kansas City: Andrews McMeel, 2012.

Maule, Tex, and Robert Riger. *The Pros: A Documentary of Professional Football in America*. New York: Simon and Schuster, 1960.

Meyers, Jeff. *Great Teams' Great Years: Dallas Cowboys*. New York: Macmillan, 1974.

Miller, Giles E. *The Dallas Texans Saga – or at the Time the New York Yanks Became the Baltimore Colts*. Dallas: Gemco, 1972.

NFL Properties. *NFL 100: A Century of Pro Football*. Edited by Rob Fleder. New York: Abrams Books, 2019.

Pomerantz, Gary. *Their Life's Work*. New York: Simon and Schuster, 2013.

Schultz, Brad. *The NFL, Year One: The 1970 Season and the Dawn of Modern Football*. Washington, DC: Potomac Books, 2013.

St. John, Bob. *Tex! The Man Who Built the Dallas Cowboys*. Englewood Cliffs, NJ: Prentice Hall, 1988.

Swift, David A. F. *Lamar Hunt: The Gentle Giant Who Revolutionized Professional Sports*. Chicago: Triumph Books, 2010.

Zullo, Allan, and Bruce Nash. *The Sports Hall of Shame*. Illustrated by Bill Maul. New York: Pocket Books, 1987. Reprinted by Tribune Media Services, 1991.

MAGAZINES, PUBLICATIONS, NEWSPAPER AND WIRE SERVICES

Girgash, Bill. "Texans Hogtie Bears, Only 2,208 See 27-23 Surprise." *Akron Beacon Journal*, November 28, 1952.

Sherrod, Blackie. "Remember the Texans?" *Dallas Times Herald*, June 7, 1982, Sports section, B.

Spong, Bob. "Six Brothers." *Texas Monthly*, October 2005.

"Yanks' Purchase Completed by Miller." *Pittsburgh Post-Gazette*, January 30, 1952, Sports section.

PERSONAL INTERVIEWS

James Curtis Sanford Jr. (son of James Curtis Sanford Sr.), Dallas, TX.

Jay Black (vice president of operations and curator, Texas Sports Hall of Fame), Waco, TX.

Joseph M. Vassalotti (coordinator, secondary education and athletics, Akron Public Schools), Akron, OH.

Ron Linger (athletic department/student services assistant, Akron Public Schools), Akron, OH.

Stewart Ransom "Rhett" Miller II (grandson of Giles Edwin Miller Sr.), Hudson Valley area, NY.

William Harlon Ray (great-grandnephew of John Harlon Ray), Dallas, TX.

REFERENCE AND OTHER ARCHIVES

Dallas Texans Memorandum of Resolutions Passed at the Meeting of Board of Directors of Dallas Texans Football Club, Inc to Jack C. Vaughn, February 18, 1952. Copy obtained from Leachman, Matthews and Gardere.

Dallas Texans Press, Radio, and Television Guide. Compiled by Tex Maule, publicity director. Dallas: Dallas Texans Football Club, 1952.

Official Game Program, Detroit Briggs Stadium. New York: Don Spencer, November 16, 1952.

Official Game Program, Dallas Cotton Bowl. New York: Don Spencer, September 28, 1952.

Official Game Program, Dallas Cotton Bowl. New York: Don Spencer, October 5, 1952.

Official Game Program, Green Bay City Stadium, New York: Don Spencer, November 23, 1952.

Official Game Program, San Francisco Kezar Stadium. New York: Don Spencer, October 26, 1952.

Sears Roebuck Company Catalog, Sports Center Football Equipment. Chicago: Buddy Young, Sears Sports Center advisory staff.

VIDEO AND AUDIO BROADCASTS

Levinson, Barry, dir. 30 for 30. Season 1, episode 2, "The Band That Wouldn't Die." 2009, on ESPN.

"Art Donovan Collection on Letterman, Part 1: 1983-1993." Don Giller, March 11, 2019, YouTube video, 2:30:44, youtube.com/watch?v=w1KXRSGjjrY.

"Art Donovan Collection on Letterman, Part 2: 1994-2000." Don Giller, March 11, 2019, YouTube video, 1:17:41, youtube.com/watch?v=i3iTye80KK0.

"Art Donovan on The Tonight Show." Mike Webb, August 15, 2010, YouTube video, 6:28, youtube.com/watch?v=7HDRLnoAY9E.

"Defunct NFL Teams: Dallas Texans." RETRO Sports, January 5, 2020, YouTube video, 3:42, youtube.com/watch?v=te5_DsKnbb0.

"NFL – 1984 - NFL Films Special - The Big Little Man Buddy Young – With Steve Sabol + John Facenda." rss empresas, October 25, 2018, YouTube video, 4:49, youtube.com/watch?v=WwWcAktxebQ.

Football Show, November 22, 2018, YouTube video, 6:08, youtube.com/watch?v=ayxZ1AyLR3I.

Miller, Rhett, and Jasmine Belcher Morris, producer. "The Texans." 2016, Los Angeles, CA, Midroll Media, Howl FM Premium Audio, original audio documentary, 27:00.

NFL Films. *The Fabulous 50's*. Volume 2, "The Dallas Texans (1952) Highlight Film." 7:00. Mount Laurel, NJ: NFL Films Archives, 1987.

Smith Barney and Co. television commercial campaign. New York: Ogilvy & Mather, 1979.

WEBSITES

The Arizona Republic. "Obituary for Donald Richard Colo." Posted June 26, 2019. https://www.azcentral.com/obituaries/par029149.Cary, David. "McLendon, Gordon Barton (1921-1986)." Texas State Historical Association. Posted April 1, 1995. https://www.tshaonline.org/handbook/entries/mclendon-gordon-barton.

Duggan, Dan. "Legendary GM George Young Earns Hall of Fame Nod after Leading Giants Return to Glory." *The Athletic*. Posted August 3, 2021. https://www.nytimes.com/athletic/2748515/2021/08/03/legendary-gm-george-young-earns-hall-of-fame-nod-after-leading-giants-return-to-glory/.

Fink, Rob. "Dallas Texans (1952)." Texas State Historical Association. Posted April 29, 2017. https://www.tshaonline.org/handbook/entries/dallas-texans-1952.

The Gridiron Uniform Database. Last updated 2024. https://www.gridiron-uniforms.com.

Horrigan, Joe. "Belly Up in Dallas." *The Coffin Corner* 7, no. 3 (1985): 1–3. Pro Football Researchers Association. https://profootballresearchers.com/archives/Website_Files/Coffin_Corner/07-03-225.pdf.

Indiana University. "Statue Dedication for George Taliaferro." IU Athletics press release. Posted November 1, 2019. https://200.iu.edu/media/news/2019/20191101-01.html.Jackson, Frank. "Burnett Field." Texas State Historical Association. Posted March 24, 2021. https://www.tshaonline.org/handbook/entries/burnett-field.

Legacies: A History Journal for Dallas and North Central Texas 17, no. 1 (Spring 2005) [full issue]. The Portal to Texas History. https://texashistory.unt.edu/ark:/67531/metapth35090/.

Morning Journal. "Akron Superintendent to Drop 'Orientals' Nickname." Posted April 27, 2010. https://www.morningjournal.com/2010/04/27/akron-superintendent-to-drop-orientals-nickname/.

Patoski, Joe Nick. "Rock 'N' Roll's Wizard of Oz." *Texas Monthly*. Published February 1980. texasmonthly.com.

Pro Football Hall of Fame. "George Young." Accessed April 1, 2024, profootballhof.com/players/george-young.

Pro Football Hall of Fame. "Gino Marchetti." Posted August 26, 2010, profootballhof.com/players/gino-marchetti.

Rosen, Ron. "Buddy Young, NFL Great, Killed in Highway Wreck." *Washington Post*. Written September 6, 1983. https://www.washingtonpost.com/archive/sports/1983/09/06/buddy-young-nfl-great-killed-in-highway-wreck/35e0c30f-50f4-43cb-bd80-b902218fda65/.

Schaefer, Bill, Rob Holecko, Tim Brulia, Austin Snelick, and John Nelson. The Gridiron Uniform Database. Accessed June 28, 2024. gridiron-uniforms.com.

Schudel, Matt. "Gino Marchetti, Hall of Fame Defensive End for the Baltimore Colts, Dies at 93." *Washington Post*. Posted May 1, 2019. https://www.washingtonpost.com/local/obituaries/gino-marchetti-hall-of-fame-defensive-end-for-baltimore-colts-dies-at-93/2019/05/01/af6eb452-6c1f-11e9-be3a-33217240a539_story.html.

Shuck, Barry. "Original Texans: 1952 Dallas Texans." Vox Media. Posted on October 13, 2017. https://www.dawgsbynature.com/2017/10/13/16469160/original-texans-1952-dallas-texans.

Simon, Harry. "Classic Induction: Art Donovan – The Man of a Thousand Questions (And They Were All 'How Much Does Fella Guy Weigh?')" Wrestle Crap–The Very Worst of Pro Wrestling. Posted on August 4, 2013. https://www.wrestlecrap.com/inductions/art-donovan/.

Sports Reference LLC. Pro-Football-Reference. [Numerous listings of past players, coaches, and staff for both the Dallas Texans as well as other franchises.] pro-football-reference.com.

Staehle, Adrian. "World Class Tragedy: The Von Erich Story." Bleacher Report. Posted on June 19, 2009. https://bleacherreport.com/articles/202380-world-class-tradgey-the-von-erich-story.

Texas Sports Hall of Fame. https://www.tshof.org.

Weiner, Evan. "Dallas is the Epicenter of NFL History." The Sports Digest. Posted on February 3, 2011. https://thesportdigest.com/2011/02/dallas-is-the-epicenter-of-nfl-history/.

Wikipedia. The following content pages were used as references, via en.wikipedia.org:
Alexander-Hamilton Hotel (San Francisco)
Baltimore Colts (established 1947–1950)
Baltimore Colts (established 1953–1983)
Bell, De Benneville "Bert"
Bellevue Stratford Hotel (Philadelphia)
Big Tex – State Fair of Texas
Boston Yanks (1944–1948)
Burnett Field
Dallas Texans (1952)
Dallas Texans (1960–1963)
Dallas Cowboys
Ewbank, Wilbur Charles (Webb)
Gino's Hamburger
Hotel Adolphus (Dallas)
Hotel Green (Pasadena)
Hotel Windermere (Chicago)
Hunt, Haroldson Lafayette (H. L.)
Hunt, Lamar
McLendon, Gordon Barton
Marshall, George Preston
Maule, Hamilton Prieleaux Bee "Tex"
National Football League Draft (1952)
New York Bulldogs (1949)
New York Yanks (1950–1951)
Northland Hotel (Green Bay)
Rosenbloom, Carroll
Rozelle, Pete
Rubber Bowl (Akron)
Schreiner University
Sheraton-Cadillac Hotel (Detroit)
Smith, Kate
SS Athenia (1922)
Texas Sports Hall of Fame

*Numerous other listings of past players, coaches, staff, ownership, and stadiums for both the Dallas Texans as well as other franchises.

Wilson, Phillip B. "Colts' Story in Baltimore Won't Go Away Anytime Soon, So Understand Both Sides of History." *Indy Star*. Posted July 17, 2013. https://www.indystar.com/story/sports/philb/1/01/01/colts-story-in-baltimore-wont-go-away-any-time-soon-so-understand-both-sides-of-history/2536173/.

Young, Avery. "Black History Month: George Taliaferro Made NFL Draft History." *Sports Illustrated*. Posted February 26, 2020. https://www.si.com/nfl/2020/02/26/black-history-month-george-taliaferro.

ABOUT THE AUTHOR

Mike Cobern grew up in the Dallas area and at an early age fell in love with the Cowboys. One of his first memories is watching Super Bowl V as his Cowboys fell to the Baltimore Colts, ironically the same team the Dallas Texans became. With his first book, he wanted to chronicle something that had never been covered before, and this goal was fulfilled in this history of the NFL's last failed franchise. Today, along with his wife, Deb, he still resides in Dallas and remains a football fan and avid historian.